Buddhist Philosophy and the Embodied Mind

Critical Inquiries in Comparative Philosophy

Series Editor: Alexus McLeod, Professor of Philosophy, University of Connecticut

This series aims to present detailed and inclusive surveys of contemporary research in multiple areas of Asian and Comparative Philosophy. Each volume outlines and engages with the current research within comparative philosophy through the lenses of traditional philosophical areas such as ethics, metaphysics, epistemology, and language/logic.

Theories of Truth in Early Chinese Philosophy: A Comparative Approach by Alexus McLeod
Moral Psychology of Confucian Shame: Shame of Shamelessness by Bongrae Seok
Buddhist Philosophy and the Embodied Mind: A Constructive Engagement by Matthew MacKenzie

Buddhist Philosophy and the Embodied Mind

A Constructive Engagement

Matthew MacKenzie

ROWMAN & LITTLEFIELD
Lanham • Boulder • New York • London

Published by Rowman & Littlefield
An imprint of The Rowman & Littlefield Publishing Group, Inc.
4501 Forbes Boulevard, Suite 200, Lanham, Maryland 20706
www.rowman.com

86-90 Paul Street, London EC2A 4NE

British Library Cataloguing in Publication Information Available

Library of Congress Cataloging-in-Publication Data
Names: MacKenzie, Matthew, 1975- author.
Title: Buddhist philosophy and the embodied mind : a constructive engagement / Matthew MacKenzie.
Description: Lanham : Rowman & Littlefield, 2022. | Series: Critical inquiries in comparative philosophy | Includes bibliographical references and index.
Identifiers: LCCN 2022005686 (print) | LCCN 2022005687 (ebook) | ISBN 9781538160145 (paper) | ISBN 9781538160138 (epub)
Subjects: LCSH: Buddhism and science. | Consciousness—Religious aspects—Buddhism. | Neurosciences—Religious aspects—Buddhism. | Mind and body. | Philosophy of mind. | Cognition.
Classification: LCC BQ4570.S3 M33 2022 (print) | LCC BQ4570.S3 (ebook) | DDC 294.3/365—dc23/eng/20220223
LC record available at https://lccn.loc.gov/2022005686
LC ebook record available at https://lccn.loc.gov/2022005687

Contents

Acknowledgments vii

Introduction 1

1 Enacting Selves 11

2 Luminosity 45

3 Agency and Other Minds 79

4 Enacting Worlds 105

5 Cultivating Compassion 131

Conclusion 159

Bibliography 165

Index 175

Acknowledgments

This book reflects more than a decade of research, reflection, and fruitful conversations, and I therefore have many people to thank. First, special thanks go to Brad Park. This project started life as a collaboration with Brad to bring both South Asian and East Asian traditions into dialogue with enactivism. His deep insights into Asian philosophy, phenomenology, and embodied cognition have profoundly shaped my thinking throughout this book. Special thanks also go to Arindam Chakrabarti for his guidance, encouragement, and constructive criticism over the years.

I would also like to thank the following for their conversation, feedback, and inspiration: Dan Arnold, Dave Chalmers, Christian Coseru, Bronwyn Finnagan, Owen Flanagan, Jonardon Ganeri, Jay Garfield, Charles Goodman, Laura Guerrero, Uriah Kriegel, Joel Krueger, Keya Maitra, Alexus McLeod, Jen McWeeney, Chakravarthi Ram-Prasad, Kranti Saran, Madhuchanda Sen, Manidipa Sen, Mark Siderits, Sean Smith, Galen Strawson, Evan Thompson, Anand Vaidya, and Dan Zahavi.

Thanks go to my colleagues at Colorado State University, especially Jeff Kasser, Katie McShane, Ken Shockley, and Beth Tropman, for their support and encouragement. I am also thankful to have received research support from the Department of Philosophy Endowment Fund.

My deepest thanks go to Ashby, Quinn, and Reid: Ashby for her steadfast love and support, without which this book (and much else) would not have been accomplished, and Quinn and Reid for their endless curiosity, good humor, and love. This book is humbly dedicated to them.

While no chapter of this book has previously been published, I have used and reworked parts of the following articles and chapters:

- "Enacting the Self: Buddhist and Enactivist Approaches to the Emergence of the Self," in *Self, No Self? Perspectives from Analytical, Phenomenological, and Indian Traditions*, ed. M. Siderits, E. Thompson, and D. Zahavi (Oxford, UK: Oxford University Press, 2011), 239–73.
- "Enacting Selves, Enacting Worlds: Reflections on the Buddhist Theory of Karma," *Philosophy East and West* 63 (2013): 194–212.
- "Reflexivity, Subjectivity, and the Constructed Self: A Buddhist Model," *Asian Philosophy* 25, no. 3 (2014): 275–92.
- "Luminous Mind: Self-Luminosity versus Other-Luminosity in Indian Philosophy of Mind," in *The Bloomsbury Research Handbook to Indian Epistemology and Metaphysics*, ed. Joerg Tuske (New York: Bloomsbury Academic, 2017).
- "The Yogācāra Theory of Three Natures: Internalist and Non-Dualist Interpretations," *Comparative Philosophy* 9, no. 1 (2018): 18–31.
- "Buddhism and the Virtues," in *The Oxford Handbook of Virtue*, ed. Nancy Snow (Oxford, UK: Oxford University Press, 2017).
- "Volition, Action, and Skill in Indian Buddhist Philosophy," in *The Routledge Handbook of Skill and Expertise*, ed. Ellen Fridland and Carlotta Parvese (New York: Routledge, 2020).

My thanks to the publishers for permission to use material from these works.

Introduction

This book offers a new way to look at the interconnected phenomena of consciousness, self, agency, and world. A central argument of the book is that an adequate understanding of these phenomena requires rejecting both substance metaphysics and strong reductionism or eliminativism. The alternative, developed in dialogue with Indian Buddhist thought and enactivist philosophy of mind, is based on a nonreductionist ontology of systems and process and a dynamic phenomenology of consciousness, embodiment, and self. Throughout, the book takes an unabashedly pluralistic, syncretic, and constructive approach to philosophy.

The book, then, has three main aims: (1) advancing the dialogue between Indian Buddhism and enactivism, (2) engaging central issues in philosophy of mind through that dialogue, and (3) developing a distinctive account of the embodied subject. Regarding the first aim, with the publication of *The Embodied Mind: Cognitive Science and Human Experience* in 1991, Francisco Varela, Evan Thompson, and Eleanor Rosch initiated a tentative conversation between proponents of embodied and enactive cognition and Buddhist philosophy (Varela et al. 2017). In the thirty years since its publication, embodied, embedded, enactive, and extended (4E) accounts of mind and experience have flourished. Moreover, during this time, there has emerged a more cosmopolitan and pluralistic approach to the philosophy of mind, drawing on analytic, phenomenological, pragmatist, and Asian sources and traditions. Throughout this book, I aim to deepen and extend the dialogue between Buddhist philosophy and enactivist philosophy of mind and phenomenology, in a philosophically and methodologically sophisticated way.

Regarding the second aim, Indian philosophers developed and defended philosophically sophisticated and phenomenologically rich accounts of mind, self, cognition, perception, embodiment, and more. As a work of comparative philosophy, the book aims to investigate the nature of mind and experience in dialogue with Indian and Western thinkers. An important implication of this approach is that the problem space and the conceptual resources available will be broadened and transformed. For example, a central theme of the book is the *luminosity* of consciousness. This metaphor of consciousness as light (*prakāśa*) or luminosity (*prakāśatā*) is at the heart of Indian thinking about the nature of the mind going back at least as far as the early prose Upaniṣads. Like a light, consciousness has (or is) the capacity to shine forth (*prakāśate*) and illuminate (*prakāśyati*) its object. Throughout the book, I take this idea and the philosophical issues surrounding it as a guiding theme for understanding the nature of mind.

Regarding the third aim, the book articulates and defends a dynamic, nonsubstantialist, and embodied account of consciousness, self, agency, and intersubjectivity. Indian Buddhist philosophy provides a deep and sustained critique of substantialism, and the views I develop here are strongly influenced by this aspect of Buddhist thought. However, many Buddhist philosophers embrace forms of reductionism, eliminativism, or antirealism that, in my view, do not do justice to the phenomena. Enactivism, with its emphasis on self-organizing systems dynamically coupled to their larger environments, provides an important alternative to both substantialism and reductionism. However, some articulations of enactivism entail a very strong form of antirealism that I think is unwarranted. Throughout the book, then, I deploy, first, a metaphysics based on processes and systems that is meant to be a middle way between substantialism and reductionism and, second, a form of pragmatic realism that is meant to be a middle way between metaphysical realism and strong antirealism.

Furthermore, the account of consciousness, subjectivity, and self developed here is grounded in the idea—found in both Indian philosophy and the phenomenological tradition—that phenomenal consciousness is self-luminous (*svaprakāśa*). That is, phenomenal consciousness is reflexive or self-presenting. Consciousness presents itself in the process of presenting its object. That it (typically) presents an object and the way that object is presented constitute the intentional character of consciousness. That it presents itself and the way it presents itself constitute the subjective character of consciousness. The reflexivity of consciousness itself constitutes the minimal *subjectivity* of consciousness. Moreover, I argue that this basic structure of consciousness is phenomenologically and developmentally prior to the sense of self. On these points, I am largely in agreement with such Buddhist thinkers as Dignāga and Dharmakīrti. However, I depart significantly from these Buddhist reflexivists in that I defend the real existence of the self as an emergent structure of the biological and psychological life of some sentient beings (such as human beings).

ON COMPARATIVE PHILOSOPHY

This book is an exercise in comparative philosophy of mind, an attempt to do philosophy of mind in dialogue with multiple philosophical traditions and methods. As Arindam Chakrabarti and Ralph Weber remark, "Comparative philosophy is all about the erecting, detecting, smudging, and tearing down of borders, borders between philosophical traditions coming from different parts of the world, different time periods, different disciplinary affiliations, and even within a single period and pedigree, between opposite or at least distinguishable persuasions" (Chakrabarti and Weber 2015, 2). Yet, on their account, there have been three distinguishable, if overlapping, stages of comparative philosophy.

According to Chakrabarti and Weber, the first stage was universalist in aspiration. The idea, roughly, was to take some central debate or issue in Western philosophy, such as the mind-body problem, and find parallels in non-Western traditions. These parallels could then establish that philosophy in some plausible sense of the term exists outside the West and that many central Western philosophical issues, in some form, are discussed in other traditions, as well. This is true, of course, but this approach has the drawback of understanding and engaging these traditions within a resolutely Western frame. The effect, intentional or unintentional, is to take the Western philosophical landscape as universal, while the African, Chinese, or Mayan landscape is taken as local and particular. A further implication is that, if a tradition does not appear to have, for example, a recognizable of version the mind-body problem, then it is to that degree less philosophical.

The second stage was more localist in aspiration. The emphasis was on important differences between traditions in their basic presuppositions, concerns, and methods. A recognition of these differences was deemed essential to a proper understanding of a tradition and also had the (potentially salutary) effect of deflating Western pretensions to universalism. Again, this stage reflected important insights into the hermeneutic complexities of cross-cultural engagement. Moreover, by better understanding traditions in their own terms, this approach also allowed comparative philosophers to engage the Western tradition in a new way. For example, if, as some have argued (Wenzel and Marchal 2017), the problem of free will was hardly known in Chinese philosophy, then perhaps this reflects a philosophical strength rather than a weakness. However, in its more extreme form anyway, this approach tended toward a view that traditions are ultimately incommensurable (Wong 1989), thereby throwing into question the very possibility of genuine cross-cultural understanding.

The third and current stage, according to Chakrabarti and Weber, exists "at the critical conjuncture between universalism and localism" (2015,

20). The idea here is to understand and engage different traditions both on their own terms, in relation to other traditions, and with an eye to how they may contribute to contemporary philosophical discussions. A central aim of this approach, then, is to accelerate the globalizing of the contemporary philosophical conversation. One might, for example, deploy a broadly hermeneutical approach whereby one attempts to develop an understanding of the particular (a text, problem, argument, etc.) in its larger context while also developing an understanding of the whole context in light of an understanding of the particular. Further, on this approach, one must recognize the inevitable situatedness of understanding while rejecting the idea that one's own background understanding is fixed. Rather, mutual understanding evolves through a more dialogical form of engagement. Alternatively, following Jonardon Ganeri (2016), one might deploy a form of epistemic pluralism inspired by the classical Jaina distinction between epistemic principles (*pramāṇas*) and epistemic stances (*naya*), both of which are parts of an epistemic culture. He writes, "A *naya* is not a proposition but a practical attitude, a strategy or policy which guides inquiry: it is an approach to the problem of producing knowledge, not a thesis about the sources of justification" (2016, 175). He goes on to articulate an inclusive approach to philosophy that is pluralistic about epistemic stances although not epistemic principles.

Chakrabarti and Weber affirm that this third stage includes "some of the best comparative philosophy written today" (2015, 20). However, they argue for the emergence and desirability of a fourth stage of comparative philosophy, which they call "borderless philosophy" (2015, 22). Here the idea is "just doing philosophy as one thinks fit for getting to the truth about an issue or set of issues, by appropriating elements from all philosophical views and traditions one knows" (2015, 22). On this approach, the qualifier *comparative* may become superfluous; one just does philosophy in a way that is mindful of the global nature and context of thinking. Likewise, Ganeri asserts that "comparative philosophy is not, I submit, a branch of philosophy nor it is a distinct philosophical method: it is an expedient heuristic introduced at a particular moment in world history as part of a global movement towards intellectual decolonization" (2016, 134–35).

Yet, on my view, even postcomparative philosophy must incorporate elements of the earlier stages of comparative inquiry. One must begin with the universalist assumption that human beings in many times and places have engaged in philosophical thinking and inquiry. In doing so, they are likely to have addressed at least some similar questions or issues, and we may benefit from coming to understand their attempted answers. As one engages in that form of inquiry, however, one immediately encounters difference and particularity. One must then engage in the hard hermeneutic (and ultimately metaphilosophical) work of building bridges between traditions and adding something of value to the ongoing global philosophical conversation of humanity. With moderate success, one may be able to do "good creative philosophy" in a global context. That is,

> Good creative philosophy in a globalized world should spontaneously straddle geographical areas and cultures, temperaments and time-periods (mixing classical, medieval, modern, and postmodern), styles and subdisciplines of philosophy, as well as mix methods, sprinkling phenomenology, and political economic analysis into analytic logico-linguistic or hermeneutic, or culture studies or literary or narrative methods—whatever comes handy. The result would be either very flaky mishmash or first-rate original work. (Chakrabarti and Weber 2015, 22)

In my view, we should strive to do good creative philosophy across cultures, traditions, and methods while avoiding the problems associated with earlier stages of comparative philosophy. That is the approach pursued in this book.

OVERVIEW OF THE CHAPTERS

Chapter 1 initiates a dialogue between enactivist and Indian Buddhist views of the self. While Buddhists and enactivists reject substantialist accounts of the self, Buddhist thinkers are further committed to a rejection of the reality of the self as such. Drawing insights from both traditions, I argue that sentient beings are best understood in terms of complex self-organizing processes, including processes of self-making. This view is contrasted with both eliminativism and substantialism about the self. In contrast to these, I argue for an enactive, emergent view of self as the embodied integration of subjectivity, ownership, agency, and valuation. Along the way, I distinguish between the basic condition of being a *subject* and the more sophisticated condition of being a *self*. On my view, sentience and subjectivity are functionally interwoven and may have coevolved. However, sentience and minimal subjectivity are necessary but not sufficient for selfhood. Rather, I argue that the emergence of the self is linked to the emergence of a degree of psychological autonomy from the biological autonomy of living systems.

Chapter 2 takes up several related issues in the philosophy of consciousness: reflexivity, temporality, subjectivity, and embodiment. Beginning with a classical Buddhist definition of consciousness as *luminosity*, it develops an integrated account of the previous issues, drawing on the general model of consciousness developed by the *pramāṇavādins*, which I call "dual-aspect reflexivism." As mentioned earlier, on this view, consciousness is by nature self-luminous—that is, self-presenting or reflexive. Reflexive awareness (*svasaṃvedana*) here is the primitive, prereflective, direct acquaintance of consciousness with itself. Moreover, a typical moment of consciousness presents two aspects: the object aspect and the subject aspect. I argue that these aspects can be understood as distinct but intertwined phenomenal modes of presentation.

On the issue of temporality, inspired by the Tibetan philosopher Mipham, I explore the possibility of combining the earlier Yogācāra idea of base consciousness (*ālayavijñāna*) with reflexivism. The view that emerges takes base consciousness to be a form of embodied, global background consciousness that preserves a degree of diachronic continuity even as the local, foreground aspects of consciousness change. In the final section of the chapter, I draw together the various strands of discussion and sketch an integrated model of consciousness. On this model, the nature of consciousness is nondual reflexive awareness, the phenomenal space within which various contents are presented but that is prior to any particular contents. It is synchronically unified and diachronically continuous. It is rooted in and emerges from the living body and in its typical form involves both subjective and objective modes of presentation.

Chapter 3 engages with problems of agency and other minds. The nature of action is a central theme in Indian Buddhist philosophy. The Buddhist theory of *karma* (*karman*, "action") addresses the short- and long-term effects of moral or immoral actions for the agent of those actions and emphasizes the interdependence of action and character. I identify four basic commitments of the Buddhist view: (1) the reality of *karma*, (2) the connection between *karma* and intending or volition (*cetanā*), (3) the efficacy of Buddhist practice to achieve liberation, and (4) the nonexistence of any substantial self or agent. Given these commitments, such Buddhist thinkers as Vasubandhu and Candrakīrti developed important accounts of agentless agency. These accounts are broadly conventionalist (in either reductionist or fictionalist ways) and show that there are powerful alternatives to the view that action requires a persisting substantial agent. However, I argue that these approaches still fall prey to the problem of the disappearing agent. In response, I examine an enactivist approach that grounds agency in the biology of cognitive systems. On this account, agency is viewed as a real, emergent capacity of certain biological systems and not merely a conventional reality. In this way, the enactive approach offers an alternative to both the substantialist agent-causal view and the reductionist (or fictionalist) view.

Turning to the issue of other minds, one of the most important insights of such Buddhist thinkers as Vasubandhu and Dharmakīrti is that the sense of self is co-constructed with the sense of independent objects and other selves. It is thus incumbent on these thinkers to specify the process or processes by which the (ultimately delusive) senses of self, objects, and other selves are constructed. And this gives rise, in the Buddhist context, to a version of the venerable problem of other minds. In this part of the chapter, I examine the approaches of Dharmakīrti and Ratnakīrti and whether they can avoid the problem of conceptual solipsism. The problem here is whether the model of the mind developed by these thinkers can account for the ability to conceive of others as self-conscious subjects (Ganeri 2012, 214). I argue that the conceptual problem of other minds is insurmountable as long as one maintains a view the mind as a self-enclosed interiority, as these Buddhist reflexivists arguably do. In contrast, I develop an account of the mind as reflexive but not self-enclosed. This requires a different approach to intentionality and embodiment, as well as seeing mentality as expressive and not merely causal. That is, as embodied subjects, our mentality is a multidimensional form of life in part constituted by and manifest in our bodily actions and expressions. On this view, the mental lives of others are not completely hidden, and our own mental lives are never fully transparent. And this is because our self-awareness and awareness of others share a basis in our nature as embodied subjects.

In Chapter 4, I argue that both Buddhists and enactivists are committed to the claim that not just ourselves but also our worlds are enacted: They are brought forth in and through action. But what could this mean? Is it simply a claim about how we perceive or conceptualize the world, or is it a strong metaphysical claim about reality? I argue that, properly understood, the idea that we enact our world (or worlds) points beyond reified forms of subjectivism and objectivism toward the deep, constitutive interdependence of mind, action, and world. The chapter begins with an examination of Buddhist and enactivist accounts of the dynamic coemergence of self and world and the denial of any metaphysical subject-object, self-world duality. I then discuss the Buddhist theory of *karma* as an account of the ongoing enaction of self and world and sketch an account of awakened agency.

Next, I take up the Madhyamaka claim that all things are empty in the context of debates over metaphysical realism. I examine both Madhyamaka and enactivist critiques of metaphysical realism as well as challenges to these views. In thinking through both the insights and the challenges of these critiques of metaphysical realism, I argue for the plausibility of a broadly pragmatist view with three main elements. The first is *ontological parity*: There is no ontologically privileged level of reality. The second is *conceptual-explanatory pluralism*: We use and *need* a plurality of conceptual and explanatory schemes. The third is *epistemological pragmatism*: An embrace of fallibilism and grounding warrant in successful practice.

I then turn to the rich view of the experiential dynamics found in the Yogācāra theory of the three natures of phenomena. I distinguish two ways of interpreting this framework, which I call the "internalist-representationalist" and the "nondualist" views. The final section of the chapter brings together the various strands of argument and interpretation and sketches a phenomenological-pragmatic realism that has the potential to move our thinking about self and world beyond the reified categories of subjectivism and objectivism and representationalist accounts of cognition.

Chapter 5 focuses on Mahāyāna Buddhist ethics as a path of moral and spiritual development. Drawing on the accounts of subjectivity, agency, and empathy developed in the previous chapters, it engages the moral psychology and phenomenology of Śāntideva's *Bodhicaryāvatāra* or *Guide to the Awakened Life*. On my view, Buddhist ethics is fundamentally a transformative path concerned with the progressive dismantling of greed, aversion, and ignorance and the progressive cultivation of the nonattachment, compassion, and wisdom of an enlightened character. This final chapter of the book aims to unpack the cognitive, affective, perceptual, bodily, and intersubjective dimensions of this path in dialogue with the enactive approach.

Śāntideva characterizes the *saṃsāric* predicament of human beings as "Hoping to escape suffering, it is to suffering that they run. In the desire for happiness, out of delusion, they destroy their own happiness, like an enemy" (Śāntideva 2008, 7). I term this sorry state of affairs the *saṃsāric* framework. It is a mode of functioning wherein our attempts to attain happiness and avoid suffering are self-defeating because they are driven by the three poisons of greed, hatred, and delusion. I argue that Śāntideva's project in *Bodhicaryāvatāra* is to dismantle the *saṃsāric* framework and develop a more wholesome or awakened cognitive, affective, and motivational-behavioral framework. The basis of this awakened mode of life, for Śāntideva and his fellow Mahāyānists, is *bodhicitta*, the "awakening mind," which he calls the "seed of pure happiness in the world and the remedy of suffering in the world" (Śāntideva 2008, 26). It is, as Jay Garfield puts it, the "commitment to attain and to manifest full awakening for the benefit of others" (Garfield 2014, 299). I argue that the basis for the cultivation of *bodhicitta* is the fundamental empathy and intersubjectivity of human consciousness discussed in chapter 3. That is, the core human capacity of empathy is the root of *bodhicitta*, and the *bodhisattva* path involves both clearing away obstructions to empathic awareness as well as developing and extending the capacity toward all sentient beings. I then turn to a discussion of a system of meditative cultivation called the "four-point mind training": meditating on (1) the equality of self and other, (2) the limits of egocentrism or self-cherishing, (3) the benefits of altruism, and (4) the exchange of self and other. This system of cognitive-affective training is designed to arouse and extend the altruistic concern of *bodhicitta* as well as the moral perception and responsiveness requisite for the path of the *bodhisattva*. Finally, I argue that the upshot of this training is to develop the ability to perceive the basic equality of self and other even across social and interpersonal difference, to perceive the emptiness and fluidity of the distinction between self and others, and to respond compassionately and effectively to others.

Chapter One

Enacting Selves

A key difficulty in the philosophy of self is that there is no consensus on what a self is supposed to be. On some views, that we are selves is taken as a datum, an experiential given for which any theory of self must account. To deny the self, then, would be similar to denying the existence of phenomenal consciousness. Eliminativism about the self would be a very puzzling denial of the obvious fact the we are selves. On other views, the self is taken not as a datum but as an ontological posit used to help explain key features of our experience and functioning. On this kind of view, eliminativism, far from being an implausible view, might even be the default assumption on grounds of ontological parsimony, among other considerations. The situation is further complicated by the fact that different accounts of the self often highlight quite different features of our experience and functioning. Is the self supposed to be associated with our core consciousness (Damasio 2000), our prereflective self-awareness (Zahavi 2008), our first-person point of view (Baker 2013), our whole being, or our self-image? If there is so little agreement on what a self would be if it were to exist, then how can we even begin to adjudicate whether it exists? As the Tibetan philosopher Tsongkhapa reminds us, we must first specify the object of negation (or affirmation) before moving on to the negation (or affirmation) itself.

Among philosophers and scientists, the conception of the self as a substance separate from the body and the rest of the natural world (e.g., the Cartesian ego) is widely rejected today. Yet many accounts of the self are developed based on assumptions, such as substantialism and objectivism, that arguably remain Cartesian. In contrast, both Buddhism and enactivism present fruitful alternatives to broadly Cartesian approaches to cognition, subjectivity, embodiment, and the nature of the self. Indeed, the enactive approach to cognition and its allied method of neurophenomenology explicitly and systematically draw from Buddhist thinkers, ideas, and practices in order to move beyond Cartesianism.

In this chapter, I take up the problem of the self in dialogue with Buddhist and enactivist accounts of the self. I begin with an examination of the Buddhist theory of no-self (*anātman*) and the rigorously reductionist interpretation of this doctrine developed by the Abhidharma school of Buddhism. After discussing some of the fundamental problems for Buddhist reductionism, I turn to the enactive approach to philosophy of mind and cognitive science. In particular, in agreement with enactivism, I argue that sentient beings are dynamic systems characterized by a high degree of self-organizing autonomy. On this view, sentient beings are not reducible to the more basic mental and physical events that constitute them. I then examine the notion of subjectivity and argue for a distinction between subjectivity and selfhood. Finally, I turn to the central question of self and, in contrast to both substantialists and eliminativists, argue for a conception of the self as constructed by an active, embodied, embedded, self-organizing process of self-making or "I"-making (*ahaṃkāra*).

NO-SELF

The doctrine of no-self (*anātman*) is perhaps the best-known and most controversial aspect of Buddhist thought. On the Buddhist view, phenomena arise in dependence on a network of causes and conditions. This is the fundamental Buddhist notion of dependent coarising (*pratītyasamutpāda*). The Buddhist analysis of any particular entity, event, or process will focus on the dynamic patterns of interaction within and through which it arises, has its effects, and passes away. It is against the backdrop of this basic analytical and ontological commitment that one can understand the Buddhist account of the self.

First and foremost, the doctrine of no-self is a rejection of the *ātman*, the enduring substantial self. On this view, the "self" (*ātman*) is not just another term for the empirical person (*pudgala*, *jīva*) but is rather the substantial, essential core of the person—the inner self whose existence grounds the identity of the person. Within the Brahmanical religious and philosophical tradition, the *ātman* is generally given a strongly metaphysical interpretation. It is the unitary, essentially unchanging, eternal, spiritual substance that is said to be one's true self. However, the ultimate target of the Buddhist theory of no-self is not the rarified spiritual conception of self commonly defended by various Brahmanical schools. Most fundamentally, the Buddhist target is a much more widely held and more deeply entrenched conception of the self. Galen Strawson's account of our basic sense of self fits well with Buddhist characterizations of the *ātman*. He writes,

I propose that the mental self is ordinarily conceived or experienced as:

1. a *thing*, in some robust sense
2. a *mental* thing, in some sense
3. a *single* thing that is single both *synchronically* considered
4. and *diachronically* considered
5. *ontically distinct* from all other things
6. a *subject of experience*, a conscious feeler and thinker
7. an *agent*
8. a thing that has a certain character or *personality*. (Shear and Gallagher 1999, 3)

Compare Strawson's view to Miri Albahari's account of the *ātman* according to early Buddhism: "A self is defined as a bounded, happiness-seeking/*dukkha* [suffering]-avoiding (witnessing) subject that is a personal owner and controlling agent, and which is unified and unconstructed, with unbroken and invariable presence from one moment to the next, as well as with longer-term endurance and invariability" (2006, 73). Here we find the self understood as an experiencing subject, owner, and controller that is bounded (or, in Strawson's terms, "ontically distinct") and enduring. Albahari also usefully distinguishes between the subject and the self. A subject is "*witnessing* [awareness] *as it presents from a psycho-physical (hence spatio-temporal) perspective*" (Albahari 2006, 8). Thus, for Albahari, while perspectival experience implies a subject, it does not necessarily imply a self, for a self is a particular *type* of subject: bounded, enduring, controlling, and so on. Central to the Buddhists, the self in the previous sense does *not* exist, and our deeply entrenched sense that we are such an entity is at the root of our existential and spiritual bondage (*saṃsāra*).

Rejecting the existence of the substantial self, the Buddhists argue the existence of a person (*pudgala*) consists in the existence of the five *skandhas* (bundles or aggregates) organized in the right way. The five *skandhas* are:

1. *Rūpa*: the body or corporeality
2. *Vedanā*: hedonic valence or affect
3. *Saṃjñā*: perception and cognition
4. *Saṃskāra*: conditioning and volition
5. *Vijñāna*: consciousness

These five *skandhas* are not to be taken as independent things but instead are seen as interdependent aspects of a causally and functionally integrated psychophysical (*nāma-rūpa*) system or process (*skandhasantāna*: an "aggregate-stream" or "bundle-continuum").

The *rūpa-skandha* (material form) refers to the corporeal aspect of the human being, including the organizational structure of the person as an organism. The *vedanā-skandha* denotes affective dimensions of the person and their experience (pleasant, unpleasant, or neutral). The *saṃjñā-skandha* denotes the more fully cognitive faculty of perception, including the ability to identify and reidentify objects of experience.[1] The operation of this capacity depends on sensory contact (*sparśa*) with the environment as well as sensorimotor skills (such as exploratory behavior) and is often taken to involve the use of concepts. Next, the *saṃskāra-skandha* (conditioning) includes the various dispositions, capacities, and formations—such as sensorimotor skills, memories, habits, emotional dispositions, volitions, and cognitive schemas—that both enable and constrain the person and their experiences. This category also includes our basic conative impulses—attraction, repulsion, and indifference—that are in turn closely tied to our feelings and the affective modalities (*vedanā*) of experience. On the Buddhist view, typically one's whole being in the world is driven by this sedimented conditioning—and not always for the better. Indeed, the basic conative impulses often manifest in pathological ways, as the "three poisons" of greed, hatred, and ignorance. As Dan Lusthaus remarks, "such predilections are always already inscribed in our flesh, in our very way of being in the world, even while we ignore—or remain ignorant of—the causes and conditions that have given rise to them" (2003, 49). Finally, the *vijñāna-skandha* denotes discerning or discriminating intentional consciousness.

Therefore, in the standard Buddhist analysis, the person is not an entity that can exist independently of the five *skandhas*. Take away the complex, impermanent, changing *skandhas*, and we are not left with a constant, substantial self; we are left with nothing. Moreover, the diachronic identity of a person consists in the appropriate degree of continuity and connectedness of the *skandhas*—that is, it is a matter of there being a causally and functionally integrated series or stream of *skandhas*.

Having briefly sketched the theory of no-self, let us examine two lines of argument against the existence of the self (*ātman*): the *criterial* argument and the *epistemic* argument. First, it is argued that none of the *skandhas* individually nor the whole complex of *skandhas* could be the self—that is, the independent, substantial, enduring, inner controller and owner of the *skandhas*. Upon examination, none of the five *skandhas* meets these criteria of selfhood.[2] The various mental factors (*nāma-skandha*) are simply too transitory, too mutable to constitute the stable, enduring essence of the person. Moreover, the mental factors are revealed in experience as a stream (*santāna*) or flow rather than as a substance or object. The body is perhaps more stable, but the fundamental problem is the same: Like any complex phenomenon, the body is in perpetual flux. How should we specify the persistence conditions of the body? One might attempt to identify the body's unique ontological boundary or some essential part of the body that explains its persistence. But neither of these strategies looks particularly viable. The physical boundaries of the body are vague, and even if one could find the essential part of the body, it is doubtful that this essential part could meet the other criteria of selfhood. Thus it appears that none of the *skandhas* individually, neither mental factors nor the body, could be the substantial enduring self.

What, then, of the *skandhas* taken together, the *nāma-rūpa*, or psychophysical, complex? Could this be the self? One problem with this response is that the psychophysical complex is the empirical person, whereas the self is posited as the essence of the person that grounds and explains the persistence of the person. The empirical person, like the individual *skandhas*, is in flux, and therefore its endurance is equally problematic. Therefore, to simply identify the self with the person as a whole would be to conflate the *explanans* with the *explanandum*. Also, the relationship between a whole and its parts is problematic, and the Buddhists deny that a complex could be the *independent* owner and controller of its parts. Therefore, the substantial, essential self is not found among the *skandhas* individually or collectively.

The second, and later, line of argument builds on the first. According to the Buddhist philosopher Vasubandhu (fourth century CE), we must apprehend the self either through direct acquaintance or through inference.[3] But, he thinks, we do not apprehend the self through either means. Therefore, we have no epistemic warrant for the existence of the *ātman*. The self is not a direct object of the five external senses or introspection. And while human beings typically have a *sense* of self, it does not follow from this that the sense of self provides direct acquaintance with an enduring, substantial self. Moreover, while it is certainly possible for the "self" to be an object of thought, again it does not follow that the self exists.

So, if the self is not known through direct acquaintance, then perhaps it is known through inference. Vasubandhu examines a valid inference to the existence of the unobservable sense faculties and then asserts that there is no such valid inference to the existence of the unobservable self. In the case of the sense faculties, there is some reasonable way to tell whether the sense faculties are present or absent (e.g., in the case of the blind person versus the sighted person). Can the same be said for the *ātman*? One might, for example, posit the existence of distinct substantial selves in order to individuate persons A and B. But because the substantial self is supposed to retain its identity independently of the ever-changing stream of mental and physical events associated with A and B, how are we to establish anything about these posited selves? As it stands, the empirical evidence (e.g., distinct bodies, various uses of names and *I*) is consistent with both the presence and the absence of the posited self as well as a single shared self or a new substantial self each moment. Hence, the inference to the existence of the *ātman* looks weak. Vasubandhu's assertion here is not decisive, but the underlying argumentative strategy is to shift the burden of proof onto the proponent of the substantial self. Is there inferential warrant for positing an enduring substantial self, or can the phenomena (e.g., memory) be accounted for in terms of the systematic relations between various mental and physical events and processes? The Buddhists, of course, opt for the latter approach on grounds of epistemic and ontological parsimony. We are, they argue, *selfless persons* (*pudgalanairātmyā*).

BUDDHIST REDUCTIONISM

The account of human beings as selfless persons is held by all major Buddhist schools, but there has been a great deal of disagreement as to the full ontological implications of the rejection of a substantial self. For the Abhidharma or Buddhist reductionist schools, the doctrine of *anātman* is at the center of a radically reductionist, antisubstantialist empiricism. Everyday entities, such as pots and people, are not ontologically basic (*dravyasat*) but rather are reducible to aggregations of basic entities. On this view, the seemingly objective, mind-independent unity of everyday composite objects is illusory—these entities have only a secondary, conceptual existence (*prajñaptisat*). The ontologically basic entities to which everyday things are reducible are called *dharmas*. These are simple, fleeting events individuated by their intrinsic defining characteristic (*svalakṣaṇa*). Moreover, the Abhidharma's basic ontology is fairly austere—according to one school, there are only seventy-five types of *dharmas*. As Vasubandhu writes in the *Abhidharmakośa*, "An entity, the cognition of which does not arise when it is broken and, mentally divided, is conventionally existent like a pot. Ultimate existence is otherwise" (AK 6.4 in Pradhan 1975, 334).[4]

This view constitutes a type of antirealism about everyday composite entities, including persons. Such entities may be pragmatically or conventionally real (*saṃvṛtisat*), but they are not ultimately real (*paramārthasat*). The being of these entities is fully accounted for in terms of more basic entities; they are fully analytically and ontologically decomposable. Thus, they have a merely derived nature (*parabhāva*) rather than their own irreducible intrinsic nature (*svabhāva*). Further, conventionally real entities must be epiphenomenal because if they were to have their own causal powers, they would not be completely reducible. Hence, according to the Abhidharmas, all causation is microcausation—that is, real causation occurs only between simple, momentary *dharmas*. Further, the genuine causal powers of these entities are determined by their intrinsic natures. Notice, then, that this two-tiered ontology rests on a radical dichotomy between the entities with a purely extrinsic nature (*parabhāva*) and those with a purely intrinsic nature (*svabhāva*).

Given such a revisionist ontology, one can see the importance of the Buddhist doctrine of two truths. On the Abhidharma view, conventional truths (*saṃvṛtisatya*) are those truths that quantify over reducible or conventionally real (*saṃvṛtisat*) entities, whereas ultimate truths (*paramārthasatya*) only quantify over irreducible or ultimately real (*paramārthasat*) entities. When using conventional discourse, one is not ontologically committed to anything but the entities mentioned in the ultimate discourse, even if conventional discourse is not analytically reducible to ultimate discourse. Further, the discourse of ultimate truth is the Abhidharma's "philosophically favored discourse"—that is, the discourse in terms of which all other discourses are ultimately to be explained (Pradhan 1975, 334).

Persons, then, are organized, temporally extended systems of mental and physical events characterized by dense causal and functional interconnectedness, including complex physical and psychological feedback loops. As Siderits characterizes the view,

> The continued existence of a person must then be said to consist in a causal series of sets of suitably arranged psychophysical elements: these body parts only exist for a while but cause similar successor parts to arise; this feeling only exists for a while but causes a successor desire, and so on. Buddhist Reductionists hold, then, that the existence of a person just consists in the occurrence of a causal series of psychophysical elements. (Siderits 2016, 265)

Psychophysical systems are also seen as deeply intertwined with and dependent on the larger environment. Indeed, for the Buddhist reductionist, there is no sharp dividing line between the collection of events labeled "person" and the collection of events labeled "environment." These terms do not carve the world at its joints; they are pragmatic, interest-relative categories. In order to understand the psychological dynamics that give rise to and perpetuate suffering, one does not look for a substantial mental self or an enduring substantial person. Instead, the Buddhist analyst attempts to understand the complex interrelations between mental and physical events over time. The rigorous Abhidharma analysis, though, goes beyond the early Buddhist shift in perspective from personal to impersonal analysis and defends a strict mereological reductionism—this position, I argue in the next section, is in significant tension with the more general Buddhist analysis of sentient beings.

FOUR PROBLEMS FOR BUDDHIST REDUCTIONISM

While Buddhist reductionism offers a powerful critique of and a sophisticated alternative to substantialist views of the self, this radical view of the human person did not go unchallenged. Indeed, both Buddhist and non-Buddhist philosophers vigorously disputed the Abhidharma or Buddhist reductionist approach. In this section, I examine four interconnected problems for Buddhist reductionism and for strongly reductionist theories of the person in general. These four problems are (1) personal and experiential continuity, (2) first-person consciousness, (3) mereological reductionism, and (4) the reification of *dharmas*. I argue that a turn to the enactive approach will contribute to the development of an antisubstantialist account of the person that overcomes these problems without reifying the self.

The first problem for the Buddhist reductionist has to do with personal continuity and, even more fundamentally, the continuity of the prepersonal body-mind stream that is the ground of personal continuity. An advocate of the self (*ātmavādin*) will want an account of diachronic personal identity (or at least personal continuity) in the absence of a self.[5] And as we have seen, the Buddhist reductionist holds that personal continuity is reducible to psychological continuity (memory, skills, habits, personality traits), which is in turn reducible to causal connections between impermanent mental and physical events. One problem for this approach is that there are just too many causal connections. By their own view, the world is taken to be a causally interdependent network of events. How are we to individuate different streams of events at a time or over time?

The Buddhist reductionist has a two-part response to this problem. At the conventional (*saṃvṛti*) level, streams are individuated by the *density* of causal connections and by the way in which some sets of interconnected mental and physical events are able to ground relatively stable capacities or functions, such as perception and motility.[6] Furthermore, at the ultimate (*paramārtha*) level, there simply is no ontologically correct way to individuate streams. Individuating streams (carving them out of the causal manifold) is an inherently pragmatic and interest-relative activity, and thus at this level of analysis, there is no fact of the matter about the identity of streams.

However, there is a deeper problem here, pointed out by a number of critics of Buddhism. For instance, the Advaita Vedānta philosopher Śaṅkara (c. 788–820 CE) argues,

> The mental impressions must have an abode. Without that they cannot exist. But the doctrine of momentariness denies permanency to everything. Even the ālayavijñāna is momentary and cannot be that abode. Unless there is a permanent principle connecting the past, present, and future, there cannot be remembrance

> or recognition of an experience originating at a particular time and place. If the ālayavijñāna is said to be something permanent, then that would go counter to the doctrine of momentariness. (II.2.31 in Vireswarananda 1982, 221)[7]

A series of momentary mental events, even if causally connected, does not yet constitute an experientially continuous stream of consciousness. And yet, the argument goes, this is what is needed for the exercise (or even possibility) of such mental capacities as recognition or memory. That is, on Śaṅkara's view, one cannot remember or recognize what one has not previously experienced. The Buddhist reductionist needs a plausible account of how to get experiential continuity from causal connectedness, and as I discuss more extensively in the next chapter, this is no easy matter. Indeed, as Śaṅkara points out here, even the later Yogācāra idea of the *ālayavijñāna*—a purportedly nongappy series of mental events—may not be able to account for experiential continuity without running afoul of the Buddhist theory of momentariness (*kṣanikavāda*).

The second problem for Buddhist reductionism involves *I* consciousness, or first-person experiences and thoughts. If a particular token of the first-person pronoun *I* does not refer to the utterer's self, then what, if anything, does it refer to? It seems obvious that when an individual correctly uses *I*, they are referring to themself. But, as the Buddhist reductionist will quickly point out, from this it does not follow that when they use *I*, they refer to a substantial self. Self-reference is not necessarily reference to an ontologically independent self. So even if one rejects the existence of such a self, one can still give an account of first-person self-reference. Perhaps the first-person pronoun is not a genuine referring term, or perhaps, as for Vasubandhu, *I* refers to the continuum in which it occurs rather than the self. The deeper problem here concerns the centrality and continuity of the sense of self (*ahaṃkāra*) and its connection to self-consciousness, or what Western phenomenologists term the "first-person mode of givenness" of experience.[8]

The great Nyāya critic of Buddhism Uddyotakara presses the difficulty in the following passage:

> The consciousness of "I," which conforms to the distinctions of the nature of the object, and which does not depend upon memory of marks, the possessor of the marks, and their relationship, is direct acquaintance just as is the cognition of physical form. Concerning what you yourself, with perfect confidence, establish to be direct acquaintance, in virtue of what is it that it is [said to be] direct acquaintance? You must establish it as being consciousness alone, which does not depend upon the relationships among marks, etc., and which is self-presenting. So then you think there is an I-cognition, but that its object is not the self? Well, then show us its object! (Kapstein 2013, 98)

As Uddyotakara points out here, first-person self-reference must be anchored in a noncriterial, noninferential mode of self-acquaintance. But if there is no-self, then what are *I* cognitions directly acquainted with? What is the subject of experience? As Uddyotakara himself mentions, one later Buddhist response to this problem is to argue that consciousness is inherently reflexive or self-presenting (*svasaṃvedana*), and this inherent reflexivity is the basis of both explicit *I* cognitions and the more inchoate diachronic sense of self (*ahaṃkāra*). That is, as in Sartre's view, consciousness is always consciousness of *itself* but not necessarily consciousness of a *self* (Sartre 2004). Later developments aside, however, it is unclear that the ruthlessly reductive, impersonalist causalism of the Abhidharma can accommodate the first-personal givenness or the first-personal continuity of human experience.

The third problem for Buddhist reductionism arises from the commitment to mereological reductionism. The properties of a whole, including causal properties, are thought to be reductively determined by the intrinsic properties of its components. Yet the thoroughgoing reductionism of Abhidharma seems to be in tension with not just non-Buddhist substantialism but also the dynamic, processual, and multilevel analysis of human beings found in early Buddhism. Dependent coarising (*pratītyasamutpāda*) is a multilevel account of interdependence, ranging from the arising of a single moment of experience to the entire cycle of rebirth. The radical interpretation of dependent origination and antisubstantialism found in Buddhist reductionism may not have the resources required to account for the dependent origination of the human person. And, in any case, as I argue later, there are good reasons to question mereological reductionism, at least with regard to some systems.

The fourth problem for Buddhist reductionism, namely the reification of *dharmas*, is closely related to the third. Recall that Abhidharma ontology rests on a sharp dichotomy between, on the one hand, those entities that have a dependent nature (*parabhāva*) and are therefore merely conventionally real and, on the other hand, those ultimately real entities that have an independent intrinsic nature (*svabhāva*). Clearly mereological reductionism requires an irreducible reduction base, and as the Abhidharmas insist, the entities that form the reduction base for everyday things must not themselves borrow their nature from other things. That is, macrolevel properties, including the properties of wholes, must reductively supervene on the intrinsic, nonrelational properties of the base level. Thus, ultimately real entities must be independent and basic, as well as individuated by their unique and intrinsic, nonrelational properties. Ultimate reality, then, is understood in terms of substance (*dravya*) and essence (*svabhāva*).[9] Therefore, the worry is that this picture constitutes an unwarranted reification of some phenomena (basic *dharmas*) and, at the same time, an unwarranted nihilism about other phenomena (conventional entities).[10] Moreover, as with the Abhidharma's mereological reductionism, I argue that there are good reasons to question this reified account of phenomena.

THE DEPENDENT ORIGINATION OF SENTIENT BEINGS

Given the shortcomings of the Abhidharma theory of persons, perhaps what is required is a middle way between their reductionist fictionalism and the substantialism of *ātman* and Cartesian ego theories. Moreover, developments in complex systems theory and biology call into question strongly reductionist approaches, such as that of the Abhidharma. For, unlike flames or chariots (two of the common analogues to the human person), biological systems display a high degree of self-organized autonomy. On the enactive approach discussed later, living beings are neither enduring substances nor merely aggregative systems but rather self-regulating unities. Of course, as we have seen, the Abhidharma analysis recognizes that psychophysical systems are self-perpetuating and characterized by functional integration and feedback loops. Yet this traditional Buddhist analysis is combined with a strict mereological reductionism that must, in the end, deny genuine causal status to macrolevel entities or structures. Therefore, to avoid this problem, in this section I turn to the theory of autonomous systems, an integral component of the enactive approach, for support in developing an antisubstantialist but nonreductionist account of sentient beings.[11]

According to both Buddhist and enactivist accounts, sentient beings are organized dynamic systems. Hence an understanding of the system requires that we pay close attention, not just to the system's components, but also to its organization.[12] We may begin with the distinction between *heteronomous* and *autonomous* systems. A heteronomous system is exogenously controlled and can clearly be modeled as an input-output system. In contrast, an autonomous system primarily is understood in terms of its "endogenous, self-organizing and self-controlling dynamics" and "does not have inputs and outputs in the usual sense" (Thompson 2010, 43). Instead of an input-output model, autonomous systems are understood in terms of perturbation and response. External factors perturb the ongoing endogenous dynamics of the system, yielding a response that must be understood in terms of the system's dynamics and its overall organization. More specifically,

> In complex systems theory, the term *autonomous* refers to a generic type of organization. The relations that define the autonomous organization hold between processes (such as metabolic reactions in a cell or neuronal firings in a cell assembly) rather than static entities. In an autonomous system, the

> constituent processes (i) recursively depend on each other for their generation and their realization as a network, (ii) constitute the system as a unity in whatever domain they exist, and (iii) determine a domain of possible interactions with the environment. (Thompson 2010, 44)

In biochemistry, Maturana and Varela (1992) call this type of autonomy *autopoiesis* (self-production). Autopoiesis involves what Varela terms a "logical bootstrap" or "loop" in which a network or process creates a boundary and is subsequently constrained by that boundary. This is the system's *organizational closure* (item ii in Thompson 2010). For instance, at the cellular level, a self-organizing process of biochemical reactions produces a membrane that, in turn, constrains the process that created it (Varela 2001). The completion of this loop gives rise to a distinct biological entity that maintains its own boundary in its environment. This new level of coherence is a "virtual identity" that is to be understood in terms of both boundary maintenance or organizational closure and a new mode of interaction with the environment. In addition, autopoietic systems are characterized by *operational closure* (item i in Thompson 2010): "the property that among the conditions affecting the operation of any constituent process in the system there will always be one or more processes that also belong to the system" (Di Paolo 2009, 15). Furthermore, autonomous systems are always coupled to their environments (item iii in Thompson 2010). As Thompson explains, "Two or more systems are coupled when the conduct of each is a function of the conduct of the other" (2010, 45). When two systems (organism and environment) develop a history of recurrent interactions leading to a "structural congruence" between them, we have *structural coupling.*

Sentient beings, on this view, are understood not as heteronomous, mechanical input-output systems but rather as dynamic, autonomous systems—necessarily coupled to the environment but also self-controlling. In addition, autonomous systems, in particular living and sentient systems, involve *emergent processes*. As Thompson describes, "An emergent process belongs to an ensemble or network of elements, arises spontaneously or self-organizes from the locally defined and globally constrained or controlled interactions of those elements, and does not belong to a single element" (2010, 60). Emergent processes and the systems in which they arise exhibit two forms of determination. Local-to-global determination involves the emergence of novel macrolevel processes and structures based on changes in the system components and relations. Global-to-local determination involves macrolevel processes and structures constraining local interactions. Thus self-organizing systems display *circular causality*: Local interactions give rise to global patterns or order, while the global order constrains the local interactions (Haken 2004).

The type of self-production and self-maintenance found in living systems goes beyond the type of self-organization seen in nonliving systems. The degree of autonomy found in living beings is, according to the enactive approach, a form of *dynamic coemergence*:

> Dynamic co-emergence best describes the sort of emergence we see in autonomy. In an autonomous system, the whole not only arises from the (organizational closure of the) parts, but the parts also arise from the whole. The whole is constituted by the relations of the parts, and the parts are constituted by the relations they bear to one another in the whole. Hence, the parts do not exist in advance, prior to the whole, as independent entities that retain their identity in the whole. Rather, part and whole co-emerge and mutually specify each other. (Thompson 2010, 65)

A candle flame (a common Buddhist analogy for nonsubstantial diachronic continuity) or a Bénard cell, as dissipative systems, displays self-organization and self-maintenance to a degree, but the key boundary conditions that keep these systems away from equilibrium are exogenous. In contrast, in truly autonomous systems, the "constraints that actually guide energy/matter flows from the environment through the constitutive processes of the system are endogenously created and maintained" (Ruiz-Mirazo and Moreno 2004, 238).

Returning to Buddhist reductionism, recall that Vasubandhu's criterion for the mere conventionality of a phenomenon was its actual or analytical decomposability. Moreover, the issue of decomposability, on the Abhidharma approach, is closely tied to reducibility. Full decomposability requires that the components of a complex entity are fully specifiable independently of their relations to one another and within the whole. Full reducibility further requires that the properties and (apparent) causal powers of the whole be determined by the intrinsic properties and causal powers of the independent and irreducible components.

However, in complex dynamic systems with *nonlinear* interactions, such as multicellular organisms, the immune system, and the brain, full decomposability is not possible. Nonlinear systems are characterized by nonadditive and nonproportional interactions (i.e., nonlinear interactions), and thus the system's properties cannot be aggregatively derived from the properties of its parts. As Thompson points out,

> An autonomous system is at least minimally decomposable, if not nondecomposable. More precisely, when one adopts an autonomy perspective, one *ipso facto* characterizes the system as at least minimally decomposable. The reason is that an autonomous system is an organizationally and operationally closed network; hence it is the connectivity of its constituent processes that determines its operation as a network. (2010, 421).

If this view is correct, then sentient beings, as living autonomous systems, are not amenable to the reductive analysis of the Abhidharma. Sentient beings are not sufficiently decomposable (if decomposable at all) to be exhaustively analyzed and explained in terms of the intrinsic properties and causal powers of independently specifiable components. In addition, the self-organizing, self-maintaining, and self-regulating capacities of living beings rely on both local-to-global and global-to-local influence, and therefore the causal capacities of the system qua system are both real and not determined by the intrinsic properties of their most basic components. In the case of such autonomous systems as human beings, we have mereological dependence without strict mereological reduction. However, it is important to note that the enactive approach is not a return to substantialism. Autonomous systems are not static, ontologically independent substances. Rather the autonomy and irreducibility of living beings derives from dense networks of relationality and interdependence. That is, autonomous systems are dependently originated (*pratītyasamutpanna*).

This tension between reductionist and emergentist approaches to sentient beings as dynamic systems, while relying on recent work in philosophy and biology, was not entirely unknown in classical Indian discussions. Indeed, as Ganeri (2013) argues, similar issues were at stake in the debate between Vasubandhu's Buddhist reductionism and the Pudgalavādins ("proponents of the reality of persons"). While the exact view of the Pudgalavādins is contentious, they arguably hold a nonreductionist or emergentist view of the person (*pudgala*) in relation to the psychophysical constituents considered both synchronically and diachronically (Carpenter 2015; Duerlinger 2003; Ganeri 2013; Priestley 1999). More specifically, they hold that the *pudgala* depends on but is not reducible to the aggregates, appealing to the analogy of fire's relation to fuel. Vasubandhu characterizes their view as follows:

> [The Pudgalavādins assert that] a person is not substantially real (*dravyataḥ*) or real by way of conception (*prajñaptitaḥ*), since he is conceived in reliance upon (*upādāya*) aggregates which pertain to himself, are acquired, and exist in the present. . . . A person is [conceived] in the way in which fire is conceived in reliance upon fuel. Fire is conceived in reliance upon fuel, it is not conceived unless fuel is present and cannot be conceived if it either is or is not other than fuel. . . . Similarly, a person is not conceived unless aggregates are present. If he were other than aggregates, the eternal transcendence theory [that a person is substantially real] would be held, and if he were not other than the aggregates, the nihilism theory [that a person does not exist at all] would be held. (Duerlinger 2003, 73–74)

So based on Vasubandhu's characterization, the Pudgalavādins hold that persons are not independent substances or ontologically basic particulars because they depend for their existence on the impersonal aggregates. However, and in sharp contrast to the Abhidharma reductionists, persons are not merely conceptual constructs imputed on the aggregates. Needless to say, this intermediate ontological status—dependent but irreducible—is perplexing to a Buddhist reductionist like Vasubandhu. As mentioned earlier, for the Buddhist reductionist, there is a dichotomy between that which is basic (*dravyasat*) and causally efficacious and that which is dependent and merely conceptually constructed (*prajñaptisat*), so there is no room in their ontology for *pudgalas* as the Pudgalavādins conceive of them.

So what kind of ontological status is the *pudgala* supposed to have here? I concur with Ganeri that the Pudgalavādins "use the term *pudgala* to refer to the macrostate of a dynamical system which is subject to a microdynamic (*pratītya-samutpāda*, 'combined origination in dependence') by which its total collective state at one time determines its state at the next" (Ganeri 2012, 139). Furthermore, in order to make good on the idea that the macrostate of the dynamic system is both dependent and irreducible, the Pudgalavādins seem committed to the claim that the *pudgala* has causal efficacy. Just how the macrostate of a dynamical system can affect the ongoing behavior of the system is a complicated matter and one that Vasubandhu was surely right to question. Indeed, I think that it is only with the development of the theory of self-organizing dynamic systems—and in particular the enactivist theory of dynamic coemergence—that we begin to see how this might work.[13] On this kind of view, the macrostate of the dynamic system emerges from the interactions of the system's components or lower-level states and in turn constrains the dynamic evolution of the system over time. So a sentient being is not an independent substance over and above the aggregates but rather a dynamic self-organizing whole, dependent on but irreducible to its parts or subsystems.

The Pudgalavādins were attempting to chart a middle way between the substantialist eternalism of Brahmanical views and the strong reductionism of Abhidharma (Duerlinger 2003). Their proposed solution was to posit the *pudgala* as a complex unity or a unity in multiplicity (Carpenter 2015) that could account for the synchronic and diachronic individuation of sentient beings without an appeal to the *ātman*. Moreover, there is an important *forensic* aspect of the person as a complex unity, having to do with the nature of *karma*. In the *Saṃmitīyanikāyaśastra* (I.165), for instance, we see the claim, "As to the deeds, one does one's own deeds. But what does self-done mean? A. It means that one receives (the fruits of one's own deeds). What does one's own deed mean? It means (to make) a distinction (between the deeds of oneself and those of another). But why? Because (the results of one's deed) do not go to another" (Carpenter 2015, 28). The Buddhist notion of *karma* requires a certain pattern of connection between intention, action, and result. One receives only the fruits of one's own deeds, yet as the Brahmanical critics of Buddhism never tired of pointing out, it is very hard to see how this *karmic* continuity is supposed to work in the absence of an enduring substantial self. The Pudgalavāda account of the person as a dynamic complex unity offers one possible Buddhist response to this difficulty. For, as Carpenter aptly puts it,

> The *pudgala* is, on this view, the mutual-relatedness of diverse kinds of elements at a time and over time. And it is just that belonging together which constitutes the possibility for moral agency, development, and unifying conceptualized reality. The capacities to serve as a moral agent and to develop are not reducible to the aggregates themselves, for all these presuppose the reality of some but not other elements' belonging together. None of this, note, implies the existence of an immaterial substantial substratum for the aggregates. (2015, 30)

SENTIENCE AND SUBJECTIVITY

The upshot of the previous section, for my purposes, is that Pudgalavāda and enactivism offer interesting and potentially fruitful accounts of sentient beings that navigate between the Scylla of substantialism and Charybdis of reductionism. In particular, with regard to sentient beings as *beings*, they offer a robust account of their synchronic and diachronic individuation. But, of course, sentient beings (let alone persons) are not merely dynamic, self-organizing systems; they are also *sentient* beings. So in this section, I take up the issue of sentience as well as the possible relationship between sentience and subjectivity.

One way to approach Buddhist accounts of sentience can be found in the *Majjhima Nikāya*:

> Dependent on the eye and forms, visual-consciousness arises. The meeting of the three is contact. With contact as condition there is feeling. What one feels, that one perceives. What one perceives, that one thinks about. What one thinks about, that one mentally proliferates. With what one has mentally proliferated as the source, perception and notions resulting from mental proliferation beset a man with respect to past, future, and present forms cognizable through the eye. (Ñānamoli and Bodhi 1995, 203)[14]

Here we find a description of the dependent origination of a complex sensory, affective, and cognitive process. Throughout the Buddhist literature, the arising of sensory awareness is analyzed in terms of six sense bases (*āyatana*). These are pairs of internal and external sensory bases: (1) eye and visual form, (2) ear and sound, (3) nose and odor, (4) tongue and taste (5) body and touch, and (6) mind and mental phenomena. Additionally, these pairs are sometimes further analyzed into triplets of sense object, sense organ, and sensory capacity. This more fine-grained analysis, then, can be deployed to cover cases of dysfunctional sense organs, such as eyes that cannot see. On the early Buddhist account, the arising of a moment of visual awareness depends on the causal contact (*sparśa*) between a (properly functioning) sense organ and a sensory object. And as we can see in the passage above, the arising of sensory awareness is closely connected to both affective response ("feeling," *vedanā*) and perceptual recognition ("perception," *saṃjñā*). So as an initial characterization of the early Buddhist account, a sentient being is one that has the requisite capacities for the arising of moments of sensory awareness.[15]

Turning to the enactive view, sentience is understood as the "feeling of being alive and exercising effort in movement" (Thompson 2010, 161). Sentience here entails a basic form of phenomenal consciousness Thompson describes as a "kind of primitively self-aware liveliness or animation of the body" (2010, 161). Further, it is closely connected to the account of cognition as sense-making. According to Thompson,

> Sense-making is threefold: (1) sensibility as openness to the environment (intentionality as openness); (2) significance as positive or negative valence of environmental conditions relative to the norms of the living being (intentionality as passive synthesis—passivity, receptivity, and affect); and (3) the direction or orientation the living being adopts in response to significance and valence (intentionality as protentional and teleological). (2011, 119)

In humans and other animals capable of phenomenal consciousness, these three aspects of sense-making are operative in sentient experience. However, it is important to note that sense-making and sentience are not coextensive. First, on the enactive view, life itself is a sense-making process, but not all life is sentient (Thompson 2010, 160–62). The E. coli bacterium that swims up a sugar gradient is sense-making, but it does not follow that it is conscious. Second, even in conscious animals, there is unconscious or preconscious sense-making. Nevertheless, on the enactive view, a sentient being is one that has a primitive phenomenal feeling of being alive, and its ongoing experience of itself and its world is structured by the previously mentioned aspects of sense making.

Furthermore, it is worth noting that both the Buddhist and the enactivist accounts of sentience involve deep interdependence between sensation, affect, and conation. As just discussed, the enactive view of sense making involves sensibility (basic sensory awareness or even just sensitivity), significance (especially affective valence), and orientation (including basic conative impulses). Likewise, according to the Buddhist twelve links of dependent origination (*dvādaśanidānāni*), sensory contact (*sparśa*) in any of the six sense bases leads to feeling (*vedanā*), which leads to craving (*tṛṣṇa*) and then to clinging (*upādāna*). In other words, a specific sensory-affective-conative dynamic is central to the Buddhist account of our (*saṃsāric*) situation as sentient beings.

In short, sentient beings are (self-organizing) dynamic systems capable of conscious sensation, feeling, and action. Understanding the life and activities of such systems requires an appeal to their sentience and sense-making capacities. And again, none of this requires appeal to substantial selves or even substantial organisms. Rather, sentient beings here are conceived as dependently originated and impermanent systems, networks of dynamic processes and relations that, partly through their own endogenous activities, maintain their organization over time within the impermanent flux of the larger environment. The crucial difference between sentient beings and other living systems, of course, is their capacity for conscious interiority, for the "feeling of being alive."[16]

Despite what I take to be the potential compatibility between these accounts of sentient beings, it is important to note that, for Thompson, sentience entails *subjectivity*, a notion that is at the very least problematic for Buddhist thinkers, for whom *anātmavāda* is axiomatic. The worry here is straightforward: Sentience entails subjectivity, subjectivity entails a subject, and a subject just is a *self*. I think things are not quite so straightforward, and the task of the rest of this chapter is to begin to trace some of the connections and differences between these terms.

At this point, the pertinent questions concern the possible relationship between sentience and subjectivity. In order to get a better handle on these questions, it is helpful to distinguish four types or dimensions of subjectivity. First, we should distinguish between *creature* subjectivity and *state* subjectivity.[17] Creature subjectivity has to do with a being (organism, person) as a whole. At this level of analysis, pertinent questions might be, Is this organism a subject of experiences? Does it use self-specifying information in its sensorimotor interaction with its environment? Does it have a (practical or phenomenological) first-person perspective? What are the neurobiological or evolutionary conditions of the emergence of (creature) subjectivity? And so on. State subjectivity has to do with the (possible) subjective character of particular mental states, events, or processes. At this level of analysis, pertinent questions might be, Do all (or any) mental states have subjective character? What is the relationship between state subjectivity and a sense of mental ownership (or agency)? What is the relationship between subjectivity and self-consciousness? Is subjectivity involved in bodily consciousness?

Does subjectivity imply a sense of self (or the existence of a self)? And so on.

The next distinction to be made here is between *phenomenal* and *nonphenomenal* aspects of subjectivity. As the term suggests, phenomenal subjectivity has to do with the qualitative and structural features of conscious experience. How, if at all, does subjectivity (creature or state) *show up* and *shape* lived experience? Nonphenomenal subjectivity has to do with those aspects of subjectivity that are not essentially understood in terms of conscious experience. Thus, for example, if there are unconscious mental states that have subjective character (on some specified analysis of subjective character), then this would be a nonphenomenal form of subjectivity. Or one may point to an organism's practical or functional grasp of itself (or aspects of itself) as forms of nonphenomenal creature subjectivity.[18]

With these initial distinctions in place, we can return to the question of whether sentience implies (some form of) subjectivity. For the Abhidharma reductionist, it would seem, the answer is a firm *no*. The basic ontology of ephemeral *dharmas* combined with a strong mereological reductionism—indeed a mereological nihilism at the ultimate level—rules out mental events either belonging to or combining to form a real subject. Thus, there occur sentient (i.e., sensory, affective, etc.) events with causal connections to other types of events, but creature subjectivity would be at best a conventional construction and more accurately construed as a manifestation of *satkāyadṛṣti* (the delusion of real individuality). Indeed, as Ganeri remarks, for the Buddhist reductionist, "There is nothing that owns mental tropes [*dharmas*,] and they don't aggregate to form subjects (it is the fundamental wrong move to think that any of the mental items, or the collective stream, *is* a subject)" (2012, 42). Another way to see the issue here is that creature subjectivity implies a degree of systemic integration ruled out by Abhidharma reductionism. Of course, a reductionist like Vasubandhu can endorse subjectivity *talk* at the conventional level, but he will give a suitably deflationary and reductionist gloss on such talk at the level of ultimate analysis.

When it comes to the issue of state or event subjectivity, again the Abhidharma reductionist will deny that mental events have a subjective character in any robust sense. Mental dharmas with certain qualitative features—say, sensory or affective—arise in dependence on their causes and conditions. In this sense, it seems the Abhidharma reductionist can affirm that these events are *like something* in the phenomenal sense. However, the classic Nagelian gloss on phenomenal consciousness includes more than this: "what it's like *for the organism*," where this implies not just that the events occur within the organism but also that qualitative events are manifest in the organism's subjective experience in the right kind of way. In short, phenomenal consciousness involves what it is like *for a subject.* On this view, states or events with a qualitative character are had from within a first-person or subjective perspective, and so we might say that qualitative character and subjective character both contribute to the overall phenomenal character of consciousness (Kriegel 2009). And it is this latter point that must be rejected by an Abhidharma reductionist. For them, subjectivity or subjective character is not a central feature of our conscious mental states but a distortion of their true character.

I have much more to say about state subjectivity in the next chapter, so here I focus on creature subjectivity. My argument is that sentience and creature subjectivity are functionally interwoven and may have coevolved. On the view I sketch later, creature subjectivity may have evolved as a solution to problems of coordinating sensation, feeling, and action in a complex and changing environment. Again, while the E. coli bacterium is sensitive to certain features in its environment (e.g., sugar), which it then seeks in order to metabolize it—that is, it engages in a basic form of sense-making—this is not yet sufficient for creature subjectivity on my view. Rather, we should look to animals with sophisticated nervous systems. A mobile animal needs to be able to coordinate perception and action in a much more flexible and adaptive fashion in order to survive. It must not only keep track of (often-changing) objects or events in its environment but must also keep track of how the sensory world changes in relation to its own actions within that world. That is, an animal that is both highly sensitive to its environment and capable of flexible mobility will encounter what Merker (2005) calls "liabilities of mobility," whereby some of the stimuli to which the animal is sensitive are caused by the animal itself. In this case, the animal needs to keep track of the difference between its *own* movements and other changes in its sensory environment. And this requires a grasp on the self-other distinction in the context of perception and action. Indeed, tracking the self-other distinction in perception and action over time is central to having a point of view. My suggestion is that this practical grasp of the self-other distinction is one of the roots of creature subjectivity.

In addition, affect and affective appraisal are also potential elements in the evolution of creature subjectivity. In this context, a *feeling* can be understood as an affective or valenced response to the organism's internal or external milieu: for instance, hunger or fear. These responses are often positive or negative and tied to motivation or action. But to see what they have to do with subjectivity, we need to look at recent work in affective neuroscience on the evolution of subjectivity (or a sense of self). Antonio Damasio, for instance, argues extensively that feelings are at the root of both consciousness and the most basic sense of self (or what I have been calling creature subjectivity).[19] For him, the root sense of subjectivity arises from the unconscious integration of information about the environment, the organism's internal milieu, and the dynamic relations between them. Indeed, "without a sense of self and without the feelings that integrate it," he writes, "such large-scale integration of information would not be oriented to the problems of life, namely survival and the achievement of well-being" (Damasio 2003, 208). This affective subjectivity is at the root of the organism's *orientation* and *concern*. He continues,

> The sense of self introduces, within the mental level of processing, the notion that all the current activities represented in brain and mind pertain to a single organism whose auto-preservation needs are the basic cause of most events currently represented. The sense of self orients the mental planning process toward the satisfaction of those needs. That orientation is only possible because feelings are integral to the cluster of operations that constitutes the sense of self, and because feelings are continuously generating, within the mind, a concern for the organism. (Damasio 2003, 208)

The basic orientation of the organism is its own continued viability, and its concerns are internal and external events or states of affairs that bear on that fundamental orientation. Here we see an important connection to the enactive account of sense-making. Damasio's notion of concern overlaps with the second aspect of sense-making, namely significance and valence. An animal has an ongoing concern to obtain sufficient food, and items (and opportunities) in its environment will have a particular significance and valence in relation to that concern. Damasio's notion of orientation overlaps with the third aspect of sense making, which Thompson also calls orientation. But the key thing to note here is the role of feelings—such as pleasure, pain, or fear—in orientation and concern. For Damasio, feelings are generally salient, motivational, and directly tied to the organism's self-concern. Furthermore, in sophisticated organisms, a sense of itself as subject (or what he calls the core self) serves to integrate the sensory, affective, and conative states and process to facilitate viable activity in a changing environment.

A closely related view can be found in the work of Jaak Panksepp and colleagues. For instance, Panksepp and George Northoff argue for a "trans-species core self." As they characterize it,

> we suggest a trans-species concept of self that is based upon what has been called a "core-self" which can be described by self-related processing (SRP) as a specific mode of interaction between organism and environment. When we refer to specific neural networks, we will here refer to the underlying system as the "core-SELF." The core-SELF provides primordial neural coordinates that represent organisms as living creatures—at the lowest level this elaborates interoceptive states along with raw emotional feelings (i.e., the intentions in action of a primordial core-SELF) while higher medial cortical levels facilitate

> affective-cognitive integration (yielding a fully-developed nomothetic core-self). Developmentally, SRP allows stimuli from the environment to be related and linked to organismic needs, signaled and processed within core-self structures within subcortical-cortical midline structures (SCMS). (Panksepp and Northoff 2009, 193)

The core self, then, facilitates adaptive organism-environment interaction by integrating environmental stimuli with affective and conative processes of the organism itself. This ongoing integration allows the organism, in a functional and pragmatic way, to make sense of its environment by connecting states and changes in that environment to its own feelings, needs, and drives.

The upshot, in my view, is that creature subjectivity—and therefore the emergence of certain complex organisms as *subjects*—is the evolved solution to a set of problems faced by motile, sensitive organisms in challenging environments. Having a sensorimotor and affective point of view that tracks internal and external events in relation to the ongoing needs and feelings of the organism itself does not imply the existence of an enduring mental substance or any kind of inner homunculus. However, it does require a high degree of self-organizing and adaptive integration of the kind seen only—so far as we know—with the emergence of life. In this sense, I agree with Vasubandhu that, as Ganeri puts it, "mental tropes don't aggregate to form subjects" (Ganeri 2012, 42). But, contra Vasubandhu, I think it is quite plausible that living systems evolve to become subjects. Moreover, whether sentience strictly speaking *entails* (creature) subjectivity or not, there is reason to think that sentience and subjectivity are functionally and developmentally interwoven in the only sentient beings we know of—that is, humans and our fellow animals.

SUBJECTIVITY AND SELF

According to the line of thinking sketched in the previous section, a sentient being is one that is capable of conscious sensation, feeling, and action. Creature subjectivity arises from and facilitates the synchronic and diachronic integration of sensation, feeling, and action and constitutes a sentient organismic perspective in and on the world. In this way, sentience and subjectivity are deeply connected, and any being that has both sentience and subjectivity is, in my terms, a *subject*. Moreover, one might reasonably treat being a subject and being a *self* as coextensive. Indeed, as mentioned in the previous section, both Damasio and Panksepp use the term *core self* to characterize what I am calling creature subjectivity or simply being a subject. However, I want to maintain a distinction between subject and self, where being a subject is necessary but not sufficient for being a self.[20] I have three main reasons for maintaining the subject-self distinction.

First, one of my goals here is to deepen and extend the dialogue between Buddhist and Western accounts of mind, self, and consciousness. Yet by defining the self too broadly, one may miss the critical power and philosophical sophistication of Buddhist no-self views. When Indian Buddhist thinkers reject any notion of self, *they really mean it*, and this uncompromising stance yields a number of powerful accounts of mind and related phenomena. Second, I am interested in the possibility of a *developmental* account of subjectivity and self. How could subjects or even selves emerge (if they do) in the course of evolution or in the life of particular sentient beings? And it seems quite reasonable that, in many cases, more sophisticated aspects or capacities of living beings build on simpler or more basic ones. On the view I develop in this section, being a self is an evolutionarily and developmentally more sophisticated phenomenon that builds on sentience and primitive forms of subjectivity. Third, I am interested in the phenomenology of subjectivity and selfhood, and as is explored in the next chapter, I think the phenomenology points to an account of the sense of self as complex and variable rather than simple and fixed. Of course, I could be wrong in all these contentions, but they motivate my exploration of the emergence of the self as a complex construct.

So, how is being a *self* different from being a *subject*? On my view, being a self involves the synchronic and diachronic integration of (at least) four paradigmatic capacities or features: (1) subjectivity, (2) ownership, (3) agency, and (4) valuation. In the normal case, there are both functional and phenomenological dimensions to the ongoing integration of these features. Further, on this view, the emergence of the self is linked to the emergence of a degree of psychological autonomy from the biological autonomy of living systems. Hence, the self is a complex or pattern of processes and capacities, not a substantial entity. It emerges from and is sustained by selfless psychobiological processes and structures. The self, then, is the ongoing functional and phenomenological integration and maintenance of subjectivity, ownership, agency, and valuation.

In line with the discussion in the previous section, (creature) subjectivity involves sentience, sensorimotor integration, and a diachronically stable organismic perspective. The function of subjectivity is to coordinate sensation, feeling, and action in motile organisms so that they may more flexibly respond to internal and external events. Thus, creature subjectivity is closely connected to the sense of agency. As Christoff and colleagues argue, "experiencing oneself as an agent depends on the existence of specific types of dynamic interactive processes between the organism and its environment. We call these processes 'self-specifying' because they implement a functional self/non-self distinction that explicitly specifies the self as subject and agent" (2011, 105). As discussed in the previous section, a sophisticated motile organism needs to be able to integrate sensory, affective, and motor stimuli. But more specifically, it must be able to functionally distinguish between sensory changes arising from the environment and sensory changes arising from its own motor actions. Christoff and colleagues further propose that in order to do this, organisms must be able to distinguish between *exafference*—afferent signals arising from environmental events—and *reafference*—afferent signals arising from the organism's efferent processes (2011, 105). The key point here is that the functional self-nonself distinction is the basis for the organism specifying itself as subject (recipient of nonself stimuli) and agent (originator of motor actions). On my account, the shift from subject to self involves incorporating this distinction into the level of conscious experience and ultimately into a diachronic sense of subjectivity and agency. That is, in order to be a self, a sentient being must (in the typical case) have a sentient perspective or subjectivity and a sense of agency, an experience of initiating and controlling actions (Braun et al. 2018).[21]

In contrast to subjectivity and the sense of agency, the sense of ownership involves the feeling of mine-ness toward one's body, feelings, thoughts, and so on (Gallagher 2000). The sense of ownership can be further divided into subcategories, including limb ownership, a sense of global body ownership, and mental state or event ownership. In the normal case, the senses of ownership and agency coincide, but they do not always do so. For instance, if I am suddenly shoved from behind, I will sense that it is *my* body that is moving, but I will not have the sense of having initiated the movement myself. Or in certain delusions of control, one might have the feeling of initiating movement in another's body or in an inanimate object. Furthermore, there can occur disruptions in different aspects of the sense of ownership, such as cases of limb disownership, wherein one may no longer feel that one of their limbs is their own while retaining a global sense of body ownership (Ataria 2015). A number of neurocognitive mechanisms for generating the sense of ownership have been hypothesized (Tsakiris and De Preester 2018), and I make no claim to any particular hypothesis. However, it is worth noting that a number of lines of evidence converge on the idea that the sense of ownership involves sensorimotor and multisensory integration, as well as the complex integration of both exteroception and interoception (Fotopoulou and Tsakiris 2017). That is, in addition to maintaining a self-other distinction in action and perception, the sense of ownership is also rooted in the internal dimensions of proprioception, interoception, and affect, which seem to provide an internal sense of the body and of feeling as one's own. My current point, though, is just that a sense of ownership is a paradigmatic feature of the overall sense of self.

Finally, in addition to subjectivity, agency, and ownership, I posit that to be a self is to engage in *valuation*. Recall that, on the enactivist account, sense-making involves significance, valence, and orientation. Furthermore, recall that, on the Buddhist account of the five *skandhas*, sentient beings interact with the world in part on the complex interplay of *vedanā* (affect, valence); *samjñā* (perception, cognition); and *samskāra* (volition, dispositions). On both accounts, an organism makes sense of its environment (or itself) in terms of the positive or negative valence of events or states of affairs and orients its own responses accordingly. What I call valuation is just this way of making sense of and interacting with the world in terms of significance and valence. Further, following Damasio, I would add a more global notion of *concern*, which can be understood as the basic orientation of the organism to its own survival and viability. Now, valuation is an aspect of sense-making, and sense-making is an aspect of living—as Thompson puts it, "living is sense-making" (2010, 158)—so all living systems engage in valuation to some degree. However, on the view I sketch here, beings that are selves are capable of *conscious* valuation, and because valuation will be integrated with more complex forms of subjectivity, agency, and ownership, such beings can guide their living in part in terms of their valuing.[22] Selves, at minimum, are organisms that can consciously value things and act accordingly.

According to the view I develop in these last two sections, sentient beings of any degree of sophistication could plausibly display subjectivity, agency, ownership, and valuation. Further, Buddhist *anātmavadins* affirm the conventional reality of sentient beings, whether they give a reductionist account of their conventional reality or not. Perhaps one should side with the no-self thinkers and affirm that there are only selfless sentient beings and no selves. Or perhaps one should side with the core self and minimal self thinkers and affirm that subjects *just are* selves. In the end, what is the real difference between (mere?) sentient beings or subjects and *selves*? On my view, the key difference between a mere subject and self comes down to increased *integration* and enhanced psychological *capacities*. A sentient being is a self when its subjectivity, agency, ownership, and valuation are integrated in such a way that it has enhanced psychological control and flexible responsiveness to its environment. In addition, the integration must be both synchronic and diachronic. Paradigmatic selves are capable of things like episodic memory, planning, and other forms of mental time travel.[23] Further, synchronic and diachronic integration is in the service of enhanced capacity. Selves can do a wider variety of things than can mere sentient beings *because* they are psychophysically integrated in the right kinds of ways.

The self is not a substantial *thing*. Rather, it is a complex structure or pattern of processes and capacities. This structure emerges from and is sustained by selfless processes and structures of the living organism. The self is the ongoing integration and maintenance of subjectivity, agency, ownership, and valuation in the life of the organism itself. In this sense, my account of the self is both emergentist and *functionalist*. A self is what it does and what it allows the organism to do. The view I sketch, therefore, is part of a broadly pragmatist tradition of understanding the self. In this tradition, the choice between a substantial self and no-self is a false one. As the twentieth-century pragmatist Risieri Frondizi puts it,

> The existence of the [self] does not depend upon any obscure or hidden substantial core, but upon what it does, what it has done, what it wants and what it is able to do. The self reveals itself by its activities; it reveals itself and constitutes itself by its doing, its behaviour. . . . The self is not something made once for all, but something that is always in the making. There is no original nucleus independent of its activities or experiences, no original stuff. If we take the activities away, the self becomes an abstraction very difficult to distinguish from a non-entity. To interpret the self correctly, we must replace, therefore, the category of substance by that of function. The concept of function connotes, in this case, those of activity, process, and relation. (2011, 445)

Of course, on a broadly functionalist account of the self, the central question is, What does the self *do*?[24] In light of the considerations introduced in this chapter, one plausible answer is that the emergence of the self amplifies biological autonomy into a form of psychological autonomy. Recall that biological autonomy, on an enactivist account, consists in autopoietic self-organization plus adaptivity. A biologically autonomous system is characterized by organizational closure, operational closure, and the capacity to regulate its own interactions with the environment (adaptivity). Adaptivity increases the system's flexible responsiveness and, according to DiPaolo, is a necessary precursor to the emergence of cognition. Psychological autonomy here involves enhanced endogenous integration, self-control, and adaptive flexibility arising from the distinctively mental capacities of the system. More complex forms of psychological autonomy are linked to such capacities as intersubjectivity, autobiographical consciousness, and sociality.

To borrow terminology from Jennan Ismael, the emergence of the self marks the transition from a self-organizing system to a *self-governing* system. As she explains,

> self-governing systems are a subclass of complex, open systems characterized by an internal dynamics that incorporates a self-representational loop and supports flexibility of response function. They store information about themselves

> in an explicit form and combine that information with new input to compute the values of self-locating parameters, which are then used to regulate responses to occurrent stimuli, making fluid change in first-order dynamical properties possible in real time. (Ismael 2011, 12)

Self-governance is a matter of degree, but the key point here is that with the emergence of the self, the system has enhanced powers of self-governance, such as conscious self-control, flexible anticipation, imagination, navigation, and planning. Presumably, the emergence of sentience allowed for greater adaptive responsiveness for organisms. Similarly, on this account, the emergence of selves allowed for even more sophisticated and diachronically integrated *psychological* capacities. There is no inner homuncular or substantial self, but being a self is more than just a phenomenological *sense* of self and more than just the *appearance* centralized integration and control in a self-organizing system. To be a self, in this enactive and functionalist sense, is to be able to experience and do things that a merely self-organizing system cannot, in virtue of the internal organization of the system's own processes and capacities. To return to Ismael, the "nice thing about this view of the unity of the self is that it doesn't require the recognition of selves as primitive constituents of the universe. Constructing a point of view that spans modalities, or spans temporal perspectives on this sort of view at the same time constitutes a self as occupant of that point of view" (2016, 48).

SELF MAKING

I have been exploring an enactivist, functionalist approach to the self as an alternative to both substantialism and eliminativism or strong reductionism. On this account, the self is neither a preexisting entity nor a mere illusion or fiction but rather an enacted, emergent construct. As is explored in chapter 4, the self is in an important sense *made* by the very system with which it comes to be identified. As a construct, the self is constructed from selfless processes and capacities. Yet I have also asserted that the self is nevertheless *real.* This enactivist view of the self as real but constructed is in contrast to Francisco Varela's enactivist account of the self a merely *virtual.*

Varela (1999a, 2001), explicitly drawing on Buddhist philosophy, argues that the human self is both emergent and *virtual* or *empty* (*śūnya*). He therefore rejects the existence of a substantial, bounded, enduring self. The self, he argues, emerges from the human organism's endogenous neurobiological dynamics and from its embeddedness in its natural and social-linguistic environment.[25] We create and re-create ourselves from moment to moment through the dynamic interaction of brain, body, language, and world. He writes,

> Why do emergent selves, virtual identities, pop up all over the place creating worlds, whether at the mind/body level, the cellular level, or the transorganism level? This phenomenon is something so productive that it doesn't cease creating entirely new realms: life, mind, and societies. Yet these emergent selves are based on processes so shifty, so ungrounded, that we have an apparent paradox between the solidity of what appears to show up and its groundlessness. (Varela 2001)

These systems behave *as if* a central agent or controller is directing them—yet no such central agent can be found. This is what Varela means by the virtual or empty self: a "coherent global pattern that emerges from the activity of simple local components, which seems to be centrally located, but is nowhere to be found, and yet is essential as a level of interaction for the behavior of the whole" (1999a, 53).

The view I have been sketching also takes the self to be a coherent global pattern, a kind of dynamic gestalt that is essential for the functional capacities of the whole system. The self is an emergent pattern that cannot be located as a substantial entity because that is the wrong ontological category for selves. So far, then, the view agrees with Varela's. However, whether the self turns out to be *śūnya* in a technical Buddhist sense is a more complicated matter, depending on which of the various and contested notions of emptiness one is appealing to. I have more to say about emptiness and its implications in chapter 4. For now, the key difference between Varela's view and my own is whether the self is *virtual*.

Varela is avowedly in agreement with the Buddhist theory of no-self. On his account, "either we are unique in the living and natural world, or else our very immediate sense of a central, personal self is the same kind of illusion of a center, accountable by more of the same kind of analysis [i.e., in terms of autopoiesis]" (Varela 1999a, 61). Moreover, "what we call 'I' can be analyzed as arising out of our recursive linguistic abilities and their unique capacity for self-description and narration" (Varela 1999a, 61). Indeed, this linguistically constructed self serves as what he terms a "virtual interface" between the body and the natural and social environment in which it is embedded. On my interpretation of Varela, there are two connected dimensions to the virtuality of the self. The first concerns the insubstantial and distributed nature of the self. The self appears to be substantial and localized, but on the enactivist view of organisms as autopoietic systems, it isn't. Varela likens the appearance of a centralized self to the illusion of a centralized controller of an ant colony. There is no such controller but only various self-organizing dynamics. The second concerns the self as a kind of illusion or fiction. Here I think he is committed to antirealism about the self, as his explicit endorsement of Buddhist *anātmavāda* and Dennett's (useful) fictionalism attest.

Varela's enactivist account of the self, then, is based on a view of sentient beings as self-organizing systems and antirealism about the "central, personal self." In contrast, the enactivist view I have been developing is based on a view of some sentient beings as self-governing systems and a form of pragmatic realism about the self. Recall that, according to Ismael, self-governing systems are a distinct subclass of self-organizing systems. Self-organizing systems, she writes, are a

> special class of dynamical systems. The hallmark of self-organization is the appearance of order in a system of interacting components without any centralized control. There is dispute about whether there is a general dynamical characterization that covers all of the central examples, but central examples include termite colonies, schools of fish, unregulated crowds, traffic systems, and free market economies. In these cases there is no real centralization of information or control, but the actions of each affect the others in a manner that produces an overall appearance of deliberately coordinated activity. (Ismael 2014, 278)

Varela seems to understand sentient beings as self-organizing systems in this sense. The autopoietic dynamics of the system give the *mere appearance* of centralized control, leading to a form of antirealism about the self as a centralized controller. However, Ismael points out,

> In a self-governing system, by contrast, there is some centralization of information and some top-down regulation of behaviour. If we were to give a formal rendering of the difference between self-organizing and self-governing systems, the crucial difference for our purposes is that in a self-governing system there is both an epistemic standpoint that synthesizes the collective knowledge and a system-wide deliberative standpoint that plays some role guiding the activity of the system in which the collective good appears explicitly as a term in the utility calculation. (2014, 278)

The payoff here, as I have suggested, is a greatly increased flexibility of response to the demands of a complex environment. The behavior of purely self-organizing systems is driven by the environment and the dynamic properties of the components. Explicit, ongoing tracking of the organism and its environment by the organism itself, however, introduces new internal variables that allow a system to respond in a way that is not entirely driven by the current environmental stimulus.

So, on my version of the enactivist view, the self—an ongoing integration of subjectivity, agency, ownership, and valuation yielding enhanced psychological autonomy—is more than just the *mere appearance* of centralized control. Rather, it is the *emergence* of some degree of centralized control and the enriched first-person perspective that goes along with it. Moreover, because the enactive self is a genuine emergence that enhances the functional capacity of the system, we should not be antirealists about the self. Instead, this enactivist view suggests a form of pragmatic realism about the self. On this view, the self is neither a ready-made entity nor a mere fiction. The self is what it does and what it allows the whole system to do, and it is always in the making. To be a pragmatic realist, then, is to affirm the existence of the self in these pragmatic, broadly functionalist terms. Furthermore, my view is enactivist in that the self emerges from and facilitates the self-organizing activity and ongoing interaction of the system in its environment.

Since the approach was first articulated in *The Embodied Mind* (1991), enactivist thinkers have developed both antirealist and realist views of the self. In a recent paper, Vishnu Sridharan takes issue with realist enactivists and argues in favor of Varela's original antirealism. According to Sridharan, realist enactivists

> argue that the same principles that Varela outlines to discuss the existence and functioning of biological processes such as cells, organs, and organisms apply with equal force to the "self." In other words, they believe that the self is empty, but only in the same manner as every-thing else is empty also (MacKenzie, 2010), and that "autonomous self-individuation is not limited to biological processes but can be found at higher levels of cognition, too" (Kyselo, 2014, p. 6). (2015, 184)

He goes on to argue that the self as understood by realist enactivists does not meet the criteria of being an autonomous system. Therefore, the proposed symmetry between the self and the organism fails, and he continues that Varela's view of the self as virtual should be maintained.

In response to this line of argument, let me return to the two dimensions of virtuality. The first dimension involves the question of how distributed or centralized is the global pattern of the emergent self. The second dimension involves realism or antirealism (including fictionalism) about the self. Sridharan interprets realist enactivists, like myself, as arguing for a double symmetry—that the self is both empty and an autonomous system, just like the organism as a whole. However, on the view I develop here, the self is not an autonomous system in its own right. It is an emergent pattern within the life of the sentient organism as a whole. In my view, what makes the self more than virtual is that it provides the sentient organism with enhanced centralized control and an enriched first-person perspective. There is an ontological asymmetry between the organism and the self, but that asymmetry is orthogonal to the questions of realism and of emptiness. This asymmetry can be obscured because of an ambiguity in how we use the term *self*: sometimes as a psychological reality and sometimes as the whole being. Again, on my view, sentient beings, including persons, are autonomous systems, but the self is the ongoing integration of subjectivity, agency, ownership, and valuation within the life of that system.

Concerning the second dimension, the fact that the self is not an autonomous system in its own right does not entail that it is merely virtual. The issue here is whether a given system is best understood as a (merely) self-organizing system, much like an ant colony, or whether, in virtue of certain emergent psychological (or psychophysical) capacities, the system is self-governing. Furthermore, whether the self should be understood as empty depends on which notion of emptiness is being deployed. From the perspective of Buddhist reductionism, emptiness entails the full reducibility of the empty, conventional thing to that which is not empty, the ultimately real *dharmas*. Because enactivists are nonreductionists about organisms, they would not count as empty in the Buddhist reductionist sense. However, Varela's antirealism about the self is consistent with the Buddhist reductionist view of emptiness. However, if one appeals to a Madhyamaka notion of emptiness, as Varela himself does, things are more complicated. Mādhyamikas hold that *all* things are empty of inherent existence, and on some prominent interpretations, this amounts to a form of global antirealism. On this interpretation of emptiness, the enactivist self is empty, but so is everything else. In this case, the empty-nonempty distinction does not track the virtual-nonvirtual distinction as Varela deploys it.

CONCLUSION

I briefly situate my view of the self in relation to Jonardon Ganeri's (2012) taxonomy of views of the self. Ganeri bases his taxonomy on the technical distinction between *āśraya* ("base") and *ādhāra* ("place") (2012, 38). An *āśraya* is an ontological support or base and can also be that which individuates an entity. An *ādhāra*, in this context, is the location or place of experience, in the sense of what (if anything) *has*, *undergoes*, or *owns* it. In short, the *āśraya* concerns individuation, while the ādhāra concerns ownership.

Ganeri derives his taxonomy of eleven possible views and four types from different possible combinations of base, place, and their relations in each account of the self. Type I views posit the same thing as both base and place of experience (Ganeri 2012, 40). A Cartesian view of the self, for instance, posits the self is both the owner ("place") and the ontological ground ("base") of experiences. Likewise, a Materialist view holds that it is the physical body that is both base and place. Type II views, in contrast, have different things playing the roles of base and place. A Phenomenal view, according to Ganeri, posits the self as place and the stream of experience as base. An Ownership view posits the self as place and the body as base. Type III views, which Ganeri associates with Buddhist thought, reject the notion of a place of experience as such. As Ganeri puts it, "The No Place View is that the happenings of the mind are not owned. The mind's ontology is one of tropes not properties. . . . So the notion of a *place* for mental states is an idle one, but the notion of individuating *base* is still available" (2012, 43). Finally, Type IV views hold that the stream of experience itself is the place or owner. Here a mental state or event is owned or finds its place in virtue of its connection to other mental events that form an ongoing mental stream or mental life. In contrast to the Phenomenal view, in Type IV views, the self is not found within the stream; rather it *is* the stream. In contrast to Type III views, the notion of a place or owner of a mental life is not an idle one.

So how does my account of an emergent, enacted self fit within Ganeri's taxonomy? It should be clear by this point that I reject the No Place, or Type III, view. On my view, there are subjects, and some subjects are selves. Because the self emerges from and is sustained by mental and biological process that are prior to the self, it cannot be a Type I, or Cartesian, view. Further, because the stream of sentient experience is prior to the emergent self both temporally and ontologically, this would seem to rule out Type IV views.[26] That leaves the Type II, or Real Self, view. For sentient beings that are selves, the enacted, emergent self is the place or owner of experience. The ongoing integration of subjectivity, ownership, agency, and valuation in experience is what makes one's mental life one's own in the robust sense we typically associate with being a self. On the question of the base, given my account of the mind as fundamentally embodied, this inclines my view toward the Ownership view—that is, to the view that self is place and the body (or living organism) is base. However, it seems to me that my view of the self is consistent with the Phenomenal view in that one might hold that the stream of mental life is the base for the self (that from which emerges and on which it depends).[27] In short, in contrast to substantialism, eliminativism, and antirealism, on my account, the self is enacted, emergent, and real.

NOTES

1. The term *saṃjñā* (*sam*: *together* + *jña*: *knowledge*) is cognate to "cognize" and can have the sense of "synthesis" as well as "association." Lusthaus translates *saṃjñā* as *associational knowledge* (2003, 47).

2. The classic version of the criterial argument occurs in *Saṃyutta Nikāya* 3.66–68.

3. This argument occurs in the "Refutation of the Theory of the Self," 1.2. See Duerlinger (2003) for a translation.

4. *'yatra bhinnena tadbuddhir anyāpohe dhiyā ca tat | ghaṭārthavat saṃvṛtisat paramārthasad anyathā ||'.*

5. Continuity is a weaker relation than identity, in that continuity comes in degrees, while identity is all or nothing. Nonsubstantialist theories of the person typically account for diachronic personal identity in terms of continuity.

6. Though the reductionist still owes us an account of how to get from causal connections to the kind of semantic and (broadly) narrative connections that seem to play an important role in any plausible account of psychological continuity.

7. *yadapyālayavijñānaṃ nāma vāsanāśrayatvēna parikalpitam, tadapi kṣaṇikatvābhyupagamādanavasthitasvarūpaṃ sat, pravṛttivijñānavanna vāsanānāmadhikaraṇaṃ bhavitumarhati; na hi kālatrayasaṅbandhinyēkasminna nvayinyasati kūṭasthē vā sarvārthadarśini dēśakālanimittāpēkṣavāsanādhīnasm ṛtipratisaṅdhānādivyavahāraḥ saṅbhavati; sthirasvarūpatvē tvālayavijñānasya siddhāntahāniḥ. api ca vijñānavādē.pikṣaṇikatvābhyupagamasya samānatvāt, yāni bāhyārthavādē kṣaṇikatvanibandhanāni dūṣaṇānyudbhāvitāni—'uttarōtpādē ca pūrvanirōdhāt' ityēvamādīni, tānīhāpyanusaṅdhātavyāni.* ēvamētau *dvāvapi vaināśikapakṣau nirākṛtau—bāhyārthavādipakṣō vijñānavādipakṣaśca;* śūnyavādipakṣastu *sarvapramāṇavipratiṣiddha iti tannirākaraṇāya nādaraḥ kriyatē. na hyayaṃ sarvapramāṇasiddhō lōkavyavahārō. nyattattvamanadhigamya* śakyatē. *pahnōtum, apavādābhāvē utsargaprasiddhēḥ.*

8. *First-person givenness* is often used interchangeably with *subjectivity*. See Zahavi (2020) for a discussion of this.

9. A *dharma* is substantial, not because it is the substratum of properties, but because it is ontologically basic and independent. It is these latter features that are rejected by Madhyamaka.

10. Of course, the Buddhist reductionist will resist these claims. The charges of reification and nihilism depend on a certain account of the relationship between the two truths that is explored later.

11. I refer to both sentient beings and persons in what follows. I take that persons are a subclass of sentient beings.

12. The following discussion of autonomous systems closely follows Thompson (2010) and Maturana and Varela (1992).

13. See also Nicholson and Dupre (2018).

14. *cakkhuñ c'*āvuso *paṭicca rūpe ca uppajjati cakkhuviññāṇaṃ, tiṇṇam saṇgati phasso, phassapaccayā vedaṇā, yaṃ vedeti taṃ sañjānāti, yaṃ sañjāṇāti taṃ vitakketi, yaṃ vitakketi taṃ papañceti, taṃ papañceti tato ṇidāṇam purisam*

papañcasaṇkhā samudācaranti atītānāgatapaccuppannesu cakkhuviññeyesu rūpesu (Nanamoli and Bodhi 1995).

15. In the current literature, sentience is sometimes explicitly tied to affective responses like suffering. My account here is primarily in terms of the capacity for sensory responsiveness, but as will become clear, on both the Buddhist and the enactive accounts, sentience is nearly always a sensory-affective mode of responsiveness.

16. As is explored in more detail in chapter 5, on the enactive account, a kind of "interiority" coemerges with life. But this interiority is not yet a form of consciousness.

17. This distinction is meant to explicitly parallel the distinction between creature and state consciousness.

18. Note that nonphenomenal forms of subjectivity may in a sense show up in experience (or become manifest as phenomenal forms), but the point is that the basic understanding of these forms of subjectivity is not dependent on whether or how they might show up phenomenally.

19. As I discuss in the next section, I set a higher bar than Damasio and others for what can count as a self or a sense of self.

20. Here I agree with Albahari in making the subject-self distinction, though as will be apparent, my way of drawing the distinction is different.

21. I say "in the typical case" here because, while a sense of agency is a paradigmatic feature of the self, certain pathologies or nonstandard experiences could alter or eliminate it.

22. In discussing valuing, I am not taking a stand on the ontological status of *values*, but see MacKenzie (2016) for further discussion.

23. I say "paradigmatic" here because an individual may not yet have developed these capacities (due to youth, for instance) or may have lost some of them while still counting as a self. However, on my view, a being that is locked in the solipsism of the present and has little or no diachronic integration will not be a self.

24. Or, alternatively, What can (beings who are) selves do?

25. On my account, the emergence of the self is prior to the development of language.

26. However, because I distinguish subjects and selves in a way that Ganeri does not, things are little more complicated here. A sentient subject that is not yet a self would still have a place of experience, which one might identify with the stream.

27. This in part depends on how one understands emergence and on somewhat-tricky questions regarding diachronic identity that I need not delve into here.

Chapter Two

Luminosity

In current discussions of the nature of consciousness, it has become commonplace to characterize phenomenal consciousness in terms of "what it is like" to experience. Yet, in my view, this gloss is incomplete. A more adequate gloss is that conscious experience, in at least the typical or paradigmatic case, involves *what it is like for a subject to be aware of something*. Based on this initial characterization, we can discern at least three aspects of phenomenal consciousness that any adequate theory will need to address. First, "what it is like" points to the qualitative or phenomenal aspects of consciousness—what it is like to see red, to feel an itch, or perhaps to puzzle though a difficult argument. Second, "for a subject" points to the subjective or perspectival aspect of consciousness—"what it is like" is more adequately "what it is like *for*" some subject and conscious appearances are "appearances *to*" some point of view.[1] Third, "aware of something" points to the intentional aspect of consciousness. Most, or perhaps all, of our states of consciousness seem to be of or about something. Finally, any adequate account will need to address the issue of the synchronic and diachronic unity of consciousness. In short, an account of phenomenal consciousness will need at least to address phenomenality, subjectivity, intentionality, and unity. Of course, a particular theory of consciousness may not affirm either the centrality or even the reality of one or more of these aspects.[2] However, given that they are widely thought to be paradigmatic features of human consciousness, an adequate theory will need to have something to say about them.

Indian philosophers developed and defended a wide range of philosophically sophisticated and phenomenologically rich accounts of the conscious mind. Central to many of these accounts is the metaphor of consciousness as light (*prakāśa*) or luminosity (*prakāśatā*), which I take to be the capacity of consciousness to present, disclose, or make manifest. Using the luminosity of consciousness as a guiding thread, this chapter explores the phenomenality, subjectivity, intentionality, temporality, and unity of consciousness. After an initial discussion of luminosity, I take up the controversy between self-illumination and other-illumination accounts of consciousness. I then explore what I call the "dual-aspect reflexivist" view of the conscious mind developed by the Buddhist *pramāṇavādins*. I argue that, despite difficulties concerning temporality and solipsism, dual-aspect reflexivism presents a rich and plausible integrated model of the conscious mind. Finally, in the last section of the chapter, I sketch my own account of consciousness as a dynamic, embodied open presence.

LUMINOSITY

The metaphor of consciousness as light (*prakāśa*) or luminosity (*prakāśatā*) is at the heart of Indian thinking about the nature of the mind going back at least as far as the early prose *Upaniṣads*. In a well-known dialogue in the *Bṛhadāraṇyaka Upaniṣad* between King Janaka and the sage Yājñavalkya, the king asks, "Yājñavalkya, what is the source of light for a person here?" In response, Yājñavalkya mentions the external sources of illumination, such as the sun, moon, and fire, as well as the illumination provided by a voice in the darkness. The king then asks,

> "But when both the sun and the moon have set, the fire has died out, and the voice is stilled, Yājñavalkya, what then is the source of light for a person here?"
>
> "The self (*ātman*) is then his source of light [svayaṃjyoti]. It is by the light of the self that a person sits down, goes about, does his work, and returns."
>
> "Which self is that?"
>
> "It is this person—the one that consists of perception among the vital functions (prāṇa), the one that is the inner light within the heart." (BAU 4.3.1–8 in Olivelle 1998, 111)

Like a light, consciousness has (or is) the capacity to shine forth (*prakāśate*) and illuminate (*prakāśayati*) its object. Indeed, just as without illumination no objects could be visible, without the light of consciousness, no object could be experienced. Thus, luminosity comes to denote the capacity to disclose, present, or make manifest. Physical light, of course, can reveal or make visible objects, but as later Indian philosophers pointed out, it can only do so to a perceiver. The luminosity of consciousness, however, is that original capacity to make experientially present some object to some subject. Yet this inner light that makes possible all experience and knowledge is itself quite elusive. Earlier in the text, Yājñavalkya remarks, "You can't see the seer who does the seeing; you can't hear the hearer who does the hearing; you can't think of the thinker who does the thinking; and you can't perceive the perceiver who does the perceiving. The self within all is this self of yours. All else besides this is grief!" (BAU 3.5.2 in Olivelle 1998, 83). On this view—widely but by no means universally held in Indian thought—the conscious subject (or consciousness itself) is not knowable in the same way as its objects. Despite its association with the elusiveness of the subject, however, luminosity also comes to be associated with the distinctive flavors (*rasa*) or qualitative features of conscious experience—that is, with the phenomenality of consciousness (Ram-Prasad 2007, 54). By the classical period, luminosity comes to denote the distinctive mark or feature of consciousness as that which reveals or discloses (to a subject), particularly in the context of distinct episodes of conscious cognition. As Chakravarthi Ram-Prasad characterizes it,

> Luminosity is the rendering of an event as subjective. It is that by which there is an occurrence, which it is like something to undergo. The subjective is the having of the experience (*anubhava*). Luminosity is the Indian metaphor for phenomenality, the undergoing by the subject of something else (its object). The philosophers are agreed on all sides that consciousness is phenomenological; it is luminous. The debate is over the constitution of the phenomenality of consciousness. The debate is about what it is for there to be subjectivity. (2007, 54)

In my view, despite their intimate connection, we should not simply identify phenomenality and subjectivity. Rather, I interpret luminosity here in terms of *phenomenal presence*—the presentation of experiential qualities or contents. This is a basic notion for understanding phenomenal consciousness meant to point to the fundamental idea of experiential manifestation, that is, of anything showing up in (or as) experience in the first place. It is then a further question of *what*, *how*, and *to whom* (or to *what*) it is showing up. One implication of this approach is that luminosity, as phenomenal presence, is related to but distinct from intentionality. That is, arguably, an experiential quality could be present in a conscious episode without that quality being the intentional *object* of the episode.[3] Yet, when an intentional object is presented in a conscious episode, that will count as an instance of luminosity in that the object is phenomenally presented. Further, if there is nonconscious intentionality, it would not count as luminosity on my interpretation.

SELF-LUMINOSITY AND OTHER LUMINOSITY

The basic divide in Indian accounts of the luminosity of consciousness is between other-illumination (*paraprakāśa*) and self-illumination (*svaprakāśa*) theories. For advocates of other illumination, the luminosity of consciousness consists in its capacity to present a distinct object. Thus, transitive, object-directed intentionality is the mark of consciousness. Conscious states, in order to be states the subject is conscious *of*, must be presented by a distinct, higher-order cognition. Hence, consciousness illuminates that which is other than itself, and conscious states themselves are apperceived by another state. In contrast, for advocates of self-illumination theories, the luminosity of consciousness consists in its being reflexive or self-presenting. Consciousness presents itself in the process of presenting its object. Moreover, just as light does not need a second light in order to be revealed, so consciousness does not need a distinct state to present itself—it is self-intimating.

A paradigmatic example of other illuminationism can be found in the Nyāya school of philosophy. The Nyāya school defends a resolutely realist, intentionalist, and first-order view of consciousness. It is realist in three relevant respects. First, Nyāya is fully ontologically realist about consciousness. Consciousness is a real, unique, and irreducible capacity of the self. Second, Nyāya is epistemologically realist in that veridical episodes of conscious cognition disclose real, mind-independent objects and properties in the word. Third, the school defends a direct realist account of perception in that veridical episodes of perception reveal mind-independent physical objects without the intermediary of conscious mental images or representations (*ākāra*). Nyāya realism is, in turn, tightly bound up with its intentionalist analysis of consciousness. It is the very nature of consciousness to be of or about an object (*svābhāvika viṣayapravaṇatvam*). Episodes of conscious cognition are individuated by their object, and the intentional object of cognition is (in the standard case) an object in the world, not any kind of mental intermediary. Thus, intentionality is the mark of the mental, and the intrinsic intentionality of consciousness is understood in externalist terms. Moreover, because consciousness is transparent (*nirākāra*, "without image/aspect"), the phenomenal features of a conscious state are grounded in (and perhaps reducible to) the way the object is presented through the state. Finally, Nyāya defends a first-order view of consciousness. The luminosity of a cognition consists in revealing its object (*arthaprakāśobuddhi*), not itself. That is, it illuminates that which is other than itself (its object) and requires a distinct, second-order cognition for a first-order cognition to be revealed.

On the Nyāya view, then, when one has a perception of a tree, one is in a conscious state with the content "there is a tree." The first-order cognition derives its content from the worldly object it discloses, and it makes no reference to either the cognition itself or its subject. The term for a first-order cognition in this context is *vyavasāya*. It presents the tree in a particular way (in terms of color, shape, and so on), but this is ultimately a function of the properties of the tree. But in what sense is this cognition conscious? It is conscious in that it makes its subject aware of the object. When one has a perception of a tree, that perception makes one conscious *of the tree*. On this view, one need not be aware of the cognition in any way in order for it to make one conscious of its object. More formally, we can call this the *independence condition*: The presence of a conscious mental state does not depend on the subject's being aware of that state (or aware of being in it). As Fred Dretske remarks, "There are, to be sure, states in (or of) us without which we would not be conscious of trees and pianos. We call these states experiences. Since these experiences make us conscious of things . . . the states themselves can be described as conscious. But we must be careful not to conclude from this that because the states are conscious, we must, perforce, be conscious of them" (1997, 100). The Nyāya school is in complete agreement with this point.

How, then, do we come to be aware of our conscious states when we are? According to Nyāya, our first-order cognitions (*vyavasāya*) are cognized by a subsequent, higher-order cognition (*anuvyavasāya*) or apperception. In the typical case of perception, a first-order cognition triggers a second-order cognition that takes the first-order cognition as its intentional object. There are several features of this view worth noting. First, this is thought to be an automatic causal process. It is causal in that, in minds like ours, the occurrence of a first-order conscious perception triggers (causes) an apperceptive metacognition. This implies, on the Nyāya view of causality, that first- and second-order cognitions (qua vehicles of content) are distinct because causation occurs between distinct existences. Second, *anuvyavasāya* as automatic metacognition should be distinguished from voluntary reflective introspection. While we do typically apperceive our basic perceptions, we do not usually go around introspecting our cognitions. Yet, insofar as the relation between *vyavasāya* and *anuvyavasāya* is causal, the Nyāya school holds that this process can be blocked or simply fail to occur. For instance, when one is fully absorbed in an object, one might have no metacognition of the perceptual cognition, or when one hears a loud noise, the sudden shift in attention might disrupt the formation of a metacognition directed at a prior visual perception. Third, while the *vyavasāya* and the *anuvyavasāya* are distinct cognitions, their content is intimately related. When a perception with the content "there is a tree" is apperceived, the content of the apperception will be "I perceive a tree." The *direct* object of the metacognition is the first-order cognition, while the *indirect* objects of the metacognition are the first-order cognition's object (the tree) and the self. Hence, while the metacognition is about another cognition, it retains reference to the first-order cognition's object of perception. In addition, the metacognition involves self-reference in that it indirectly refers to the self as the subject of the state. It does not, however, refer to *itself*, as all cognitions reveal only that which is *other* than the cognition itself.

Whereas the Nyāya school identifies intentionality as a fundamental aspect of consciousness, the Advaita Vedānta school takes self-luminosity to be the essence of consciousness. Consciousness (*cit*) in its fundamental nature is pure reflexive subjectivity. What we normally think of as the intentionality of consciousness itself actually arises from the association of pure nonintentional consciousness with certain noncognitive mental states (*vṛtti*). As Ram-Prasad characterizes it,

> This Advaitic conception of consciousness as essentially reflexive in fact is tantamount to saying that it is purely reflexive. Indeed, this is the idea behind the conception of consciousness as "witness" (*sākṣin* . . .). Just as onlookers do not engage in the events they are witnessing, so witnessing-consciousness does not engage with objects. It is present, but it is transparent to content, not itself intentionally directed towards (i.e. "engaged with") objects. (2007, 80)

Moreover, it is important to note that, for the Advaitin, the *ātman* is not a substantial self, such as was defended by the Naiyāyikas, but rather, the self is pure reflexive transcendental subjectivity. That is, the *ātman* is not an individuated, enduring entity. It is the witnessing subjectivity that can never be objectified. Thus, in contrast to the Buddhist theory of reflexive awareness, for the Advaitin, it makes no sense to say that individual mental states or events are self-luminous. Conscious mental states are immediately present, not needing an additional second-order mental state to reveal them. They are, therefore, self-presenting in a derivative sense in that they need no further cognitions to reveal them. They are not, however, present *to themselves*, as in the Buddhist view. Rather, conscious states are immediately present to *the self* as pure witnessing subjectivity. The *ātman*, as pure consciousness, is the self-luminous source of illumination for any phenomenon whatsoever, "internal" or "external," and cannot itself become an object of cognition. As the condition of the possibility of any presentation of an object, consciousness is not one object among others, yet it is indubitably present. So, while the Buddhist view of luminosity focuses on the internal structure of individual, empirical cognitive events, the Advaita account of luminosity focuses on a transcendental notion of subjectivity in which the subject is distinct from any empirical entity.

The Advaita philosopher Citsukha, for instance, carefully defines *self-luminous* as that which is immediately evident (*aparokṣa*) but not an object of knowledge. It is immediately evident in the sense that we cannot be mistaken about whether we are conscious. The earlier Advaitin Śrī Harṣa unpacks this familiar Cartesian point in terms of three absences. First, there is the absence of doubt over whether one is having an occurrent conscious cognition. Second is the absence of a metacognition that one has no first-order cognition, when one does have a first-order cognition. Third is the absence of a metacognition that one does not have a first-order cognition when one has no first-order cognition. Whatever we make of Śrī Harṣa's view, the basic point is straightforward: We have an immediate and indubitable acquaintance with at least the existence of our occurrent consciousness. For the Advaitin, we can be mistaken about the contents of consciousness in a variety of ways, but the fact that we cannot be mistaken about whether we are conscious at all just supports the distinction between consciousness itself (*cit*) and its various contents (*viṣaya*) and modifications (*vṛtti*). Citsukha is keen to maintain that consciousness is never its own object because it is never an object at all. On this view, an object is that which is revealed by consciousness, and that which is revealed is distinct from that which reveals. Indeed, on this account, what it is to be an object is to be presented as distinct from the experience of it. In this way, it is similar to the phenomenological notion of an object as a *Gegenstand*—that which stands against one's awareness of it. If consciousness were to know itself as an object, then it would thereby falsify itself by occluding the revealing of that object in the knowing itself. Hence, *cit* is self-conscious without positing itself as an object. As the source of all revealing, then, consciousness is pure unobjectifiable subjectivity.

DUAL-ASPECT REFLEXIVISM

On my account, the luminosity of consciousness is its capacity to present qualities or objects. It can then be inquired *what* is presented. Only that which is other than the moment or act of consciousness? The moment or act itself? Both? Furthermore, it can be inquired *how* consciousness presents. Does it present its object by way of an intermediary phenomenal form or mental image (*sākāra*)? Or does it present its object immediately and without a form or image (*nirākāra*)? In the case of Nyāya, we have a view that consciousness (or the self that is conscious) only reveals that which is other and does so without need of mental intermediaries. In the case of Advaita, we have a view of consciousness as ultimately pure reflexivity or self-luminosity. In this and subsequent sections, I take up a distinct third view developed by the Buddhist *pramāṇavādins*, starting with Dignāga, which I call "dual-aspect reflexivism."

On this view, consciousness has both a reflexive structure and a two-fold form or content (*dvairūpya*). As Dignāga puts it [PS(V) 1.9a], "Every cognition is produced with a twofold appearance, namely that of itself (*svābhāsa*) and that of the object (*viṣayābhāsa*)." The object appearance or object aspect is the presentation of the intentional object in cognition. It is what the experience is *as of*.[4] Whatever the further status of the intentional object, insofar as it is given in experience, there is an object appearance. There are then further questions, such as the relation between the object aspect and the object that is the cause of the cognition. Dignāga argues for a theory of experience whereby the intentional object of an experience (its object aspect) is logically independent of its cause and wherein the experience can be *as of* an object that does not in fact exist, as in, for instance, a vivid hallucination of a pink elephant in the room when there is no pink elephant in the room. Further, the identity of the cognition is partly constituted by its object aspect, and so it can be individuated in terms of its intrinsic intentionality. Indeed, its being a cognition is often characterized in terms of its grasping an object (*viṣayagrahaṇam*).[5] That is, a cognitive episode's being *as of* a tree is intrinsic to it, whether there is a cognition-independent tree or not.

For the dual-aspect reflexivists, one role of the object aspect is to mediate and facilitate cognitive access to the world. The object aspect provides the cognitive link or mode of presentation of the external object within the medium of consciousness.[6] In this way, the object aspect is an answer to what Michelle Montague terms the "access problem": "How does one achieve access to the things with which one stands in perceptual intentional relations? When one perceives some particular thing, what makes it the case that one has that very thing in mind? What mechanism determines which object a perception is of?" (2016, 142). In other words, it is the problem of how exactly a cognitive event or system achieves (cognitive or conscious) access to its intentional object. Further, Montague distinguishes between two common but opposed approaches to the access problem, which she terms "internalist" and "externalist." According to the externalist, the "phenomenon of having an object in mind" is explained "*solely* in terms of external relations (causal or historical) that hold between a thinker's relevant mental state and the relevant object in the world" (2016, 143). As Dretske characterizes the externalist view, "When I am experiencing an object, nothing in my experience of it determines which object I'm experiencing anymore than there is something about a gauge's representation of a tire's pressure that determines which tire it is registering the pressure of" (1997, 33; quoted in Montague 2016, 143). In contrast, according to the internalist, the explanation of having an object in mind must include an internal condition on access. As Montague puts it, "The fundamental idea behind the internal approach to the access problem is that thinking of a particular object essentially involves conceiving of it in some particular manner, or characterizing it in some fashion, and that reference to the particular manner involved is essential for determining which object is being thought of" (2016, 142). It is important to note that the internalist condition, beyond thinking and conceiving, can apply to other modes of intentionality, including perception. The key claim is that, in addition to whatever external conditions may be required, there is something about the particular way of cognizing the object that (at least in part) explains having that object in mind.

On my interpretation, dual-aspect reflexivists, such as Dignāga and Dharmakīrti, hold an internalist view, and the object aspect of the cognition plays the role of the internal "particular-way" condition. For instance, as Dignāga affirms in his *Ālambanaparīkṣā*, Buddhist thinkers generally held that there are two conditions on a genuine perceptual cognition. First, the object perceived must be the cause of the perceptual cognition. This is an external condition on the perception. Second, the object must *appear* in the perception. When I see a tree, the tree appears to me visually, and the tree has caused me to be in that perceptual state. But what is it for that tree to appear in the perception? For *sākāravādins*, it is for the visual consciousness to take on the phenomenal form of the tree, like a clear mirror reflects the form of an object in front of it. The aspect or phenomenal form here is the internal "particular-way" condition that in part determines that the perception is of the tree. In contrast, *nirākāravādins* reject the need for an internal aspect to mediate cognitive access to the intentional object.

On the dual-aspect view, however, a cognition is not exhausted by its presentation of an intentional object. It also presents a subject aspect (*svābhāsa*), which for Dignāga means the way the cognition presents *itself*. When one has an experience as of a tree, on this view, the experience presents both the tree (the object aspect) and the experiencing of the tree (the subject aspect). As Dignāga asserts, "That cognition has two aspects is [known] from the difference between the cognition of the object and the cognition of that [cognition]" (PS 1.11ab). This view of cognition is similar to that of Colin McGinn. On McGinn's view, "experiences are Janus-faced: they point outward to the external world but they also present a subjective face to their subject; they are of something other than the subject and they are like something for the subject" (1993, 29). On the dual-aspect view of consciousness, the phenomenal character of experience involves both how the object is presented and how the experience itself is presented. This entails a phenomenological distinction between what the object is like and what it is like to cognize the object. For instance, what it is like to see a bright yellow lemon may be different from what it is like to *imagine* the lemon or to *remember* it, even if the lemon itself is presented in the same way (as bright yellow, etc.) in each cognition (Zahavi 2020, 23) . Indeed, Jonardon Ganeri characterizes the subject aspect simply as "whatever it is in virtue of which attending to one's experience does not collapse into attending to the world as presented in experience" (2012, 170).

For Dignāga, the available features of the cognition itself include subordinate mental factors. He writes, "The mental [perception] which, taking a thing of color, etc., for its object, occurs in the form of immediate experience (*anubhava*) is also free from conceptual construction. The self-awareness (*svasaṃvedana*) of desire, anger, ignorance, pleasure, pain, etc., is [also recognized as] mental perception because it is not dependent on any sense-organ" (PSV 1.11ab). That is, for Dignāga, we have direct self-awareness of certain features of our own mental states. In particular, Dignāga here is appealing to the more general Buddhist *citta/caitta* model of cognition. Here *citta* refers to the moment of cognition as such, whereas the *caitta* or mental factors are analytically discernable aspects of the cognition. On the standard analysis, there are five omnipresent mental factors: sensory contact (*sparśa*), affect (*vedanā*), cognition (*saṃjñā*), conition (*cetanā*), and attention (*manaskāra*). That is, the basic nature of the cognition is shaped by sensory, affective, cognitive, conative, and attentional factors. Further, for the dual-aspect reflexivist, these mental factors contribute to the *svābhāsa*, the way the cognition presents itself in addition to the way it presents its object. There is a discernable phenomenological difference between a vivid, pleasant, attentive, and desirous cognition of a bright yellow lemon and an unfocused, nondesirous, unpleasant cognition of that same bright yellow lemon.

Now, I have suggested that the object aspect is meant to solve the problem of cognitive access to objects. What about the subject aspect? Here I want to suggest that there is a different kind of access problem for the cognition itself. That is, there is an *intramental* access problem, namely, how can one become directly aware of one's own cognitive states or their (intrinsic) features? Indeed, Dignāga's two main arguments involving the subject aspect—the introspection argument and the memory argument—concern the possibility of intramental access.[7]

Dignāga's introspection or metacognition argument for the dual-aspect view (*dvyābhāsatā*) is that if cognitions are transparent, then there would be no distinction between a cognition and the cognition of that cognition (Kellner 2010, 210; PS 1.11). That is, if a cognition of a tree (C1) has no form other than its object, and a metacognition of C1 (C2) is also transparent, then while C2 has as its object C1, C1 has no form other than the form of the tree. Therefore, C2 will collapse into just another cognition of the tree. However, if C1 has two faces, then we can make sense of what C2 grasps when it cognizes C1, namely, the subject aspect of C1. C2 will also grasp C1's object in grasping C1, but it will not collapse into it. Whatever one makes of the soundness of this argument, the point here is that the subject aspect facilitates intramental access, just as the object aspect facilitates extramental access.

In his memory argument, Dignāga states that one cannot remember what one has not experienced before. But we can remember our own previous experiences—that is, we can remember not just the *object* of a previous experience but also the previous experience itself. Thus, the experience must itself have been experienced. If the prior cognition is cognized by a distinct cognition, as in the higher-order view, then there would occur an infinite regress. This is because, according to Dignāga, the higher-order experience, too, can be remembered and so must itself have been experienced and so on. To avoid the regress, he argues, we must hold that experiences are reflexive—that is, that the awareness of the experience is not separate from the experience itself. To be sure, this is a controversial argument, but my point here is that Dignāga is appealing to the subject aspect to mediate intramental access. Of course, the intra*mental*-access problem is different from the object-access problem. There is no ontological gap between consciousness and external objects to overcome.[8] Rather, the role of the subject aspect is to account for the direct availability of cognitions in a way that avoids collapsing the distinction between cognitions and metacognitions (memory, introspection) or setting off a vicious regress of cognitions.

So, on this interpretation of the dual-aspect theory of consciousness, the object and subject aspects of experiences are *phenomenal modes of presentation*. The object aspect presents the object (e.g., as being yellow and oblong), while the subject aspect presents the experience itself (e.g., as being a pleasant, focused, visual experience, as well as being a cognition of a yellow lemon). They are *phenomenal* modes of presentation in that the object and the experience are presented qualitatively. In modern parlance, we can say that there is something it is like to be aware of a yellow lemon and there is also something it is like to live through an involuntary, attentive, pleasant, visual experience of a yellow lemon.

Yet while the aspects are both phenomenal modes of presentation, there is, I think, an important distinction between them. On the dual-aspect view, both aspects belong to a single cognition. However, as distinct modes of presentation, they must present differently. The object aspect purports to present an object distinct from the cognition itself, that is, by way of transitive intentionality. In perceiving a pot, the pot is presented as being distinct from the perception and external to the perceiver. This may ultimately be an error or illusion if the object is really itself an immanent mental image. However, the error or illusion itself is based on the gap between how the object is given (*as* independent and external) and how it is understood to be on further analysis.

In contrast, the cognition itself, presented through the subject aspect, is presented as within, as immanent rather than transcendent.

The phenomenological difference here is between presentation as *object* and presentation as *subject* (Legrand 2007). For a thing to be given *as object* is for it to be given as distinct from the experience that presents it. For a thing to be given *as subject* is for it be given as nondistinct from the experience that presents it. Of course, some philosophers in India and the West have deployed this kind of distinction to support the existence of an independent self. However, in the Buddhist context, the subject is clearly the individual cognitive episode, not a self. Furthermore, it is important to note that these modes of presentation (as object and as subject) can present one and the same entity. For instance, take Wittgenstein's example of *seeing* a broken arm and *feeling* a broken arm. In the case of seeing the arm, one might be mistaken about whether the perceived object is one's own. In the case of feeling the arm, it is not clear that one can be mistaken about whether one is feeling one's own arm. One can be mistaken about whether the arm is really broken but not, it seems, about whether it is painful or whether it is one's own arm being felt. In this case, the same object (the arm) is presented exteroceptively (as object) and interoceptively (as subject). Likewise, I suggest that on the dual-aspect view, the same entity (the cognition) is presented both as object and as subject, and yet it is only the cognition presented as subject (the subject aspect) that is given *as itself*.

So, for Dignāga and his successors, the dual aspects of experience are *appearances* (*ābhāsa*), and arguably, it is a feature of the conceptual grammar of "appearance" that it is always "appearance to." Indeed, insofar as our discussion of luminosity has taken it to be a form of phenomenal presentation, the very idea of consciousness as presentation seems to presuppose presentation to. This fits well with views that accept the self (*ātman*) as the enduring subject of experience but seems to present a problem for Buddhist philosophers for whom *anātmavāda* (the doctrine of no-self) is foundational. In short, if both the objective and subjective aspects are presentations, then to whom or to what are they presenting?

For Buddhist reflexivists like Dignāga, the answer is *svasaṃvedana* (self-awareness). Here "self-awareness" or "reflexive awareness" denotes the primitive, direct acquaintance one has with one's own experience. To be presented an object in experience is to be aware of the object as it is given in and through that experience, whether one thematizes the object *as* experienced or not. To experience an object is also to live through the experiencing directly. In both cases, we may say, there is something it is like to have the experience and that is a function of how the experience presents the object and how it presents itself. Reflexive awareness, then, is the direct awareness one has of that which is presented (objectively or subjectively) in experience. It is, in other words, the basic awareness of the objective and subjective faces of each cognitive episode.

The Buddhist reflexivists, then, are committed to something like what David Rosenthal (1997) calls the *Transitivity Principle*, according to which a subject is in a conscious state *M* only if the subject is, in some suitable way, aware of *M* (or of being in *M*). The subject need not be *reflectively* or *attentively* aware of *M* but must only be aware of it "in some suitable way." The Transitivity Principle does not entail reflexivity because one might, like Rosenthal, hold the higher-order representationalist (HOR) view that *M* is represented by a distinct, second-order state. It does, however, entail a rejection of the *independence condition* maintained by Nyāya. What is distinctive about the reflexivist view is that self-awareness is *not* a distinct higher-order state but a feature of the same state of consciousness. It is a same-order view of prereflective self-awareness. Moreover, such dual-aspect reflexivists as Dharmakīrti and Śāntarakṣita hold that this reflexivity or self-luminosity is the very nature of consciousness. As Dharmakīrti asserts, "Just as an illuminating light is considered to be the illuminator of itself, because of its nature, just so, awareness is aware of itself" (PV 3.329).[9]

The Buddhist reflexivists, then, are committed to three key ideas. First, they hold that all conscious awareness by its nature involves awareness of itself (awareness of awareness). Second, they hold that any conscious mental state presents itself. And, third, they hold that the presentational content of the state and the reflexive awareness of the state are features of the same state or episode of consciousness. In short, the object aspect, subject aspect, and reflexive awareness are features of a single episode of consciousness. As Dignāga characterizes the view, "That whose appearance [cognition possesses] is the object that is validly cognized. The form as apprehending and [reflexive] awareness, again, are the means of valid cognition and the result. Therefore, these three [aspects of cognition] are not separate [from one another]" (PS 1.10). In this way, dual-aspect reflexivism is what David Woodruff Smith (2016) calls a modal model of consciousness, whereby one can analytically distinguish various aspects or factors in the phenomenological structure of a typical act or event of consciousness while denying that these factors are ontologically distinct or separable (proper) *parts*.

As mentioned previously, Dignāga's main argument for *svasaṃvedana* is the memory argument. However, Dharmakīrti deploys a different line of argument that, in my view, links reflexive awareness to the two access problems already mentioned. In his *sahopalambaniyama* argument, Dharmakīrti states,

> Blue and its cognition are not different because they are necessarily perceived together.
>
> For someone who does not perceive perception, the perception of the object is not established either. (PVin 1.54a–d)

Here, "blue" is the object aspect of the cognition, while "its cognition" is the cognitive state itself in which blue is presented. The claim is that, because they must be given together, they are aspects of a single state. And, as we see in the next line, his reason for this is that, without an awareness of the perception, the perceptual object is not established. He elaborates in the autocommentary,

> To explain: (1) a perception of an object is not due to the existence of the object, but due to the existence of its perception. (2) And if the existence of the object's perception is not established by a means of valid cognition (*aprāmāṇika*), then it does not attach itself (*anuruṇaddhi*) to forms of behavior that presuppose existence (*sattānibandhanān vyavahārān*). (3) If the perception is then unestablished, then the object is also unestablished, so that everything would go asunder, for (4) even if something exists, it cannot be treated as existent unless it is established. Therefore, someone who does not perceive the awareness of something is not aware of anything at all.[10]

The idea here seems to be that perceptual access to an object requires that the perceiver be in a particular perceptual state. But in order for that perceptual state to do its cognitive work, the cognizer must somehow *register* that it is in that cognitive state. Otherwise, Dharmakīrti argues, the percept would not be available for downstream operations like behavior.

Here we see a clear contrast between dual-aspect reflexivism and first-order other-illuminationist (or first-order representationalist) views of cognition. Recall Dretske's view that a conscious perceptual state is one that makes the subject aware of objects but that one should not conclude that the subject must therefore be aware of the perceptual state itself. The perceptual state is something the subject is *conscious with*, not something the subject is *conscious of*. Moreover, in a contemporary context, the issue is complicated by the important distinction between conscious and unconscious cognition because an unconscious cognition may be available for certain downstream functions even when the subject is not conscious of the cognition or its object. Take, for instance, the phenomenon of blindsight. A lesion in the primary visual cortex (V1) causes a blind spot in the visual field. The subject reports not consciously seeing anything in the blind spot. However, the subject does have access to visual information about what is in the blind spot. In particular, the typical person with blindsight is capable of accurately guessing the presence or absence of the stimulus; movement detection; as well as reaching, pointing, and avoidance behavior.

So in the blindsight case, there is some degree of cognitive and behavioral access to an object in the absence of any reported conscious awareness of the object or the cognition. This weakens Dharmakīrti's argument but may not defeat it. There are important differences between blindsight and normal sight. First, the degree of access is significantly diminished in the blindsight case. Subjects possess some visual information about the blind spot, but it is impoverished and unavailable to many typical mental functions, such as verbal report, voluntary attention, or fine-grained sensorimotor tasks. Second, based on the first-person reports of blindsight subjects, the visual information is not phenomenally conscious. There is nothing it is like for the subject to perceive an object in the blind spot, in marked contrast to other objects in the conscious visual field. Plausibly, an object in the blind spot is only partially established in terms of access and entirely unestablished in terms of phenomenal presentation. Indeed, blindsight provides a plausible demonstration of the distinction between conscious and unconscious cognition. So, while Dharmakīrti's argument is not successful as it stands, his point about the connection between reflexive awareness and *conscious* cognition may yet stand. Indeed, one could argue that the blindsight phenomenon bolsters the transitivity principle. A cognition of which the subject is unaware is, like as in blindsight, an *unconscious* cognition lacking in phenomenal character and to which the cognizer has limited, if any, voluntary direct access.

Again, in sharp contrast to the first-order other-illuminationist view, Dharmakīrti posits a deep link between conscious *content* and reflexive awareness. Consider what Montague terms the Conscious Content Principle: "If a mental state S is conscious, the (representational) content of that mental state must be consciously entertained (we may say that in this sense the content of a mental state must be conscious). And conversely, if some (representational) content is consciously entertained, the mental state S of which it is the content must be conscious" (2016, 55). The idea here is that consciously occurrent content implies a conscious state and vice versa. In the blindsight case, it seems we have neither conscious content nor conscious state. On my reading, though, Dharmakīrti is concerned with the epistemic status of conscious content, and according to the conscious content principle, this implies a conscious cognition. And in virtue of what is the cognition conscious? Dharmakīrti argues that the cognizer must "perceive the perception"—that is, they must be directly, noninferentially aware of it.

So, we might reconstruct his argument as follows:

1. (Conscious) perception of an object entails a perceptual state directed at the object.
2. If the object is consciously occurrent (if it is phenomenally present), then the perceptual state must be conscious. By the CCP.
3. If the object is *not* consciously occurrent, the cognizer will not have full epistemic access to the object.
4. A cognition of which the cognizer is unaware is not a conscious cognition, as in blindsight.
5. Therefore, in order to have full epistemic access to the perceptual object, the cognizer must be aware of her own cognition of the object.

Now proponents of a first-order view of consciousness, in keeping with the independence condition, can respond that the perception is conscious just insofar as it makes the cognizer conscious of its object. Nothing more. But how is a mental state of which the subject has absolutely no awareness different from the blindsight case? On the first-order view, in the blindsight case, the state does not succeed in phenomenally presenting the object, and in the normal case, it does. In neither case does the subject need to be aware of her *perceiving*. What, then, differentiates an unconscious mental state from a conscious mental state for the first-order view? Here a proponent of the first-order view could appeal to a functional notion of access or availability. A mental state is conscious (makes its subject conscious of its object) just in case it is, say, widely available for things like action guidance, belief formation, and verbal report. As we have seen, this is a concern for Dharmakīrti, as well. However, while there does seem to be an important link between consciousness and wide access, this purely functional account is not yet sufficient to explain state consciousness.

A further objection to the first-order view is that it is no longer clear that it is accounting for *phenomenal* consciousness at all. Let us suppose that a mental state M makes its subject S conscious of O. What does it mean to make S conscious of O? Is there something it is like for S to be conscious of O? If there is not, then phenomenal consciousness has not been accounted for, and this case is not fundamentally different from a case of blindsight. S may have information about O that is available to guide behavior or form beliefs, but O will not be phenomenally present, and there will be no *viṣayābhāsa*, no object appearance. However, if there is something it is like for S to be conscious of O, then there is something it is like for S to be in M—M will have phenomenal character. Now, as a pure representationalist, Dretske (and the Naiyāyikas) will argue that what M is like for S is strictly a function of what O is like for S—that is, the first-order representationalist will appeal to the (alleged) transparency of experience. On this view, phenomenal character is explained as representational content, such that there can be no more to the phenomenal character of experiencing O than the features one's experience represents O as having. Moreover, introspection will not reveal any intrinsic features of M that are not experienced as properties of O. However, even if the phenomenal character of M is a function of the representation of O, then it is still the case that it is like something for S to be in M. Now, as Greg Janzen (2008) argues, it is a plausible principle that in order for X to be like something for S, S must be aware of it. That is, in order for an object, such as a pot, to be like something for S, S must be aware of the pot. If S is entirely unaware of X, then X cannot be like anything for S. It is up to the representationalist to show that X could be like something for S without S being aware of X. So, according to Janzen's Symmetry Principle, if M has phenomenal character (even if that character is constituted by M's representation of O), then S must be aware of M (2008, 75). However, if the first-order representationalist says that it is O that has phenomenal character, not M, then we are back to the idea of M as not phenomenally conscious.

Furthermore, there are at least three ways in which this pure representationalist account of phenomenal character looks incomplete. First, both phenomenological and conceptual considerations support the idea that the overall character of the experience is not exhausted by its representational *content* (i.e., what is represented). In phenomenal consciousness the object, O, must be represented by way of a phenomenal mode of presentation. Indeed, this mode of presentation seems to play a crucial role in determining both *what* object is represented and *how* it is represented in experience, that is, its very contentfulness (*viṣayābhāsatā*). As Jinendrabuddhi points out (in commenting on Dignāga), "there can be no awareness (*saṃvitti*) of anything apart from cognition." He continues, "Suppose there are external objects; even so an object of awareness (*viṣaya*) is ascertained only according to experience (*yathāsamvedanam eva*)" (Arnold 2014, 176). An object of experience must be given some way or other in experience, and this mode of presentation is a feature of the experience, not the object. Moreover, modes of presentation can vary independently of objects of presentation. My experience can present the green grass as red. It will then be *of* green grass (its representational object or content) but *as of* red grass [its (re)presentational character or mode of presentation]. Moreover, Jinendrabuddhi argues,

> In this regard, with respect to an accusative such as form, a cognition (which consists in resemblance) must have a nature (*svabhāva*), comparable to an instrument (*karaṇabhūta*), as being experienced—[an experiential nature] owing to which there is effected an ascertainment of various cognitions as distinct, such that we can be aware: "this is a cognition of blue, this of yellow." (Arnold 2014, 170)

That is, the phenomenal character of experience must be such that the subject can ascertain first-personally the differences in the qualitative character of distinct states. Thus the object appearance (*viṣayābhāsa*) contributes to the overall phenomenal character of the experience, is available for reflection, and provides a basis on which the subject can discern distinctions in both qualitative character ("this is a cognition of blue, this is of yellow") and, arguably, sensory modality ("this is a cognition of blue, this of a high-pitched tone"). When the Buddhist epistemologists insist that the intentional object is always given through the cognition and more specifically through the cognition's *ākāra* (aspect), I take them to be making a point about the centrality of experiential modes of presentation (*ābhāsa*, "appearance," or *ākāra*, "aspect") in the analysis of an experience's having intentional content. This is one way that the phenomenal character of experience involves more than its representational content.

Second, as a number of phenomenologists have argued, in addition to ways the object is presented, features of the experiential acts themselves figure into phenomenal character. The intentional object may be seen or visualized or remembered. In each case, the object may be presented as having the same features, but the experience will be different. What it is like to *see* green grass is different from what it is like to *visualize* or *remember* green grass. As Thompson points out, the "visual perception feels voluntary and effortless, whereas the visualization feels voluntary, effortful, and needing to call upon memory" (2010, 285). In addition, we may appeal to the *citta-caitta* structure of experiential episodes. In addition to being luminous and cognizant, an episode of awareness may be pleasant or unpleasant, focused or unfocused, calm or agitated, and so on. These mental factors (*caitesika*) contribute to the global phenomenal character of the episode and are available for reflection by the subject—that is, they are prereflective aspects of the experience. These features of the experiencing rather than the object experienced are, as discussed previously, part of what Dignāga terms the *svābhāsa*, the "self-appearance" or subject aspect of the cognition. Thus, the subject aspect contributes to phenomenal character, is available for reflection, and provides a basis on which the subject can discern distinctions in cognitive activity (e.g., remembering vs. visualizing).

On my account, these mental factors or subsidiary mental processes are constitutively embodied. Each moment of experience is grounded in and arises from ongoing (somato) sensory contact (*sparśa*) between the sentient being and its environment and is structured by affective, cognitive, conative, and attentional factors. These factors, while analytically divisible, are mutually specifying and reinforcing and operate below the level of reflective attention. Thus, for instance, the mental factor of attention is shaped by the affective and motivational factors. What grabs our attention or what we choose to attend to is frequently biased by the hedonic valence (or expected hedonic valence) of sensory stimuli, as well as by basic action tendencies, drives, or practical goals. Note also that the omnipresent factors involve the integration of exteroceptive processes (sensory contact) with interoceptive processes of affect (*vedanā*), attention (*manaskara*), and motivation (*cetanā*). Further, the basic conative orientation of the sentient being on this view—that is, approach/avoid/ignore—suggests that the integration of exteroceptive with interoceptive information primarily would be within an egocentric rather than allocentric spatial framework in order to be relevant for action. Hence, we can understand the dual-aspect view of cognition in terms of the integration of self-specifying and other-specifying information within a single conscious point of view. Further, a number of researchers on the neuroscience of consciousness (Damasio 2000; Merker 2007; Parvizi and Damasio 2001) argue that this kind of self/other information integration within an egocentric model of the organism in its environment is central to many forms of subjective experience.

Third, the subject aspect of an experience involves the first-person perspective. It is the "face" that the cognizing presents to the cognizer and is available within the first-person perspective. As an *ābhāsa* (appearance) or *ākāra* (aspect) of experience, the subject aspect is a mode of presentation, but unlike the object aspect, which purports to present an intentional object distinct from the cognition itself, the subject aspect presents the very experience it partly constitutes. That is, the phenomenal experience, on this view, is its own mode of presentation and is therefore self-luminous. Furthermore, the subject aspect of experience qua subject aspect must present the experience as the subject's own, at least in the minimal sense of perspectival ownership. It will then be an implicitly *de se* mode of presentation that is immune to error through misidentification—an experience presented to the subject through its subjective face is the subject's own. Drawing these strands together, then, we have an account of the rich phenomenal character of experience as involving a world-presenting aspect coupled with a subject-presenting aspect with the subject's awareness of these two faces understood as a form of prereflective self-awareness.

In his *Pramāṇavārttika*, Dharmakīrti asserts that the "mind is by nature luminous cognizance (*prabhāsvara*)" (PV 2.210cd–211ab in Dunne 2004, 372).[11] It is the very nature of mind (*citta-prakṛti*) to reveal. At the level of phenomenal consciousness, luminous cognizance could be considered a form of phenomenal intentionality. As Horgan and Nichols recently put it, "phenomenality is inherent to consciousness, and intentionality is virtually always inherent to phenomenality" (2016, 145). That is, consciousness is luminous in that it is essentially characterized by the capacity for phenomenal presentation, including both interlocking modalities of self-presentation and other presentation. It is cognizant (*jñānatā*) in that it is essentially characterized by the capacity to apprehend, to constitute as significant, aspects of the experienced world, including itself. These two features of consciousness are primordial forms of phenomenality and intentionality, the intertwined operation of which constitute the basic mark or nature of conscious experience.

TEMPORALITY

As William Waldron argues, we may think of Buddhist accounts of consciousness as operating in two distinct but intertwined dimensions. The first, synchronic or *dharmic* dimension, involves "dissecting experience into its discrete and momentary elements [*dharmas*], [and] understand[ing] the internal relationships within and between these momentary processes" (Waldron 2003, 55). The second, diachronic or *santāna* (stream) dimension involves the "indispensable relationship between causal conditioning and temporal continuity, of how the past continues to affect the present" (Waldron 2003, 56). Both dimensions are necessary, but as Hindu critics of Buddhist thought are quick to point out, they are in tension with one another.

Most Buddhist discussions of reflexive awareness involve the *dharmic* dimension because it is each moment of consciousness that is reflexive and these moments constitute the stream of consciousness (*citta-santāna*). However, reflexive awareness may be central to understanding consciousness diachronically, as well. To bring this out, I focus on the two tightly related problems of objective synthesis and the diachronic continuity of the stream of consciousness itself. The problem of objective synthesis "has to do with how the mind can perceive the change or persistence of temporal objects" (Gallagher 1998, 8). The succession of consciousness is not consciousness of succession, so how can the stream of consciousness—which is made up of distinct moments of consciousness—be aware of objects through time? How can one hear a melody *as* a melody and not simply disconnected notes? How can one recognise that it is the same object experienced through time? The problem of diachronic continuity has to do with how the moments of consciousness can be connected so as to constitute an organized and experientially continuous flow. How does one moment flow into the next? How can one recognize that an object is the one previously experienced *by me*? So, while the first problem concerns how the stream of consciousness can be aware of *objects* through time, the second problem concerns how it can be aware of *itself* through time.

As discussed in chapter 1, we can see both problems raised by Śaṅkara in his critique of the Buddhists. In the Buddhist Abhidharma and Yogācāra, the stream of consciousness is constituted by—and indeed reducible to—a causal sequence of discrete mental events. Yet while it may be the case that the stream is a causally connected process, the appeal to causal connectedness, according to Śaṅkara, is not sufficient to address the problems of objective synthesis and diachronic continuity. He writes,

> The mental impressions must have an abode. Without that they cannot exist. But the doctrine of momentariness denies permanency to everything. Even the ālayavijñāna is momentary and cannot be that abode. Unless there is a permanent principle connecting the past, present, and future, there cannot be remembrance or recognition of an experience originating at a particular time and place. If the ālayavijñāna is said to be something permanent, then that would go counter to the doctrine of momentariness. (Deutsch and Dalvi 2004, 137)

The relevance of memory for accounts of diachronic continuity is well known, but what about recognition? Śaṅkara argues that the phenomenon of recognition refutes the momentariness of both object and subject:

> [Śaṅkara]: Your statement that every moment a different jar in contact with light is produced, is wrong, for even at a subsequent moment we recognise the same jar.
>
> [Buddhist]: The recognition may be due to similarity, as in the case of hair, nails, etc. that have been cut and have grown anew.
>
> [Śaṅkara]: No, for even in that case the momentariness is disproved. . . .
>
> In the case of a jar etc. we perceive that they are identical. Therefore the two cases are not parallel.
>
> When a thing is directly recognised as identical, it is improper to infer that it is something else, for when an inference contradicts perception, the ground of such inference becomes fallacious. Moreover, the perception of similarity is impossible because of the momentariness of knowledge (held by you). The perception of similarity takes place when one and the same person sees two things at different times. But according to you the person who sees a thing does not exist till the next moment to see another thing, for consciousness, being momentary, ceases to be as soon as it has seen some one thing. To explain: The perception of similarity takes the form of "This is like that." "That" refers to the remembrance of something seen: "this" to the perception of something present. If after remembering the past experience denoted by "that," consciousness should linger till the present moment referred to by "this," then the doctrine of momentariness would be gone. If, however, the remembrance terminates with the notion of "that," and a different perception relating to the present (arises and) dies with the notion of "this," then no perception expressed by, "This is like that," will result, as there will be no single consciousness perceiving

> more than one thing. Moreover, it will be impossible to describe our experiences. Since consciousness ceases to be just after seeing what was to be seen, we cannot use such expressions as, "I see this," or "I saw that," for the person who has seen them will not exist till the moment of making these utterances. (*Bṛhadāranyakopaniṣadbhāṣya* 4.3.7 in Deutsch and Dalvi 2004, 137)

In this dense passage, Śaṅkara is making the following points. First, in the case of a (seemingly) persisting object, such as a jar, we perceive that it is identical, not merely similar. When one looks at a jar, looks away, and then looks at it again, the two perceptions of the jar are given as perceptions of one and the same jar. Moreover, when one walks around a jar, each profile is perceived as a profile of the same jar. Second, the Buddhist is faced with a dilemma. Because perception of similarity (or identity) requires comparison between an earlier and a later percept, either there is a single enduring consciousness that has both perceptions and the doctrine of momentariness is false, or there is no enduring consciousness and each perceptual event is locked in the solipsism of the present moment. In the latter case, no perception of similarity is possible. Third, Śaṅkara argues that if consciousness is momentary, then there can be no diachronic continuity of the first-person perspective. Furthermore, note that Śaṅkara sees very clearly the deep phenomenological connection between the experience of persisting objects and the experience of oneself as a persisting subject. Thus, on Śaṅkara's view, one must either accept an enduring self or consciousness or be faced with an experientially disconnected series of mental events.[12]

The Buddhist reflexivist response to this kind of objection is to appeal to both the causal and cognitive relations between mental events in a stream. The connection between a current mental event and its immediate condition (*samanantarapratyaya*)—that is, the immediately prior mental event—is causal but also synthetic. It is these synthetic cognitive relations rather than the positing on an enduring self that explain the synthetic cohesion (*pratisandhāna*) of the stream. It is the intrastream relations between events that ground synthetic cohesion, and according to the Buddhist reflexivist, to infer an enduring ontological ground behind the stream imputes a false substantial unity on a series of momentary events. However, while a substantial self or changeless witness consciousness may not be necessary to account for diachronic continuity, it remains unclear whether an account based on causal and cognitive connections between moments of reflexive awareness will be up to the task.

Another alternative, mentioned by Śaṅkara in the passage, is to appeal to the Yogācāra idea of the *ālayavijñāna*, the base or storehouse consciousness. Yogācāra thinkers, such as Vasubandhu and Asaṅga, distinguish eight modes or aspects of consciousness. The first five modes are the basic forms of sensory awareness. The sixth dimension is called "mental consciousness" (*manovijñāna*) and has to do with ideation, thinking, and so on. These six types or aspects of consciousness are accepted throughout Indian Buddhist philosophy of mind, but thinkers associated with Yogācāra posit two more types of awareness: afflictive mentation (*kliṣṭamanas*) and base or store consciousness (*ālayavijñāna*). On this account, the seventh consciousness (*kliṣṭamanas*) is the source of the basic sense of self, the felt sense of mental ownership that is built into our default mental architecture. The *ālayavijñāna* forms the most basic stratum of the stream of consciousness (*cittasantāna*) against the background of which the other seven types of awareness operate. Unlike the discontinuous flow of the manifest types of awareness (*pravṛttivijñāna*), the base consciousness is taken to be a diachronically continuous flow in that it is a nongappy series of momentary mental events. It is also the store or repository of the various habits, dispositions, and latent propensities that shape the experience of the individual. Finally, according to the Yogācārins, the base consciousness is central to the explanation of the synchronic coherence of consciousness. In phenomenological terms, the *ālaya* is a sedimented retentional continuum, an egoless streaming (Zahavi 2010).

On either approach, the task for the Buddhist is twofold. First, they must account for the *santāna* dimension, the temporal continuity of consciousness, without appeal to a substantial self. Second, their account must be consistent with the doctrine of momentariness (*kṣaṇikavāda*), which states that nothing really persists. Furthermore, recall that it is phenomenal continuity and not merely causal connection that must be explained. These are not easy tasks, and as I now argue, a nonsubstantialist approach may require combining insights from the reflexivists and earlier Yogācārins while softening or rejecting the commitment to momentariness.

The Tibetan Buddhist philosopher Jamgon Mipham (1846–1912), in his brilliant and at times idiosyncratic commentary on Śāntarakṣita's *Madhyamakālaṃkāra*, provides a philosophically rich fusion of aspects of reflexivism, early Yogācāra, and Madhyamaka. Of particular interest here is his combination of a reflexivist analysis of the nature of consciousness with a theory of the *ālayavijñāna*. According to Mipham, the ālayavijñāna is the basal background field or continuum of awareness and is understood as "mere luminosity and cognizance," where *luminosity* here means *self-luminosity*. "It is," he writes, "an awareness of the mere presence of objects and it arises as a continuity of instants," and "it does not have a specific object of focus but observes the world and beings in a general, overall manner" (Śāntarakṣita and Mipham 2005, 238). The *ālaya*, then, is characterized by luminosity, both in the sense of phenomenal presence and in the sense of reflexivity. It is also characterized by cognizance or intentionality but of a different sort than the manifest modes of awareness that arise from it. In contrast to the thematic and transitive modes of intentionality to be found in the *pravṛtti-vijñāna*, the cognizance of the *ālaya* is nonthematic—a basic openness or open presence to the world of experience, corresponding somewhat to Thompson's sense making as sensibility. Mipham further elaborates that the base consciousness must be understood in terms of two distinct but inseparable aspects: the "seed aspect" and the "maturation aspect." The seed aspect corresponds to the retentional function of the base consciousness.[13] It is the synchronic and diachronic basis for the various habits and propensities that condition experience. The maturation aspect functions as a "potential (a power source) for the seven kinds of consciousness and their attendant mental factors, which rise and fall like waves on the sea" (Śāntarakṣita and Mipham 2005, 238).

So while some have understood the *ālaya* as a form of unconscious cognition, here I follow Mipham in taking it to be prereflective global background consciousness. Further, this background open presence is fundamentally bodily. In the Yogācāra tradition, base consciousness is said to pervade the body and to differentiate the living body from a corpse. Phenomenologically, we may see this as linking base consciousness to the lived, animate body—that is *Leib* rather than *Körper*.

This Yogācāra account of the stream of experience is based on what I call horizontal and vertical dynamics. The basic temporality of experience is constituted by the causal, cognitive, and phenomenal connections between moments of consciousness in the base consciousness. This horizontal form of dynamism roughly corresponds to what Mipham calls the seed aspect of the *ālaya*. Second, experience involves the vertical dynamic between the more passive background and the more active and explicit foreground of conscious activity. The foreground here, though, is not constituted by the ever-changing objects of experience but rather the manifest mental processes, such as perceiving, imagining, or thinking. In Buddhist terms, this is the ongoing reciprocal dynamic between the *ālayavijñāna* and the *pravṛttivijñāna* and what Mipham calls the maturation aspect of base consciousness. Thus, for instance, as Thompson puts it, the "antecedent and 'rolling' experiential context of perception modulates the way the object appears or is experientially lived during the moment of perception, and the content of this transient conscious state reciprocally affects the flow of experience" (2010, 355).

This rich account of the temporal dynamics of the stream has, in my view, strong resonance with the classic phenomenological analysis of time consciousness. And by bringing the phenomenological account into conversation with this Buddhist view, we may better see the connection between reflexive awareness and the temporality of consciousness. On the Husserlian view, the basic unit of temporal experience has a threefold structure of *protention–primal impression–retention*. As Husserl explains,

> In this way, it becomes evident that concrete perception as original consciousness (original givenness) of a temporally extended object is structured internally as itself a streaming system of momentary perceptions (so-called primal impressions). But each such momentary perception is the nuclear phase of a continuity, a continuity of momentary gradated retentions on the one side, and a horizon of what is coming on the other side: a horizon of "protention," which is disclosed to be characterised as a constantly gradated coming. (Hua IX, 202, quoted in Zahavi 2020, 66)

The primal impression is restricted to the now phase in a sequence. In listening to a melody, the primal impression is directed to the currently sounding note. Retention is directed toward the just-elapsed note. The elapsed note is not actually present in consciousness but is retained intentionally.[14] Protention is directed toward the future, the next note about to be heard. Where the currently sounding note is given in the vivid immediacy of the present and the just past note is determinately retained, the upcoming note is not given in a fully determinate manner.

This threefold structure forms a unity, the continuous operation of which allows for the experience of temporal continuity. The structure constitutes the *living present* within which temporal experience "wells up." Further, on Husserl's view, the primal impression–protention–retention structure of consciousness accounts for the temporal unification of the stream of consciousness itself. Retention retains the prior phases of the stream, while protention reaches out toward future moments of consciousness. It is through this process, which he calls "longitudinal intentionality," that consciousness is self-affecting or temporally given to itself. Furthermore, longitudinal intentionality makes possible what Husserl calls "transverse intentionality." It is the transverse intentionality of time consciousness that allows for the continuous experience of a temporal object, such as a melody or a persisting jar. Because the now phase of consciousness takes an object (for example, a note) and is retained in the stream, so, too, is the object of the now phase of consciousness. In sum, the threefold structure of time consciousness is the condition of the possibility of both the diachronic continuity of the stream of consciousness and the objective synthesis of temporal objects.

Husserl's analysis of time consciousness implies that consciousness is recursive. Consciousness takes in its impressions and retains them, marking the impression as past and making the past impression available for the ongoing flow of consciousness. Indeed, the process of retention is iterative in that not only "pastness" but also the degree of "pastness" is marked within this retentional continuum. The temporal flow of consciousness involves retentions of retentions, thereby allowing the experience of a temporal *sequence*. Moreover, this recursive process is reflexive. As James Mensch explains,

> In retention the subject does not just have the experience of the retained, it experiences itself having this experience, i.e., as retaining the retained. Accordingly, when it grasps an object through a series of retained contents, it prereflectively grasps itself in its action of retention. This grasp is a grasp of itself as having experience, i.e., of itself as a subject. Such self-experience implies that the self-referential character of retention grounds the subject as nonpublic, i.e., as referring (or being present) only to itself. (2010, 107)

Thus, on Husserl's view, time consciousness entails reflexive awareness.[15] When one is aware of the melody, one is prereflectively aware of one's ongoing experience of the melody.

External temporal objects are constituted for consciousness through transverse intentional acts that have the threefold structure of time consciousness. But we also experience those acts of consciousness themselves as unfolding through time. Both the melody and the hearing of the melody are experienced as having duration. How can one be aware of the temporality of one's own stream of thoughts, sensations, and so on? Must one posit a distinct intentional act with its own threefold structure directed toward one's own first-order mental state? And does this second-order act have its own immanent temporality?

To avoid the looming regress, Husserl posits what he calls absolute consciousness or the absolute flow. This is the deepest level of time consciousness, and every other layer of consciousness presupposes it. It is absolute in that it is not constituted by any deeper layer of consciousness. It is neither a substance nor an unchanging witness consciousness but rather a primordial flux. Husserl writes,

> The flow of consciousness that constitutes immanent time not only *exists* but is so remarkably and yet intelligibly fashioned that a self-appearance of the flow necessarily exists in it, and therefore the flow itself must necessarily be apprehensible in the flowing. The self-appearance of the flow does not require a second flow; on the contrary, it constitutes itself as a phenomenon in itself. (Hua X, 83, quoted in Zahavi 2020, 75)

So for Husserl, the "flowing consciousness . . . is necessarily the consciousness of itself as flowing" (Hua XXXIII, 48, quoted in Zahavi 2020, 75). Here again, we see the close connection between consciousness as self-presenting—that is, as reflexive or luminous—and its immanent temporality or diachronic continuity. Moreover, note that Husserl's absolute consciousness is not a pure, unchanging witness above the stream of consciousness. Rather, it is a continuum of reflexive awareness, akin to *ālayavijñāna* (Larrabee 1981).

Taking stock, recall that Śaṅkara argues that "unless there exists one continuous principle equally connected with the past, the present, and the future, or an absolutely unchangeable (Self) which cognizes everything, we are unable to account for remembrance, recognition, and so on" (Vireswarananda 1982, 221). In my view, Śaṅkara is right that any view that attempts to *reductively* analyze consciousness into discrete, merely causally connected moments will not provide an adequate account of the diachronic functions of consciousness. However, Mipham's account of the *ālaya* as embodied, reflexive, global background consciousness presents a promising alternative. Furthermore, incorporating to the phenomenological analysis of the structure of time consciousness provides both a fine-grained analysis of the structure of the horizontal dimension of base consciousness and a connection between temporality and reflexive awareness. Indeed, the phenomenological view that prereflective self-awareness and basic temporality are two aspects of the same feature of consciousness bolsters the Buddhist reflexivist view that *svasaṃvedana* is the very nature of consciousness. In response to the demand for a continuous principle to account for the diachronic aspects of consciousness, one may respond that the principle is not a substantial self but rather the primordial reflexive, recursive, and dynamic structure of consciousness itself.

On this hybrid view of time consciousness, a moment of consciousness is not an isolated experiential atom but rather is phenomenally and intentionally connected past and intentionally connected to the anticipated subsequent moment. Is the doctrine of momentariness preserved on this account? Monima Chadha (2015) defends a sophisticated constructive account inspired by both Abhidharma and Yogācāra that aims to maintain strict momentariness. However, for Husserl, "each such momentary perception is the nuclear phase of a continuity, a continuity of momentary gradated retentions on the one side, and a horizon of what is coming on the other side" (quoted in Zahavi 2020, 66). On my reading, the classical phenomenological account suggests that moments of consciousness are not basic independent units but rather analytical abstractions from a more fundamental continuity. Likewise, in Śāntarakṣita's Yogācāra-Madhyamaka, while an appeal to basic moments of experience may be warranted in arguing against the existence of an enduring substantial self, it is a mistake to reify the mental events in the stream by treating them as irreducible atoms of experience. He therefore deploys his standard neither-one-nor-many argument to prove that moments of consciousness, too, are empty of inherent existence. In his commentary on Śāntarakṣita's argument, Kenchen Thrangu makes the point:

> Examining the successive manner in which consciousness perceives objects, we might be led to believe that each "flash" of awareness, each moment of consciousness, is a fundamental unit of time, comparable to the indivisible particles of matter already discussed. However, if we could ever isolate such a single unit of time, we would see that it could only occur within a framework of ongoing consciousness, because awareness is never static and hence each moment is linked to a previous and a future moment. That is, such a moment would not be an inseparable whole but rather would consist of three parts: past, present, and future. (2013, 48)

On this account, that moments of consciousness are not simply strung together like pearls on a string. Each moment is inseparably a part of a larger process. Indeed, temporal part and temporal whole are interdependent and mutually specifying. The stream is not simply a series of moments but a genuine process.

DYNAMIC EMBODIED NONDUAL AWARENESS

At the beginning of this chapter, I point out that a standard gloss on consciousness—that consciousness involves "what it is like for a subject to be aware of something"—invokes a number of key features that an adequate theory of consciousness must account for. "What it is like" points to the qualitative or phenomenal aspect. "For a subject" points to (minimal) subjectivity. "To be aware of something" points to the intentionality or cognizance of consciousness. Moreover, a theory of consciousness must address the synchronic unity and (at least) diachronic continuity of consciousness, as well. In this final section, I draw together the strands of the discussion and argue that the broadly reflexivist view of consciousness presents an interesting and promising integrated model of consciousness. (Fair warning: The following remarks are explicitly synthetic and constructive.)

On a dual-aspect reflexivist (DAR) account, the qualitative features of an experience can be considered differential manifestations of the basic luminosity of consciousness itself. That is, luminosity as the capacity for phenomenal presentation entails different ways that things may be present, including the whole range of phenomenal qualities or qualia.[16] Further, on DAR, the global phenomenal character of an experience is constituted by features of its object aspect and its subject aspect. What it is like to experience a sunset involves both how the sunset is phenomenally present to the experience as well as how the perceiving is phenomenally present. As discussed previously, this can include the ways that, for instance, sensory, affective, conative, cognitive, and attentional factors of experience modulate its overall phenomenal character. Moreover, while both the subject pole and the object pole contribute to the phenomenal character, in the typical case, an experience is attentionally structured into a foreground and a background.

The cognizance (*jñānatā*) of consciousness is its capacity to grasp or apprehend its object. This aspect, then, is linked to the intentionality of consciousness, the "aware of something" part of our slogan. Conscious states not only present phenomena but also are contentfully directed to objects (*viṣayatā*). Further, consciousness is implicated in the capacity to identify, reidentify, and understand its objects (*saṃjñā*). In a contemporary context, I suggest that the cognizance of consciousness could be understood in terms of the enactivist account of sense-making. As we see in chapter 1, according to Thompson,

> Sense-making is threefold: (1) sensibility as openness to the environment (intentionality as openness); (2) significance as positive or negative valence of environmental conditions relative to the norms of the living being (intentionality as passive synthesis—passivity, receptivity, and affect); and (3) the direction or orientation the living being adopts in response to significance and valence (intentionality as protentional and teleological). (2011, 119)

On this account, an episode of conscious experience is luminous and cognizant in that it paradigmatically involves phenomenal presentation, significance, and valence. Further, on the Buddhist view, any particular episode of experience is understood as the confluence of a complex network of conditioning factors, including subpersonal mental processes.

Reflexive awareness accounts for the minimal (state) subjectivity of consciousness. Reflexive awareness constitutes the minimal phenomenal point of view within which various phenomenal contents are present. Both objective and subjective appearances appear within the condition of reflexive awareness. And, according to DAR, without consciousness's fundamental self-presence, no other phenomenal contents could be present. Furthermore, as the basic condition within which anything can be present, reflexive awareness also constitutes the synchronic unity of consciousness. As Śāntarakṣita writes in *Madhyamakālaṃkāra* 17–18a,

A mind that is by nature one and without parts
Cannot possess a threefold character;
Self-awareness thus does not entail
An object and an agent as real entities.
Because this is its very nature,
Consciousness is apt for self-cognition. (Śāntarakṣita and Mipham 2005, 201)

Here Śāntarakṣita is responding to the objection that reflexive awareness is incoherent because it implies the conflation of agent (*kartṛ*), object (*karman*), and activity (*krīyā*). Just as a knife does not cut itself and a finger does not point at itself, so a moment of consciousness cannot be conscious of itself. However, for Śāntarakṣita, consciousness has a synchronic unity that makes inappropriate the usual language of agent, action, and object. Again, Mipham's commentary is helpful:

> By excluding all that it is not (namely, all other things), self-cognizing consciousness constitutes a single entity. This being so, it is necessarily without aspects that are different from itself. It is therefore unacceptable to say that it really has a threefold nature. . . . Therefore, when it is said that consciousness is self-knowing, this is not meant in the sense of an axe chopping wood. It does not mean that consciousness apprehends itself as something really other than itself, or that consciousness as the subject and consciousness as the object of the act of cognition are being considered as real and separate entities. To know is simply the nature of consciousness, and for this reason it is acceptable and correct to consider consciousness auto-cognising. (Śāntarakṣita and Mipham 2005, 202)

In this way, for DAR, *svasaṃvedana* is the very nature of consciousness. However, while reflexive awareness may constitute minimal (state) subjectivity, it does not entail the richer notions of subjectivity or the sense of self discussed in chapter 1. Rather, richer aspects of subjectivity and the sense of self would be features of the *svābhāsa*.

According to Dharmakīrti and his commentator Śākyabuddhi, reflexive awareness is more basic than the subject-object structure and intentionality of consciousness.[17] Transitive intentionality presupposes subject-object duality, but on this view, the subject-object duality is a cognitive distortion, not a real feature of consciousness. Reflexive awareness, however, is the very nature of consciousness and is therefore nondual and nonintentional. As Śākyabuddhi puts it,

> Since an agent and its patient are constructed in dependence upon each other, these two [i.e., subject and object] are posited in dependence on each other. The expression "subject" does not express mere reflexive awareness, which is the essential nature of cognition itself. The essential nature of cognition is not construed in mutual dependence on something else because it arises as such from its own causes. The essential nature of cognition is established in mere reflexive awareness (*svasaṃvedanamātra*). Since it is devoid of the above-described subject and object, it is said to be non-dual. (quoted in Dunne 2004, 407)

On this view, reflexive awareness is the fundamental nondual space or matrix within which various contents can arise but that is, in its nature, prior to any given content (MacKenzie 2012). Indeed, as Dunne argues, the Buddhist nondual contemplative tradition of Mahāmudrā has its philosophical roots in the dual-aspect reflexivist tradition developed by the *pramāṇavādins* (Dunne 2011). Drawing on this tradition in his work on the neuroscience of consciousness, Zoran Josipovic proposes that the nature of consciousness is a "non-conceptual nondual awareness, in itself empty of all other phenomenal content, yet reflexively self-aware" (2019, 1). More fully, it is a

> nonconceptual nondual awareness (NDA) that abides, ordinarily unrecognized, in the background of all conscious experiencing. This background awareness appears in meditation to be unitary and unchanging—a cognizance that is in itself empty of content, yet clearly aware and blissful—whereas various sensory, affective, and cognitive contents, and the various states of arousal appear to it as dynamic processes or, as a well-known metaphor states, like images in a mirror. NDA is characterized, among others, by its reflexive property—it knows itself to be conscious without relying on subsequent moments of conceptual cognition. (Josipovic 2014, 2)

Here the nature of consciousness is reflexive nondual awareness, the basic open self-luminosity that is the condition of any other phenomenal appearance. No phenomenal appearance can be given apart from this basic condition. The dual aspects of a typical moment of experience, then, are manifest *aspects* of this more fundamental nondual matrix. Subject and object are not reified independent substances but rather corelative and mutually specifying modalities of experience.[18]

So far, then, we see a philosophically rich integrated account of the qualitative, intentional, subjective, and synchronically unified aspects of consciousness. In the remainder of this section, I take up the dynamic or temporal and embodied aspects of consciousness. And as I discuss in earlier sections, the Yogācācara account the *ālayavijñāna* nicely fits the bill.[19] Recall that, on this account, the *ālaya* is the embodied, temporal background awareness that provides the "seed bed" and context for the transient manifest contents of consciousness. Like Thompson's notion of background consciousness, it is the "antecedent and 'rolling' experiential context of perception" (Thompson 2010, 355). I further suggest that a contemporary reconstruction of the horizontal or diachronic dynamics of the *ālaya* could appeal to the classical phenomenological analysis of time consciousness.[20] Furthermore, for both Mipham and the classical phenomenologists, the basic structure of time consciousness is closely tied to its reflexive self-affection.

With regard the embodiment of background or base consciousness, Thompson argues,

> Background consciousness is inextricably tied to the homeodynamic regulation of the body and includes primary affective awareness or core consciousness of one's bodily selfhood. Background consciousness in this fundamental sense is none other than sentience, the feeling of being alive, the affective backdrop of every conscious state. Sentience—or primal consciousness or core consciousness—is evidently not organized according to sensory modality, but rather according to the regulatory, emotional, and affective processes that make up the organism's basic feeling of self. (Thompson 2010, 354–55)

I take background consciousness to have a field-like topology. That is, base consciousness opens up or constitutes a synchronically unified phenomenal space within which phenomena can be given. This space is implicated in the appearance of anything within it but cannot itself be found among the objects it allows to appear. And because it is a phenomenal space, it is perspectivally structured—it is characterized by a genitive-dative or *of-to* structure. Note also that the phenomenal field is not a hidden Cartesian theater across which mental representations parade. Rather, it is the phenomenal-intentional openness to the world of an embodied, situated conscious agent. Recall further that the *ālaya* is partly constituted by a felt sense of the body as lived and therefore constitutes a basic form of nonobjectifying bodily self-awareness. It therefore exemplifies—in its own inchoate and prereflective way—the Janus-faced structure of phenomenal consciousness more generally.

Moreover, it is interesting to note that the functions associated with base consciousness—basic bodily awareness, affect, and self-regulatory functions, for instance—are subserved by midbrain and brainstem structures (Parvizi and Damasio 2001) and are not organized according to sensory modality (Damasio 2000). In contrast, the various more transient sensory states associated with the foreground of consciousness crucially involve thalamo-cortical structures (among others), damage to which can leave intact background awareness and core self-consciousness (Philippi et al. 2012). This is one reason, as Thompson argues, the "search for content NCCs in a particular sensory modality such as vision runs the risk of missing the biologically and phenomenologically more fundamental phenomenon of sentience, whose affective character and ipseity (nonreflective self-awareness) underlie and pervade all sensory experience" (2010, 355). That is, if this model of consciousness is on the right track, then our empirical and philosophical attempts to account for local phenomenal *state* consciousness will need to take more seriously the more fundamental modes of global background and creature consciousness and the reciprocal dynamics between these aspects of conscious experience. In Buddhist terms, we need an account of the vertical dynamics between the *ālayavijñāna* and the *pravṛttivijñāna*. In addition, if it is the case that base consciousness is reflexive, then it would make sense to look for the roots of reflexive phenomenal subjectivity, not so much in features of local, transient phenomenal states, but rather in basic features of bodily creature consciousness.

On the picture that emerges, then, reflexive or self-luminous nondual awareness is the nature of consciousness. As sentience, it is rooted in the self-regulatory, sensory, affective, and conative functions of the body. As base consciousness, it is the continuous embodied global background context for the transient local states of consciousness. As temporal, it has the standing-streaming structure that constitutes both the living present and the dynamic flow of the stream of consciousness. As reflexive, it is at the root of both creature subjectivity and the minimal phenomenal point of view (*svasaṃvedanamātra*) in each moment of manifest consciousness. Finally, as the reflexive matrix or phenomenal space of awareness, it is the ever-present horizon within which any and all phenomenal forms come to presence.

NOTES

1. As Thomas Nagel puts it, "But fundamentally an organism has conscious mental states if and only if there is something that it is like to be that organism—something it is like *for* the organism" (1974, 436).

2. For instance, as is discussed in this chapter, most Buddhist philosophers strongly deny the diachronic unity of consciousness and many also deny subjectivity.

3. For instance, on some accounts of consciousness, an experiential quality might be an aspect of the *mode* of presentation rather than the object presented.

4. Both *ākāra* ("phenomenal form") and *ābhāsa* ("appearance") are used to refer to these "aspects."

5. See Dharmakīrti PV 2.206.

6. For purposes of this discussion, the ultimate status of external objects or the external world for these thinkers are left aside. I treat the *pramāṇavādins* external realists who deploy an indirect realist account of perception.

7. On my interpretation, the introspection or metacognition argument is meant to establish the subject aspect, while the memory argument is meant to establish reflexive awareness and in doing so relies on the accessibility of the subject aspect of prior states.

8. Ultimately, of course, Dignāga will deny any such ontological gap even in the case of the perceptual object.

9. *prakāśamānas tādātmyāt svarūpasya prakāśakaḥ / yathā prakāśo 'bhimatas tathā dhīr ātmavedinī.*

10. *kiṃ tarhi tadupalambhasattayā/ sā cāprāmāṇikā na sattānibandhanān vyavahārān anuruṇaddhi / tadaprasiddhau viṣayasyāpy aprasiddhir ity astaṅgataṃ viśvaṃ syāt / sato 'py asiddhau sattāvyavahārāyogyatvāt / tasmān nānupalabhamānaḥ kasyacit saṃvedanaṃ vedayate nā ma kiṃ cit.*

11. *prabhāsvaram idaṃ cittaṃ prakṛtyāgantavo malāḥ*. "This mind is by nature luminous; its defilements are adventitious."

12. As Śaṅkara argues later in the same passage, mere causal connection between mental events is not sufficient to give experiential continuity.

13. The idea that the *ālaya* carries seeds (*bīja*) for future experience goes back to early Yogācāra.

14. This is an important point. Because it is retained intentionally rather than actually, the note does not need to exist in order to be retained.

15. Retention is not the source of reflexive awareness for Husserl but rather presupposes it. The nature of consciousness involves primordial self-givenness. Moreover, unconscious retention is not possible.

16. This gloss would rule out pure qualia externalism but is consistent with projectivist and relationalist accounts of qualia. It is also consistent with the view that the qualitative features of experience causally depend of the neurobiology of the organism and its interactions with the environment. See MacKenzie (2016) for more on a pragmatist and enactivist approach to the qualitative dimension of experience.

17. There is significant debate among Buddhist reflexivists about the relationship between the aspects and the nature of awareness. Some argue that there is no awareness without the aspects, while others argue that the aspects themselves are in some sense an illusion. See Dreyfus (1997) for an extensive discussion.

18. In the context of this discussion, I take this to be a strictly phenomenological claim about the nature and structure of conscious experience, not a metaphysical claim about either organisms (as subjects) or objects in the world.

19. I leave aside discussion of the *kliṣṭa-manas*, but see MacKenzie (2015).

20. Such a reconstruction could also appeal to the neurophenomenological view of the underlying brain dynamics (Varela 1999b), but that is outside the scope of this chapter.

Chapter Three

Agency and Other Minds

The Buddhist project centrally concerns understanding and removing the causes and conditions that give rise to and perpetuate suffering (*duḥkha*). Indeed, the basic analysis of the human situation is that we are trapped in *saṃsāra*, a self-reinforcing, self-perpetuating cycle of frustration and dissatisfaction, not just within a single lifetime, but across multiple lifetimes. The root causes of this sorry situation are the three poisons of attraction (*rāga*), aversion (*dveṣa*), and delusion (*moha*), which are dysfunctional forms of our basic conative framework, on the basis of which we respond to changing circumstances, seeking happiness and trying to avoid suffering. Because these basic forms of reaction are distorted or dysfunctional, as long as we are bound to them, our attempts to secure the lasting happiness we desire are doomed to fail. And yet, on the Buddhist view, because suffering is dependently originated (*pratītyasamutpanna*)—that is, it arises on the basis of specific causes and conditions—one can be free of suffering by understanding and removing its causes.

KARMA

Action (*kriyā*, *karman*) plays a central role in the classical Buddhist analysis of the human situation and its prescribed path to liberation from *saṃsāra*. The word *karma* originally derives from the Sanskrit *karman* (√*kṛ*), meaning "action," and in particular referring to a properly performed ritual action (Chapple 1986). By the time of the *Upaniṣads*, we find the meaning of the term expanded to cover moral actions and, by extension, the fruits (*phala*), or consequences, of those actions. Further, we can distinguish between what Roy Perrett (1998) terms the "general" and the "special" theories of *karma*.

The general theory concerns the relations between one's actions and one's well-being and character in one life, while the special theory concerns relations between successive lives of the same individual (or mental continuum). The two theories are logically independent, and the general theory does not require belief in rebirth. Here I am concerned with the general theory of *karma*, unless otherwise specified.

In the *Bṛhadāranyaka Upaniṣad*, we find an early statement of the general theory of *karma*: "According as one acts, according as one conducts himself, so does he become. The doer of good becomes good. The doer of evil becomes evil. One becomes virtuous by virtuous action, bad by bad action" (Hume 1921, 140). This core conception of *karma* is likewise accepted in the Buddhist tradition. For instance, in the *Majjhima Nikāya*, the Buddha explains, "Student, beings are owners of their actions, heirs of their actions; they originate from their actions, are bound to their actions, have their actions as their refuge. It is action that distinguishes beings as inferior and superior" (MN 135: III 202–06 in Bodhi 2005, 166).

The core conception or general theory of *karma* deals with the short- and long-term effects of moral or immoral actions for the agent of those actions. Wholesome (*kuśala*) actions tend to have positive consequences for oneself in this life, while unwholesome (*akuśala*) actions tend to have negative consequences. It is thus claimed that there is a reliable causal connection between virtuous action and long-term well-being, a claim that is at the center of Buddhist ethics and soteriology.

Furthermore, the Buddhist theory of *karma* emphasizes the deep interdependence of action and character. Unskillful actions plant *karmic* seeds (*bīja*) in one's stream of consciousness that, given the appropriate internal and external conditions, grow into negative consequences (*phala*, "fruit"; *vipāka*, "result") for the agent. That is, one's actions affect one's character, habits, and dispositions over the long term. Each time the thief steals, they may find it that much easier to steal (or that much harder to avoid stealing) in the future. An action performed once might be said to be out of character for an individual, but if repeated, it becomes less appropriate to say that it does not reflect the individual's true character. Moreover, insofar as an individual's attitudes, habits, perceptions, desires, values, and so forth are interconnected, unwholesome actions may have rather pervasive or unexpected negative effects. In any case, the key point here is that, as a part of Buddhist moral psychology, *karma* focuses on the often subtle and intricate feedback mechanisms in the human psyche, emphasizing the ways in which action, intention, and character are mutually reinforcing.

Another key point to recognize about the theory of *karma* is that it involves both descriptive and normative claims. There is no discernable fact-value dichotomy in the Buddhist tradition, and the theory of *karma* is meant to provide a framework for interpreting the complex relations between the moral dynamics of human experience and the larger causal order. Specifically, as we have seen, Indian Buddhists understand sentient beings and their world in terms of dependent origination (*pratītyasamutpāda*). The focus, then, is on patterns of dependence between events or processes rather than on, for instance, the operation of external forces on ontologically independent objects. The world is understood as a dynamic network of interdependent events, and the sentient beings within it are understood in the same terms.

Moreover, one may interpret the theory of *karma*, in addition to positing certain kinds of causal connections, as expressing a commitment to a fundamental, internal relation between virtuous action and genuine well-being. The specifics of this connection may rest on empirical claims about human action and psychology, but commitment to the internal relation itself will not be a merely empirical generalization. In the final analysis, then, the general theory of *karma* expresses a regulative normative commitment to the idea that, as Aristotle put it, "activities in accord with virtue control happiness, and the contrary activities control its contrary" (Aristotle 1999, 1100b7–11). According to the doctrine of *karma*, virtues are both means to the end of genuine happiness or well-being (*sukha*) and partly constitutive of the end itself. Thus, vices are harmful to oneself in that they detract from one's objective well-being. In addition, vices tend to undermine one's ability to enjoy other things of value, such as worldly happiness or wealth.

Given this framework, Indian Buddhist thinkers share four basic commitments. First, they are committed to the reality of *karma*. Second, they are committed to an understanding of *karma* as deeply connected with intention or volition (*cetanā*). Third, they are committed to the idea that, through Buddhist practice, one may become liberated from the afflictions of craving, aversion, and ignorance and achieve *nirvāṇa*. Thus, it is not surprising that the relationship between volition, action, and the results of action for the agent constitutes a central theme of Indian Buddhist philosophy. Fourth, while Buddhist philosophers are committed to the reality of action and its results, they are also committed to the unreality of any substantial self or agent of actions. How can one affirm the reality of volition, action, efficacious practice, and liberation while denying the existence of agents, practitioners, or liberated beings? Reconciling the doctrine of no-self (*anātman*) with an account of agency and *karma* was a central task of such great Buddhist philosophers as Vasubandhu.

AGENTLESS AGENCY

Buddhist discussions of morality, cultivation, and the path make liberal reference to intentions, actions, agents, and a variety of capacities—attention, deliberation, self-control—associated with agency. However, this way of talking about the Buddhist path as one in which individuals, through effort and training, come to gain increasing awareness and self-mastery, leading ultimately to awakening, appears to be in significant tension with the central idea of *anātman* generally and the Buddhist reductionist project specifically. For instance, the *Vissudhimagga* boldly states, "There is suffering but none who suffer, there is action but no agent, there is *nibbāna* but no one who is released, there is a Path but no goer on it" (Buddhaghosa 1999, 97).

Buddhist reductionists attempt to resolve this tension by appealing to the conventional-ultimate distinction. As discussed in previous chapters, on the Buddhist reductionist analysis, the existence of the individual person just consists in the existence the right kind of system of subpersonal events. Persons are conventionally real (*saṃvṛtisat*) but not ultimately, irreducibly real (*paramārthasat*). Furthermore, given their rejection of the enduring substantial self and their reductionist account of persons, it should not come as a surprise that Buddhist reductionists also reject agent causality. Ontologically, there being no enduring substantial entity that could exercise agent-causal power, our naïve sense that we and others are such agents is an illusion. Just as Buddhist reductionist thinkers reject the self and reduce the person to a complex stream of events, so, too, will they give an account of action, not in agent-causal, but in event-causal terms.

For instance, Vasubandhu in chapter 9 of the *Abhidharmakośabhāṣya* confronts the objection:

> [Opponent:] If there is no-self, who is the agent of an action, and who is the recipient of the consequences of the action?
>
> [Vasubandhu:] What do you mean by "agent" and "recipient?"
>
> [Opponent:] He who acts is the agent; he who receives is the recipient. . . . In common usage, for example, Devadatta is said to have the independent power of bathing, sitting, walking, and so on.
>
> [Vasubandhu:] What being are you calling "Devadatta"? Is he the self? But that's just what you have to prove! Now, is he the totality of the five aggregates? We would consider that to be the agent. Action is of three types: bodily, vocal, and mental. Bodily action is dependent on the functioning of the mind. The functioning of the mind as regards the body is dependent on its own causes in the same way. Nothing has any kind of independence. All beings arise in dependence on contributing causes. Even if we were to admit that the self is not caused and doesn't depend on anything, that would not prove that something has independence. Therefore, this characteristic of "independence" does not apply

> to any agent at all. Whatever is the principal cause of an action, that is called the "agent." And the self has no causal efficacy at all. Therefore, the self should not be considered an agent. From memory arises intention; from intention, thought; from thought, exertion; from exertion, a wind in the body; and from this wind comes the action. What does the self do in this process? (Goodman 2009, 305)

According to Vasubandhu, then, the locus of agency is not an enduring self but a highly complex psychophysical system (the "five aggregates"). Despite our sense that proper names, the first-person pronoun, and terms like *agent* (*kartṛ*) refer to an enduring self that is the locus of experience and will, these terms in fact refer to an interlocking network of events. In explaining action, we need only refer to the mental and physical events (memories, intentions, bodily impulses) that arise within a relatively causally and functionally integrated system. As Vasubandhu asks, "What does the self do in this process?"

On this view, the sense of being a stable self arises from and is sustained by a complex set of impersonal causes and conditions that are not transparent to the system itself. The sense of self functions as a kind of user illusion, and it is ultimately maladaptive according to Buddhist thought. The system comes to represent and experience itself as if there were a homuncular, enduring self that is an owner, subject, and agent. Yet, this representation of a self obscures the complex psychophysical processes that actually drive experience and action.

In this regard, then, Buddhist thinkers like Vasubandhu are similar to contemporary skeptics concerning the experience of agency. For example, Daniel Wegner writes,

> The real causal sequence underlying human behavior involves a massively complicated set of mechanisms. . . . Each of our actions is really the culmination of an intricate set of physical and mental processes that correspond to our traditional concept of will, in that they involve linkages between our thoughts and our actions. . . . However, we don't see this. . . . The illusion of conscious will may be a misapprehension of the mechanistic causal relations underlying our own behavior that comes from looking at ourselves by means of a mental explanatory system. We don't see our own gears turning because we're busy reading our minds. (Wegner 2003, 26–27)

For both Wegner and Vasubandhu, our experience of ourselves as conscious agents obscures the incredibly complex causes and conditions that give rise to our actions. For Vasubandhu, agency is a psychophysical process with no substance at its base or center. "From memory," he writes, "arises intention; from intention, thought; from thought, exertion; from exertion, a wind in the body; and from this wind comes the action" (Goodman 2009, 305). The self is not the agent. If one wants to use the term *agent*, on Vasubandhu's account, then one can apply the term to the complex system or process as a whole or to the principal cause of the action. What counts as the agent is a matter of general usage or explanatory utility, but in either case, there is no substantial thing that is the agent. Furthermore, both thinkers agree that we interpret both others and ourselves through the framework of agency. Our (mis-)interpretation of ourselves and others as enduring, conscious, agential selves is of a piece. Indeed, according to Vasubandhu, the fundamental basis for our false construction of the world of everyday experience is the representational (*vijñapti*) construction of entities (*bhava-kalpanā*), such as the self, others, and objects.

Clearly, then, the Buddhist reductionist rejects the existence of the self as agent and of agent-causal accounts of action and agency. Yet Vasubandhu also gives an account of action and agency in terms of causal connections between mental and physical *dharmas*. Indian thinkers identified three criteria for being an agent. The agent must be (1) the performer of the action and (2) the owner (*svāmin*) of the action, and (3) the action must be within the agent's own power (*svātantrya*) to enact. For Vasubandhu, "that which is the chief cause (*pradhāna-kāraṇa*) of [the action], is said to be its agent (*kartṛ*)" (Hanner 2018, 598). The performer of the action is not a persisting agent but a prior event in the causal stream of aggregates (*skandha-santāna*). Furthermore, he argues that the cause of the action, in exercising control over the effect, is also the owner. Of course, this is an impersonal description of a psychological causal process. Vasubandha also allows that, speaking conventionally, we may say things like "Caitra remembers" or "That is Caitra's memory." This is because we have conventions for naming and tracking streams of aggregates as persons. But on his reductionist view, these are merely convenient labels for the complex impersonal causal processes of the aggregates, which are themselves reducible to the causal flow of momentary *dharmas*. Finally, Vasubandhu simply rejects the idea of *svātantrya* as an independent power on the grounds that any such independent power would be incapable of interaction and so causally inert. Indeed, the idea of *svātantrya* here seems to be one of agent causation and so precisely what Vasubandhu's selfless, reductionist alternative must reject.

But here the Buddhist reductionist theory must grapple with the "disappearing agent problem." Take David Velleman's account of what he calls the "standard story of human action":

> There is something that the agent wants, and there is an action that he believes conducive to its attainment. His desire for the end, and his belief in the action as a means, justify taking the action, and they jointly cause an intention to take it, which in turn causes the corresponding movements of the agent's body. Provided that these causal processes take their normal course, the agent's

> movements consummate an action, and his motivating desire and belief constitute his reasons for acting. (Velleman 1992, 123)

The problem here, according to Velleman, is that the standard story fails to include an agent or, more precisely, "fails to cast the agent in his proper role. In this story, reasons cause an intention and an intention causes bodily movement, but nobody—that is, no person—does anything" (Velleman 1992, 189). More specifically,

> various roles that are actually played by the agent himself in the history of a full-blooded action are not played by anything in the story or are played by psychological elements whose participation is not equivalent to his. In a full-blooded action, an intention is formed by the agent himself, not by his reasons for acting. Reasons affect his intention by influencing him to form it, but they thus affect his intention by affecting him first. And the agent then moves his limbs in execution of his intention; his intention doesn't move his limbs by itself. The agent thus has at least two roles to play: he forms an intention under the influence of reasons for acting, and he produces behavior pursuant to that intention. (Velleman 1992, 189–90)

So, what's the problem? For Vellemans, the problem with causal-reductive accounts of action and agency is that they require psychological states and events to, as it were, play their usual roles in an activity while also playing the role of the agent in relation to them. The agent is responsive to reasons, forms intentions, and produces behavior. States like intentions and desires have their role to play here but only in relation to the central role of the agent themself.

Helen Steward provides another way to think about the problem. Our folk psychological notions of belief, desire, intention, and the like are person-level concepts that cannot be translated without loss into the framework of impersonal events and causes. And at the personal level, the agent themself plays the central role in the very intelligibility of the concepts of action, agency, and so on. On her view,

> one cannot give a pure event-causal story in which the antecedent causes of bodily movements are said to be things like beliefs, desires, and intentions. These concepts are part and parcel of a way of thinking about action from which the agent and her doings cannot simply be banished, for the way of thinking is designed in the first place to be a story in which the agent and her acting essentially features. If there is a pure event-causal story to be told about action (and I do not at this stage want to rule this out as a possibility), it has to be told at a quite different ontological level from this, one involving, say, neural firings and muscle contractions. It cannot be a story in which the role we normally suppose action to have in the production of voluntary movement is simply taken over by

> states like intentions, even what have come to be known as "immediately executive" intentions. Even an immediately executive intention has to be executed. (Steward 2012, 64)

In terms of Buddhist reductionism, we see by now a familiar problem emerge. Can the Buddhist reductionist both preserve the conventional reality of agents, agency, and actions and give a purely impersonal event-causal account at the ultimate level? Of course, when giving an account of different ontological levels, it isn't surprising that what shows up at one level might not show up at another. Even if agents and agency are real, we shouldn't necessarily expect to find them at the microphysical level, for instance. But the Buddhist reductionist needs more than this. Vasubandhu attempts to give an impersonal, event-causal account of what agency amounts to. So the impersonal level of *dharmas* and *skandhas* (along with our conventions) must in some way ground and explain the conventional reality of agency. But if, as Steward and others assert, this renders the personal level of agency unintelligible, then the attempted reduction fails. The alternatives, it seems, would be to embrace the reality of agency and agents or to eliminate them.

However, another option would be to treat the conventional reality of agents and agency along fictionalist lines. On this approach, ultimately there are no agents and no agency—events just *happen* in a vast network of causes and conditions. Yet, such fictions as "person," "agent," and "action" have dependently arisen and can be skillfully redeployed toward more liberatory aims. In this sense, agency and agents are merely skillful means (*upāya kauśalya*) toward awakening, after which they are to be abandoned as the illusions they always were (Goodman 2016). Whatever the merits of this position, though, it is in tension with Vasubandhu's reductionist program, which needs to both deflate substantialist notions of agents and agency and ground or explain the conventional reality of agency in terms of impersonal causal processes. Indeed, the fictionalist approach sits better with a Madhyamaka account of the conventional. As Jay Garfield argues, "An account of agency and responsibility in Madhyamaka only addresses the realm of dependent origination, of conventional truth. . . . [T]hey will ascribe agency and responsibility to nominal entities, evaluating actions without ultimately existent agents" (2016, 52). The key difference here is that persons, agents, and actions are understood as mere conceptual constructions without appeal to any ultimate metaphysical or explanatory ground.

Garfield's own Madhyamaka-inspired account rests on the constructive processes of appropriation and narration. The fictional self is constructed by the appropriation of the aggregates as belonging to a self, as "mine." And the aggregates over time are constructed in relation to the fictional self to which they "belong." In this respect, Garfield faithfully follows Candrakīrti. However, he also draws on more recent narrative approaches to identity:

> To act is for our behavior to be determined by reasons, by motives we regard as ours. For Madhyamaka, it is for the causes of our behavior to be part of the narrative that makes sense of our lives, as opposed to being part of the vast uninterpreted milieu in which our lives are led. This distinction is not *metaphysical* but *literary*, and so a matter of choice, sensitive to explanatory purposes. That means the choice is not *arbitrary*. We can follow Nietzsche here. For what do we take responsibility and for what are we assigned responsibility? Those acts we interpret—or others interpret for us—as ours, as constituting part of the basis of imputation of our identities. (Garfield 2016, 54)

In contrast to Vasubandhu's Buddhist reductionism, this view is both deflationary and nonreductive. It is deflationary in that agency and responsibility are not metaphysical but, as Garfield puts it, *literary* (i.e., narrative). It is nonreductive in that it eschews the attempt to give an explanatorily robust, bottom-up account of these phenomena. Rather, agency and responsibility emerge as fluid, constructed aspects of the distinctively human forms of life.

ENACTIVE AGENCY

For both the Buddhist reductionists and the Mādhyamikas, agency is a conventional construction carved out from the larger network of dependently originated events. In contrast to both of these strongly conventionalist approaches, the enactivist approach grounds agency in the biological nature of cognitive systems. As discussed in chapter 1, on the enactive theory, living things are self-organizing, autopoietic, and biologically autonomous systems. Unlike nonliving self-organizing systems, such as tornados, living systems are both self-maintaining and self-producing. Furthermore, at least many forms of living systems display adaptivity, the capacity to self-regulate with respect to their conditions of viability (Di Paolo 2005). On the enactive theory, agency is a real, emergent biological capacity rather than a mere convention, much less a convenient fiction.

According to Barandiaran, Di Paolo, and Rohde, "agency involves, at least, a system doing something by itself according to certain goals or norms within a specific environment" (2009, 2). They continue, "From this description, three different though interrelated aspects of agency follow immediately: (i) there is a system as a distinguishable entity that is different from its environment, (ii) this system is doing something by itself in that environment and (iii) it does so according to a certain goal or norm" (Barandiaran, Di Paolo, and Rohde 2009, 2). On this enactive account, a theory of agency will need to account for these three features of individuality, interactional asymmetry, and normativity.

As discussed in chapter 1, the enactive notion of individuality is grounded in the theory of biological autonomy. Thompson writes,

> Individuality in this case [i.e., of an autopoietic system] corresponds to a *formal self-identity*—to an invariant dynamic pattern that is produced, maintained, and realized by the system itself, while the system undergoes incessant material transformation and regulates its external boundary conditions accordingly. An autopoietic system is thus an individual in a sense that begins to be worthy of the term *self*. (2010, 75)

The key requirement here is that the system defines itself as a system in relation to its environment, and it does so through its own endogenous powers and capacities. As observers, we can categorize groups or systems as individuals for any number of reasons or even just arbitrarily. However, biological individuality is grounded in the self-producing and self-maintaining capacities of the system itself. On the enactive approach, living individuality is an emergent biological phenomenon, not a mere convention or fiction.[1]

Of course, the enactivist view of individuality is not that of an atomistic or ontologically separate substance. Rather, the living individual is a dynamic, self-organizing system that is necessarily coupled with its environment. Further, as is discussed in the next chapter, the enactive approach entails the coemergence and mutual implication of the organism and its world, or *Umwelt*. Yet in order for a living being to count as an agent, there must be an asymmetry in its active relation to its environment and its conditions of viability within it. As Stapleton and Froese remark, "The key point here is that agency requires that the adaptive regulation of agent environment interaction is realized by the agent rather than resulting only from contributions of the environment" (2016, 119). It is not enough that the system is mobile or that some subsystem drives its movement. The adaptivity underpinning agency requires that movement is deployed to regulate the system's ongoing interaction with the environment. Dynamic self-organizing systems are always coupled to the environment, but *agents* must have the endogenous capacity to modulate that coupling in order to preserve their own conditions of viability *as* individual systems.

The third requirement of biological agency is normativity. Here normativity concerns goal-directed adaptive behavior. An agent is an individual that can modulate or regulate its own interaction with its environment and can do so in relation to its own goals. These goals must not be simply externally imposed (or arbitrarily attributed), but rather they must be grounded in the self-production and self-maintenance of the individual. However, at the level of biological agency, it is not necessary that the individual explicitly represent the goal in order for its actions to count as goal directed. Finally, "[s]uch goals or norms emerge within the living system as a result of the autonomous or adaptive dynamics (metabolic or otherwise) attempting to keep the system within its boundaries of viability" (Stapleton and Froese 2016, 119).

The enactivist view, then, is importantly different from the reductionist, event-causal account of action and agency. Agency requires not simply the right causal chain of events but also the existence of biological individuals and their endogenous capacities to adaptively regulate their interactions with the environment in relation to their needs and goals *as* biological individuals. Therefore, the agent does not go missing but remains an essential feature of the account. Of course, the enactivist view here concerns biological agency, not the sophisticated forms of psychological agency discussed by Vellemans and Steward. A fully worked out enactivist view needs an account of the emergence of cognitive agency from biological agency and personal agency from cognitive agency. I do not attempt that here, but the discussion in chapter 1 of the emergence of psychological autonomy from biological autonomy gives at least part of an account.

The enactivist view is also importantly different from the substantialist, agent-causal view critiqued by Vasubandhu and other Buddhist philosophers. The agent here is a dynamic, self-organizing system, a complex multilevel process, not a stable enduring substance. There is no substantial core of the system that could be that type of agent. Rather, part and whole are dynamically coemergent. As discussed in chapter 1,

> Dynamic co-emergence best describes the sort of emergence we see in autonomy. In an autonomous system, the whole not only arises from the (organizational closure of the) parts, but the parts also arise from the whole. The whole is constituted by the relations of the parts, and the parts are constituted by the relations they bear to one another in the whole. Hence, the parts do not exist in advance, prior to the whole, as independent entities that retain their identity in the whole. Rather, part and whole co-emerge and mutually specify each other. (Thompson 2010, 65)

Agency here is a system-level capacity, and action is an emergent process. They exist and operate at the level of the whole organism, but the organism as a whole coemerges from and is interdependent with the parts.

On the enactivist view, then, the problem with Vasubandhu's event-causal reductionism about agency isn't that it neglects the agent-causal powers of a substantial self. The problem is that the microdynamics of the system—in this case, the causal chain of simple *dharmas*—are not sufficient to explain the behavior of the system as a whole. Furthermore, the microlevel interactions occur as they do in part because of the relational context of the meso- and macrodynamics. In other words, the whole is not a mere epiphenomenon of the parts and their interactions. Rather, living systems are constituted by the processes of local-to-global determination, whereby novel processes and structures, such as actions, arise, and by global-to-local determination, whereby emergent processes and structures constrain local interactions. Agency, as a system-level capacity, is not found at the microcausal level but rather at the level of the organism dynamically and adaptively coupled to its environment. And here again, we see a fundamental tension between Buddhist reductionism and the enactivist process emergentism. Agents and agency, for the enactivist, are dependent but irreducible and so not merely a conventional fiction or construct. However, as we have seen in our prior discussion of the ontological status of persons, this intermediate category makes no sense in the Buddhist reductionist framework.

PSYCHOLOGICAL AGENCY

The enactivist view discussed in the previous section concerns biological agency. However, the notion of agency addressed by Vasubandhu, Vellemans, and Steward is psychological. We experience ourselves not just as organisms interacting with our environments through metabolism or movement but also as mental agents who engage in thinking, feeling, and intending. Indeed, the main thrust of the denial of agent causation concerns this sense of being a kind of (inner) mental agent as the author and owner of intentional actions. Ganeri characterizes the view: "Let me call any view according to which agents are compositionally irreducible substances and that causation by agents is an ontological primitive in intentional action an 'Authorship View' of self. The Authorship View is the view that selves just are the agents posited by agent causationists" (2017, 16). Ganeri further points out, and I agree, that Buddhist *anātmavāda* explicitly rejects this view of the self. I have already discussed Vasubandhu's reductionist objections to agent causation. But even going back to the Buddha, we see a rejection of the self as a stable locus of self-control. On the Buddhist view, the dynamic flow of our mental lives is not centered on or organized by a self. Rather, the stream of consciousness is dependently originated, structured by the causal and functional connections between mental events. And like other self-organizing systems, such as schools of fish or ant colonies, the dependently originated flow of mental life can give the appearance of centralized self-control, when in fact there are just causal-functional patterns of decentralized mental events.

Ganeri's own objection to the authorship view it that "it commits one to a particular account of the nature of mental action, to a polarization of mental life into voluntary events that are 'under one's control' and all else that just happens in the mind, now seen as mere occurrence" (2017, 18). More specifically, the particular account of mental action here is just the causal theory of action, whereby actions are understood as events that are caused by (an agent's) intentions in the right sort of way. Such events are "willed" or "intended," but other events, even ones we would consider forms of behavior, are ultimately mere happenings. Note then, that Vasubandhu's account of agentless agency, as I interpret it here, is also a form of the causal theory. And by maintaining a causal theory while rejecting the need for an agential self, Vasubandhu's theory threatens to collapse the distinction between actions and mere happenings. Ganeri's "attentionalist" view is in part inspired by the Theravāda philosopher Buddhaghosa, for whom "there is no-self as controlling agent of thinking, believing, and feeling. Attention instead is what explains the activity of thought and mind" (Ganeri 2017, 31). So unlike the top-down authorship view or the bottom-up reductionist view, attentionalism holds that the dynamic autonomy of mental life is sui generis (Ganeri 2017, 23).

I find much that is attractive in the attentionalism of Buddhaghosa and Ganeri. In particular, I agree that an adequate alternative to both the authorship and reductionist views should affirm the endogenous dynamism and self-regulating autonomy of mental life. As Ganeri puts it, "our conscious mental lives are controlled neither from *outside* nor from *below*" (2017, 23). However, to sketch my own enactivist alternative, I return to a theme introduced in chapter 1, psychological autonomy as self-governance. Recall Jennan Ismael's description of a self-governing system:

> self-governing systems are a subclass of complex, open systems characterized by an internal dynamics that incorporates a self-representational loop and supports flexibility of response function. They store information about themselves in an explicit form and combine that information with new input to compute the values of self-locating parameters, which are then used to regulate responses to occurrent stimuli, making fluid change in first-order dynamical properties possible in real time. (2011, 12)

In chapter 1, I argue that the emergence of the self is bound up with the emergence of self-governance and psychological autonomy from more basic forms of biological autonomy. Psychological autonomy is characterized by enhanced endogenous integration, self-control, and adaptive flexibility arising from the distinctively mental capacities of a system. In human beings, psychological autonomy enables, for instance, conscious self-control, flexible anticipation, imagination, navigation, reasoning, and planning.

The key point here is that both mindedness and agency emerge from the self-organizing and self-regulating processes of life and are themselves higher-order self-regulation processes. Our conscious mental lives are not controlled from the outside—either by exogenous factors or by a separate substantial self—because the "mind" is a dynamic, self-regulating process. Our conscious mental lives are not controlled from below because self-regulating processes necessarily involve both "bottom-up" and "top-down"—or, better, local-to-global and global-to-local—processes. As Ismael puts it, "When we look at the fine-scale material structure of the brain, we find neurons connected in complex networks that regulate the voluntary and involuntary movements of the body, but no *thing*—no indivisible nugget of selfhood—that receives the signals coming in from the senses and orchestrates the motor activity" (Ismael 2014, 276). Rather,

> In a self-governing system, there is some *one* making the choice, some *one* exercising control, some one making judgments and undertaking commitments. The one here is not an individual substance or material particular lurking inside the system, it is a point of view (or, if you like, is the formal subject of a point of view, the occupant, or the possessor), and it is a kind of formal *one-ness* that is the product of, rather than a precondition for, the collectivization of epistemic and practical deliberation (Ismael 2014, 286).

The emergence of the agent, then, is the emergence of a deliberative standpoint within a self-regulating system. In other words, the self as agent is *enacted*, just as it in turn *enacts*.

OTHER MINDS

In discussing a Mādhyamika view of the self, Garfield writes,

> [S]elves are *constructed* through the appropriation of aggregates, through recognizing a body, thoughts, values, dispositions, and intentions as *mine*. In turn, those physical and cognitive processes are constructed in relation to that appropriating self. That appropriation and narration of a life is not a solo affair. We narrate and construct each other in the hermeneutical ensemble act of social life. (2016, 53)

The constructed self is a social self. The construction of a self is a co-construction of and by other selves. And precisely because the self here is constructed, we need an account of the emergence of both the sense of being a self and the sense of others *as* other selves.

This is no small task, of course, and Indian Buddhist philosophers developed deeply sophisticated accounts of this (ultimately delusive) co-construction process. One of the most important insights developed by such thinkers as Vasubandhu and Dharmakīrti is that the construction of the self is inextricable from the construction of both objects and other selves. I have more to say about the co-construction of self and world in Madhyamaka and Yogācāra in the next chapter. Here I want to focus on the problem of how (or whether) the experience of others as other subjects or selves might emerge.

The Yogācāra school, broadly construed, offers a radical critique of the subject-object framework of experience. That is, the various thinkers associated with this tradition develop both positive accounts of the co-construction of subjects and objects and negative accounts of the ultimately delusory nature of both subject and object. Indeed, as I interpret it, the ultimate philosophical and soteriological aim of Yogācāra is the radical transcendence of the subject-object framework. One approach to this deconstruction project—what in the next chapter I call the *internalist-representationalist* approach to Yogācāra—finds expression in such Buddhist epistemologists as Dharmakīrti, Prajñākaragupta, and Ratnakīrti. The reduction of subject and object to mere virtual images (*ākāra*) internal to a moment of consciousness, coupled with Buddhist nominalism and mereological reductionism, makes the problem of other minds particularly challenging. As Ganeri argues, Buddhist reflexivism must confront the problem of conceptual solipsism. The problem, as Ganeri states it, is "whether a mind constructed according to reflexivist principles would actually be able to sustain first-person phenomena" (2012, 213). His answer is no because "in depriving the subject of the conceptual resources for genuine first-person reference, the subject has also been deprived of two abilities that are constitutive of a first-person stance, the ability to conceive of one's experiences as *one's own*, and the ability to conceive of *other subjects* of self-conscious experience" (Ganeri 2012, 214).

Now, concerning the problem of other minds, Dharmakīrti argues in his *Santānāntarasiddhi* that other mind streams can be inferred on the basis of observed speech and action. He writes, "Observing that the appearance of our bodily and verbal actions is preceded by our minds, we infer the existence of other minds from the appearance of other persons' bodily and verbal actions" (quoted in Inami 2001, 466). One has (noninferential) epistemic access to the arising of mental events in one's own mind stream and can observe the causal connection between intentions and actions or speech in our own case. On this basis, one can infer the existence of mental states on the basis of the perceived actions or speech of others. In other cases of valid inference, such as inferring the existence of fire from the perception of smoke, it is also possible to gain perceptual knowledge of the inferred phenomena. Seeing smoke on the hillside and inferring fire, one can subsequently gain perceptual confirmation of the fire's existence by going to the hillside. However, in the case of other minds, Dharmakīrti holds that they are imperceptible (*adṛśya*). So how is the inferential link established? First, following the Sautrāntika view, Dharmakīrti holds that one can perceive or be aware that a certain observed action was *not* caused by one's own intending, desiring, and so on. Second, for Dharmakīrti, the inference to other minds is established as trustworthy or nondeceptive (*avisaṃvāda*) because it is a fitting guide to action (*arthakriyā*). Furthermore, because the other's mind is established by inference and not perception, what comes to be known is not token mental events themselves (as *svalakṣaṇas*) but only types of mental events (as *sāmānyalakṣaṇas*). In correctly inferring that another is feeling hunger by observing their behavior, one is not directly acquainted with their hunger but only that they are feeling a mental event of the type "hunger." Therefore, even though we can gain knowledge of other minds, on this view, we cannot know the minds of others directly or noninferentially in the way we know our own.[2]

In contrast, Ratnakīrti, in his *Santānāntaraduṣaṇa*, contends that Dharmakīrti's arguments fail and that there is no epistemic warrant for the existence of other mind streams. He argues that Dharmakīrti faces a dilemma. He asks, "Is the volition that is being established as the cause of the phenomena of language and behavior something perceptible by the inferrer or is it volition as such, [something] which is independent of the properties of visibility and invisibility?" (quoted in Ganeri 2012, 206). If the other's mental state is perceptible by the inferrer but unperceived, then on Ratnakīrti's view, its existence would be disproven by that very nonobservation. If, on the other hand, it is perceived, then inference is redundant and does not establish the existence of the other mind. Now, if it is not the perceptible mental event that is inferred but rather the general type, Ratnakīrti argues that there will be no basis for establishing the casual connection between volition in general and speech or action. This is because, on his view, the volition in general, unlike an unobserved fire on the hillside, is not the kind of thing that could be perceived. There is, therefore, no way to establish the necessary causal connection (*tad-utpatti*).

Having cast doubt on the inferential warrant for other minds, Ratnakīrti then turns to a disproof of other minds. He argues, "If there were another stream, there would, of necessity, be a difference between it and one's own stream" (quoted in Ganeri 2012, 209). Otherwise, there wouldn't be distinct, individuated mind streams. He then questions whether this difference is manifest or unmanifest. As a reflexivist, he holds that the "difference certainly should be manifest when one's own stream is manifest, as it is the very being (*svabhāva*) of the stream [to be manifest]" (quoted in Ganeri 2012,

209). That is, one's own mental states are self-manifest or self-presenting, and it seems for Ratnakīrti, they are manifest *as one's own*. But, he argues, if another's mental states are manifest to one, then they must be manifest *as another's*. Are they? Ratnakīrti states, "[T]his difference is not manifested. For if the differences were thought to be manifest, the other stream would incontrovertibly too, as its boundary," which he denies (Ganeri 2012, 209). Thus, he argues,

> Just as when only one's own stream of experience is manifest, difference from a non-manifest hare's horn does not appear, so likewise difference from a manifest other stream does not appear. Not even the slightest difference appears between one's own and another stream, just as there is none between one's own mind and a hare's horn. In the case of one's own experience, the hare's horn and another mind are on a par. It is not the case that either difference or non-difference appears in relation to the hare's horn, and similarly it is not possible to establish that difference appears in relation to another stream. (Ganeri 2012, 209–10)

Ratnakīrti's idea here seems to be that, unlike one's own stream, which is by nature manifest, other streams are not manifest, and there is no experiential basis for streams different from one's own. Nothing truly shows up *as* the mental life of another in our own experience, and any inference to posited but unobservable other minds is ultimately unwarranted, even if practically useful. The reflexivist view of mind gives an account of immediate access to one's own mental life and an account of how experiences *as of* external objects and other minds are constructed. Yet the constructed forms, while they appear to be external to the mind, are on this view immanent to reflexive consciousness. For Ratnakīrti, the reflexive mind is ultimately *self-enclosed*, and so solipsism—at the ultimate level anyway—is an implication of the nonduality of consciousness. Prajñākaragupta gives a bracing summary of this more radical type of view:

> There is neither an "I" nor a "he" nor a "you" nor even an "it"; neither the thing, nor the not-thing; neither a law nor a system; neither the terms nor the relations. But there are only the cognitive events of colourless sensations which have forms but no names. They are caught for a moment in a stream and then rush to naught (Ganguli 1963, 193). Even the stream is a fiction. That sensum of the moment, the purest particular, that *advaya*, the indivisible unit of cognition, that is the sole reality, the rest are all fictions, stirred up by time-honoured convention of language which is itself a grand fiction. (quoted in Ganguli 1963, 193)

Each moment of cognition is an indivisible unit of reflexive awareness that appears as if structured into subject and object. But these are mere appearances or forms within the nondual moment of consciousness, which is the "sole reality" relative to which everything else is a "fiction."

At this point, one can see the force of Ganeri's argument that reflexivism entails conceptual solipsism. However, the idea that consciousness or even mindedness more broadly is reflexive is not limited to the radical reflexivism of later Buddhist epistemologists. Indeed, I present a version of reflexivism in chapter 2, and to put it mildly, I am not prepared to embrace philosophical solipsism. So, it is worth asking whether and how a broadly reflexive theory of the conscious mind can account for intersubjectivity and the existence of other minds.

On my view, there are three key areas to address in order to give a broadly reflexivist account of intersubjectivity and other minds. The first concerns the nature and relationship between reflexivity and intentionality. The second has to do with the role of embodiment in an account of the conscious mind. The third concerns the nature of mental life in relation to our embodiment and the possibility of a noninferentialist account of intersubjectivity.

As discussed in chapter 2, the Buddhist dual-aspect reflexivist theory of mind posits mental episodes with (the appearance of) complex internal structure. A moment of reflexive awareness is typically characterized by an object aspect, a subject aspect, and its fundamental reflexivity or reflexive awareness. The subject aspect presents aspects of the mental episode itself, whereas the object aspect presents an object. Further, I argue that these aspects can be understood as distinct modes of presentation—"as subject" and "as object"—that are immanent structures within the reflexive mental episode. On this view, the role of the object aspect is to provide cognitive access to (what appears to be) an independent object. In this way, the object aspect is an immanent intentional structure that presents an object. Finally, I argue that this form of dual-aspect reflexivism has an internalist view of intentionality. According to Montague, on the internalist view, "thinking of a particular object essentially involves conceiving of it in some particular manner, or characterizing it in some fashion, and that reference to the particular manner involved is essential for determining which object is being thought of" (2016, 143).

For the internalist, then, some immanent aspect or structure of intentionality is necessary for determining the intentional object. But the internalist is not committed to the stronger claim that the internal aspect is also sufficient. The internalist need not deny that in the case of veridical intentional awareness, one is aware of an independent object. Their claim is only that there is an internal condition on determinate *access* to the object. However, Ratnakīrti's internalist-representationalist view does seem to be committed to these claims. On my interpretation, he holds a radically internalist view of intentionality according to which a moment of reflexive awareness is only ever aware of itself. The dual aspects are the faces of the moment of awareness itself and only present the false or fictional appearance of that which is other. Given this radical internalism, it is not surprising that Ratnakīrti insists that another's stream would need to appear explicitly *as other* and that there is no observed boundary between the manifest contents of one's own experience that of the (purportedly) other. In short, any mental state that shows up in experience would be one's own, and any state that does not show up is no different from the hare's horn. Ultimately, for him, the nondual sphere of experience is unbounded.

A reflexivist theory of intersubjectivity, then, should reject this radically internalist account of intentionality. What the reflexivist is committed to is that consciousness is self-luminous or self-presenting, not that it is exclusively so. Indeed, the central insight of the phenomenological tradition, as I see it, is that the intentionality is fundamentally *openness to the world.* Whatever the metaphysical status of the world, rigorous phenomenological analysis of intentionality reveals that intentionality can only be understood as consciousness pointing beyond itself. Indeed, the life of consciousness is intentionally directed toward a world of transcendent objects through transverse intentionality, and it is interwoven with past and future acts of consciousness through the horizontal intentionality of time consciousness. Now, there are a number of competing accounts of intentionality among the classical phenomenologists, and I won't here enter into the details of that debate. The important point is that intentionality is not like a mirror reflecting oneself back on oneself, but rather it is a mode of engaging the world.

Likewise, the enactivist account of intentionality holds that it is a mode of open engagement with the world. Recall that the three aspects of basic sense making are (1) sensibility as basic openness to the world, (2) significance as positive and negative valence relative to the norms of the living being, and (3) orientation in relation to the significance and valence of the world. Each of these is an aspect or form of intentionality, the intertwined operation of which constitutes a sentient being's sense-making of and in its environment. Crucially, sense-making is neither purely internal nor restricted to a single moment of experience. Rather sense making is an ongoing way that a living, cognitive being engages its world. It is transactional and world-involving from the start. On this kind of view, it is hard to see how solipsism could gain a foothold.

On my view, the Buddhist reflexivists offer a plausible and philosophically attractive account of the reflexive dual-aspect structure of consciousness. And they do so while avoiding ontological commitment to enduring substances. This kind of reflexivism also provides crucial insights into the dynamic construction of self and world within experience. However, the radically internalist approach to intentionality ultimately leads to intractable problems of skepticism and solipsism. Ratnakīrti, of course, boldly embraces this at the ultimate level. But I cannot help but take the implication of solipsism to be a reductio ad absurdum. In this regard, then, the phenomenological and enactivist approaches to intentionality have the advantage.

If one posits intentionality as openness to the world, then how should one think about reflexivity? I discuss this issue in detail in chapter 2, so here I take up the question in the context of emotion and affective intentionality. Classical Indian thinkers posited a set of basic, stable emotions (*sthāyi bhāva*) while recognizing that emotions themselves are quite complex phenomena. I take emotions to be affective responses (to objects, events, situations, etc.) that reflect the concerns of the subject. Furthermore, emotions typically involve bodily changes (often including expressive changes) and motivation to specific behavior. More specifically, I take emotion and affective responsiveness to be fundamental aspects of embodied sense-making.

The affective subject is sensitive to the environment in that she can detect certain features of the environment, of course, but also in that she can be affected or *moved* by those environmental features. Certain objects, events, or states of affairs have significance or valence for the subject and evoke an affective response in the subject. This response can then (re-)orient the subject in relation to the environment and motivate an appropriate response. The affective subject is moved and can move in response. For instance, an animal may detect a sudden movement that it perceives as a potential threat. This evokes an affective response of fear, which includes a suite of bodily responses that partly constitute the fear. The fear response motivates, say, a cautious attention to the environment and then a hasty escape.

On this view, emotions involve a form of nonpropositional affective intentionality. Feelings like fear or delight are directed toward or about salient features of the subject's environment (or the subject's own condition). And affective responses disclose these features as relevant and valuable for the subject (as, for example, dangerous or delightful). They are a form of embodied appraisal. Moreover, affective intentionality is reflexive. As Fuchs and Koch put it, "Affective intentionality is thus twofold: it discloses an affective or value quality of a given situation as well as the feeling person's own state in the face of it. . . . To be afraid of an approaching lion (world-reference) means at the same time being afraid for oneself (self-reference)" (2014, 3). In this way, the embodied subject is disclosed to herself in her affective engagement with the world.

The reflexivity of consciousness, then, is not itself a form of intentionality, but neither is it a replacement for it. In the typical case, a conscious subject is aware of the world by way of their own sense-making activity, but it is nonetheless the *world* of which they are aware. And in being consciously aware of the world, they are also prereflectively aware of themself or their own states and activities. Intentional objects are presented *as objects*, that is, as *other* than the acts through which they are presented. The subject's own states and activities are present *as subject*, not as distinct from the subject themself. Both modes of presentation are presented within or to a basic phenomenal point of view constituted by reflexive awareness. Reflexive awareness is the condition of the possibility of both modes of presentation, but this does not imply that these modes are fictions or that they do not in fact *present* objects or the states and activities of the subject. On this account, experience is not a self-enclosed domain of reflexivity, like a hall of mirrors. Rather, the embodied subject is reflexively open to the world.

This account of intentionality and reflexivity crucially depends on understanding us as *embodied* subjects. Our sense-making is a complex form of adaptive activity by a living organism in relation to its environment. It is, in Dewey's terms, transactional. A series of causally and functionally connected moments of consciousness alone cannot fully capture our way of being in the world. In this sense, Ratnakīrti is quite right that, based on the object aspect of a moment of cognition alone, one would not have epistemic warrant for the inference that there are other subjects (or, for that matter, an external world). But on the embodied and enactive view of subjects, this restriction makes little sense. Instead, the enactivist approach holds that cognition is essentially embodied. There is a "unique, non-trivial, and cognitively limiting role for the body in the determination of mental states" (Kiverstein and Clark 2009, 2), and the structure and dynamics of the living body are partly constitutive of cognition.

As *embodied* subjects, we experience ourselves as in the world, and the world becomes intelligible and makes sense in and through our embodied comportment and our cognitive engagement with it. A single moment of consciousness is neither the ontological nor epistemic ground for our experience of otherness. Rather, it is an abstraction from the complex activity of our biological and cognitive life. As embodied *subjects*, we are disclosed to ourselves as living subjects in and through our conative, affective, and cognitive engagement with the world in and through the living and lived body. The key point for the current discussion is that embodiment is a condition of the possibility of our being *in* the world, *open* to the world, and subjects *to which* the world is disclosed.

On this picture of embodied subjects, mental life is more than "only the cognitive events of colourless sensations which have forms but no names . . . [which are] caught for a moment in a stream and then rush to naught." Rather, the mental life of an embodied subject is partly constituted by its overall pattern of adaptive responsiveness in and to the world. It is, as Michelle Maiese puts it concerning the self, "nothing more and nothing less than *a dynamic structure of an essentially embodied process*—in effect, a *life form*, or a *form of life*" (2016, 51). Furthermore, the form of life of embodied subjects like us is affective, conative, and expressive. For better or worse, we are feeling and desiring beings, and these feelings and desires find their expression in our embodied form of life.

As Thompson observes, "emotion is a prototype whole-organism event, for it mobilizes and coordinates virtually every aspect of the organism" (2010, 363). The emergence of an emotion is a fully psychosomatic event, including a suite of neuroendocrine, visceral, and motor processes. It also involves the modulation of feeling, attention, and appraisal. And the event finds expression in the body, face, and comportment of the subject. In this regard, the central dualism to be overcome here is not that between aspects of a moment of cognition but rather the duality between an "inner" mind and an "outer" body. Emotions are fundamental aspects of our form of life, and emotional processes span the neurobiological, psychological, and phenomenological dimensions of our being.

On this view of emotions, the problem of other minds is transformed. The mental life of embodied subjects is not fundamentally *hidden* from others in some purely private realm. Yet by the same token, mental life is not fully *transparent* to the subject. Rather, it is a multidimensional form of life that spans or even undercuts any simple inner-outer duality. And this is especially apparent when it comes to emotional expression and intentional action. Merleau-Ponty argues,

> If the subject's only experience is the one I obtain by coinciding with it, if the mind, by definition, eludes the "outside spectator" and can only be recognized inwardly, then my *Cogito* is, in principle, unique—no one else could "participate" in it. . . . What spectacle will ever truly be able to induce me to posit outside of myself this mode of existence whose sense requires that it be grasped inwardly? If I do not learn within myself to recognize the justification of the for-itself and the in-itself, then none of these mechanisms that we call "other bodies" will ever come to life; if I have no outside, then others have no inside. If I have an absolute consciousness of myself, the plurality of consciousness is impossible. (2013, 391)

According to this line of argument, we are not merely subjects that have bodies. Rather, our subjectivity is a *bodily* subjectivity, shaped and expressed in and through our embodiment and embeddedness in the world. And because our mental life is bodily and expressive in this way, we are not necessarily hidden from one another. We are embodied subjects among other embodied subjects.

Now, if this is on the right track, it opens up the possibility of a noninferentialist account of the awareness of other minds grounded in *empathy*. On a phenomenological view, empathy is a distinctive form of intentionality, a conscious openness to the experience of the other as other. It is distinctive in that it is constitutively second-personal in its mode of disclosing its object. Thus, while empathetic awareness of the joy or pain of another, on the phenomenological account, is like perception in that it is direct rather than inferential, it is unlike perception in that the joy of another is not presented as a distinct, concrete thing (Stein 1989; Thompson 2010). That is, when one perceives an object, it is given as concretely there before one as a distinct thing—a tree, a sunset, and so on. In contrast, the joy of one's friend is presented noninferentially *in and through* the joyful expression and comportment of one's friend. In this respect, the other's experience is *appresented*: It is given in the perception of the other without being *explicitly* presented in a way that is analogous to the hidden profiles of a perceived object. When I perceive a concrete object, I see only part of it at any given time, but I take it to be more than any one of its profiles. The hidden profiles are implicated or appresented in the perceptual constitution of the object as an object. Similarly, I am aware of my youngest child's joy in and through my perception of his animate body, even if I can't perceive joy in the way I perceive, say, his eyes. Importantly, though, on the phenomenological account, appresentation is a form of perceptual givenness, not an inferential representation added to perception. Furthermore, the awareness of another's joy is an awareness of an experience (not merely a certain facial expression). In this respect, empathy is like one's first-person awareness of one's own experience. Yet, unlike first-person awareness of experience (i.e., the awareness one has of an experience by living through it oneself), in the second-person mode of empathy, one is aware of the experience *as* another's. Thus, for such phenomenologists as Edith Stein, empathy takes its place along with other basic modalities of intentionality, such as perception, memory, and imagination.

Furthermore, this mode of intentionality is closely linked with awareness of others as agents. With the development of joint attention at nine to fourteen months, children show awareness of the gaze of others within a shared situation. By around eighteen months, children show awareness of others' actions and some understanding of the intentions of others, including the ability to complete the incomplete goal-directed behavior of others (Gallagher and Zahavi 2012, 211). Arguably, this grasp of others as agents is based on perception and interaction within a shared pragmatic context rather than implicit or explicit inference to unobservable mental states (Gallagher and

Hutto 2008). Older children, of course, do develop more sophisticated "mentalizing" modes of understanding. However, this more abstract mode for understanding others is arguably parasitic on the more basic empathetic and pragmatic forms of understanding (Trevarthen and Bullowa 1979). I discuss these modes of intersubjectivity more extensively in the next chapter. The point here is that, on this account of us as embodied subjects, we have noninferential access to others as other subjects and agents, despite the remaining asymmetry between first- and second-person modes of access to mental life.

Now, this proposed form of noninferential second-person intentionality does not fit well within the categories of Buddhist epistemology. It is not strictly speaking a form of perception (*pratyakṣa*) because it is arguably conceptual. And it is, by hypothesis, not a form of inference (*anumāna*), like inferring the existence of fire from the perception of smoke. Perhaps this form of intentionality is closest to what Buddhist epistemologists call a *niścayapratyaya*, a "perceptual judgment" or "ascertaining cognition." This form of cognition is based on a prior nonconceptual perception but involves the deployment of concepts. For instance, when one perceives smoke on the hillside, one may then form the determinate perceptual judgment that "there is smoke on the hillside," which could then feed into the inferential process of concluding there is a (unobserved) fire on the hillside. In this way, cognizing the other as other would not be a form of raw perception, but neither would it be a form of inference to what is unobserved (or even unobservable).

To sum up, in order to avoid the problem of conceptual solipsism, a reflexivist must distinguish reflexivity from intentionality while affirming that they are deeply interwoven. The life of consciousness consists in its openness to the world and its immanent presence to itself. As Merleau-Ponty puts it, "Self-consciousness is the very being of the mind at work" (2013, 390). And this is possible because the conscious mind is embodied and embedded in the world. As embodied subjects, our mental life is not simply an inner private domain. Rather it is a multidimensional form of life that is in part constituted by and manifest in our bodily actions and expressions. This means that, in spite of the self-presenting nature of consciousness, we are never fully transparent to ourselves. There is always more to our mental lives than is available within a moment of consciousness. And yet, by seeing the conscious mind as rooted in the body, not simply constructed from the flow of distinct moments of consciousness, we can see that our self-awareness and our awareness of others share the same basis: the life of the embodied subject.

CONCLUSION

The problems of agency and of other minds discussed in this chapter are deeply linked. In the context of Buddhist thought, both problems stem, in part, from an underlying (reductionist) causalism. The contingency and lack of observed covariance between mental states and outward movement pointed out by Ratnakīrti—and the need for Dharmakīrti to appeal to inference in his response to solipsism—are based on the causal theory of action. This view, combined with mereological reductionism, effectively dissolves subjects/agents into casually connected flows of the events. But as these thinkers and their critics realize, this threatens to make individuation of sentient beings or even streams of consciousness impossible. Further, the austere and radically internalist form of reflexivism lacks the resources to explain the emergence of a strong first-person and second-person stance. Indeed, as these thinkers agree, the conventional world is structured as a triangular affair: First-, second-, and third-person phenomena (subjects, others, and objects) are mutually constituting. The problem is that radical reflexivism cannot give a plausible account of how this conventional world arises. However, this is not to say that the Buddhist tradition more generally lacks such an account. Indeed, in the next chapter, I examine robust accounts of the arising of the conventional world as understood in early Buddhism, Madhyamaka, and Yogācāra.

NOTES

1. Of course, as I take up more fully in chapter 4, the ontological status of the conventional is complex. Even within the domain of the conventional, we can distinguish categories that are more or less arbitrarily constructed. Thus, even if biological individuality is still conventional and not ultimate, it should have an ontological status on par with other biological phenomena.

2. It is important to note, however, that a Buddha is thought to be able to know other minds directly.

Chapter Four

Enacting Worlds

In chapter 1, I argue that the self is not an independent substance but rather a complex process that emerges in dependence on the recursive, reflexive, self-organizing aspects of life. Indeed, we *enact* ourselves—actions (or interactions) and their effects are central constituents of the self-organizing processes that we label the "self." As the Buddha pointed out, we "originate from our actions" (Bodhi 2005, 166), and as Hans Jonas observes, "our being is our own doing" (Jonas 1996, 86).

Yet, both Indian Buddhists and enactivists go further. It is not just we ourselves who are enacted, but so, too, are our *worlds*. Vasubandhu goes straight to the heart of the matter. "The world (*loka*) in its varied forms," he writes, "arises from action (*karma*)" (AKBh *ad* V 1).[1] Likewise, Thompson writes, "The conviction that motivates the enactive approach is that cognition is not the representation of an independent world by an independent mind, but the enactment of a world and a mind on the basis of a history of embodied action" (1996, 128). What does it mean to claim that the world arises from action, that we enact worlds? At first glance, the claim may sound like a particularly outrageous form of subjective idealism. But in this chapter, I argue that, properly understood, the Buddhist and enactivist assertion that we enact our world (or worlds) points beyond the reified forms of subjectivism and objectivism that are so deeply entrenched in contemporary philosophy and the cognitive sciences and toward the deep, constitutive interdependence of mind, action, and world.

I begin with an examination of Buddhist and enactivist accounts of the dynamic coemergence of self and world and the denial of a subject-object, self-world duality. I then move on to a discussion of the Buddhist theory of *karma* as an account of the ongoing enaction of self and world and sketch an account of awakened agency. Next, I return to the Madhyamaka claim that all things are empty, this time in the context of debates over metaphysical realism. I examine both Madhyamaka and enactivist critiques of metaphysical realism as well as challenges to these views. The final section brings together the various strands of argument and interpretation and sketches a phenomenological-pragmatic realism that has the potential to move our thinking about self and world beyond the reified categories of subjectivism and objectivism and representationalist accounts of cognition.

THE COEMERGENCE OF SELF AND WORLD

For both Buddhists and enactivists, action (*karman*) plays a central role in the account of the coemergence of self and world. For instance, in the *Saṃyutta Nikāya*, we find the origin and passing away of the world linked to the *karmic* process in terms of the twelvefold chain of dependent origination:

> And what, monks, is the origin of the world (*loka*)? In dependence on the eye and forms, eye-consciousness arises. The meeting of the three is contact. With contact as condition, feeling [comes to be]; with feeling as condition, craving; with craving as condition, clinging; with clinging as condition, existence; with existence as condition, birth; with birth as condition, aging-and-death, sorrow, lamentation, pain, dejection, and despair come to be. . . .
>
> [And so on for the six sensory modalities.]
>
> And what, monks, is the passing away of the world? In dependence on the eye and forms, eye-consciousness arises. The meeting of the three is contact. With contact as condition, feeling [comes to be]; with feeling as condition, craving. But with the remainderless fading away and cessation of that same craving comes the cessation of clinging. [And so on for each link in the chain.] Such is the cessation of this whole mass of suffering. This, monks, is the passing away of the world. (SN 12:44, II.73–74, in Bodhi 2005, 358–59)

Here we see the Buddhist concept of a world (*loka*) is in an important sense subject relative. The arising and passing away of the world depends on such things as sense consciousness, feeling, craving, and clinging. Indeed, the *loka* is a domain of sensory, cognitive, affective, and conative interactions. Furthermore, the specific character of a subject's world depends in part on the subject's psychophysical makeup and *karma*. Hence, the term *loka* does not denote an objectivist world of entities whose existence and properties can be specified independently of a subject; rather, a *loka* is a world of experience, activity, and meaning—that is, a *lifeworld* (*Lebenswelt*). On the Buddhist view, we find ourselves in a world of persons, objects, events, and situations that are directly experienced as attractive, repellent, or indifferent; that are identified as "self" or "not self"; and that are, ultimately, unsatisfactory (*duḥkha*). But the more fundamental claim is that, at bottom, both subject and world arise with the *karmic* process, that is, from action and the effects of action. Thus, sentient beings enact themselves and their lived worlds in dynamic interdependence over time.

According to the enactive approach, the emergence of the self qua living being entails the emergence of a world. Thompson argues, "To exist as an individual means not simply to be numerically distinct from other things but to be a self-pole in a dynamic relationship with alterity, with what is other, with the world" (2010, 153). The key to this view is Varela's maxim, "living is sense-making." Thompson elaborates,

1. *Life = autopoiesis and cognition.* Any living system is both an autopoietic and a cognitive system. (Henceforth, I will use "autopoiesis" widely to include cognition and adaptivity.)
2. *Autopoiesis entails the emergence of a bodily self.* A physical autopoietic system, by virtue of its operational closure (autonomy), produces and realizes an individual or self in the form of a living body, an organism.
3. *Emergence of a self entails emergence of a world.* The emergence of a self is also by necessity the co-emergence of a domain of interactions proper to that self, an environment or *Umwelt.*
4. *Emergence of a self and world = sense-making.* The organism's environment is the sense it makes of the world. This environment is a place of significance and valence, as a result of the global action of the organism.
5. *Sense-making = enaction.* Sense-making is viable conduct. Such conduct is oriented toward and subject to the environment's significance and valence. Significance and valence do not preexist "out there," but are enacted, brought forth, and constituted by living beings. Living entails sense-making, which equals enaction. (2010, 158)

The emergence of an autonomous (i.e., organizationally and operationally closed) organism entails the emergence of a field of possible interactions between that organism and the larger environment. Some interactions will allow the organism to continue and even thrive, while others can harm or kill it. The environment takes on significance and valence: Some events are dangerous for the organism, some things are food, and so on. What *we* label the organism's environment becomes for *it* an *Umwelt*, a world. Coemergent with sentient and mobile beings is a sensorimotor world, which in turn shapes the ongoing dynamics, structure, and viability of the organism. To be alive is to come into being in the midst of this circular process. To remain alive entails making sense of (i.e., acting appropriately in relation to) the significance and valence of one's world.

The organism engages in sense making at a variety of levels. First, the very sense of the world is partly a function of the structure, capacities, and evolutionary history of the organism. Second, sense (significance and valence) is enacted and transformed through the organism's action in the world, for example, in exploration of the sensorimotor environment. Third, the organism makes sense of its world through *viable* conduct, which is, arguably, the most primitive form of circumspection or understanding. The viable organism "knows" its way around its world.

On my interpretation, for both the Buddhists and the enactivists, a sentient being's world (*loka*, *Umwelt*) is a domain of interactions structured by significance and valence that is inseparable from the structure and actions of that being. Indeed, the inextricable interdependence between self and world arises out of the structural coupling of the dynamic systems we come to see as the organism and its environment.[2] The deep interdependence between the embodied subject and its world is seen as so important in early Buddhism that the Buddha repeatedly states, "I further proclaim, friend, that it is in this very fathom-long body with its perception and thoughts that there is a world, the origin of the world, the cessation of the world, the path leading to the cessation of the world" (*Anguttara Nikāya* II, 48, in Bodhi 2012, 438). And yet, the embodied subject itself is a dynamic system that arises in dependence on a vast network of worldly causes and conditions. Thus, the world is "in" the body, just as the body is "in" the world—they are interdependent and mutually implicative.

On my enactivist interpretation, then, the Buddhist theory of action (and result) highlights the recursive, autopoeitic character of our existence. Indeed, one's accumulated *karma* is the experientially embodied record of the "history of embodied action" that is the basis from which the self is enacted. Or, as Varela puts the point, the "cognitive self is its own implementation: its history and its action are of one piece" (1999a, 54). At the very root of our embodied existence is a form of living organization that simultaneously constitutes an interior (a living being) and an exterior (a world—*Umwelt* or *loka*) and an internal relation between the two. Indeed "interiority," "exteriority," and the relations between them are not defined primarily in spatial or physical terms but *biologically* and *psychologically*. And with the emergence of biological and psychological interiority comes a deeply ambivalent relation to the larger environment. The environment becomes both the source of survival (*self*-preservation) and the greatest threat to it. Correspondingly, the emergence of the sentient being leads to the development of behaviors geared toward survival and self-protection, such as attraction and aversion. At the level of the human being, the emergence of sentient individuality, coupled with past conditioning (*vāsanā*), yields a deeply entrenched sense of an independent self (*ātma-dṛṣti*). And this deep sense of an independent self is the linchpin of *saṃsāra*.

ENACTING WORLDS

As pointed out previously, on the Buddhist theory, one's world is somehow dependent on one's *karma*. That is, it is not just one's situation in a world or even into which world (of all the possible realms) one might be reborn but the world itself that is a product of *karma*. For instance, as we saw in the *Saṃyutta Nikāya*, we find the origin and passing away of the world linked to the *karmic* process in terms of the twelvefold chain of dependent origination.

Here are two different depictions of the *karmic* mode of dependent origination:

> Dependent on the eye and forms, visual-cognitive awareness arises. The meeting of the three is contact. With contact as condition there is feeling. What one feels, that one apperceives. What one apperceives, that one thinks about (*vitakketi*). What one thinks about, that one conceptually proliferates (*papañceti*). With what one has conceptually proliferated *as the source* (*nidāna*), apperceptions and notions tinged by conceptual proliferation beset a man with respect to past, future, and present forms cognizable through the eye [and so on, up to] mind-objects cognizable through the mind. (Waldron 2003, 163)[3]

And:

> In dependence on the eye and forms, eye-consciousness arises. The meeting of the three is contact. With contact as condition, feeling [comes to be]; with feeling as condition, craving; with craving as condition, clinging; with clinging as condition, existence; with existence as condition, birth; with birth as condition, aging-and-death, sorrow, lamentation, pain, dejection, and despair come to be. (Bodhi 2005, 358)

Clearly, these two formulations point out different aspects of the process that keeps beings bound to *saṃsāra*. The first emphasizes the role of conceptual proliferation (*prapañca*), while the second emphasizes the role of distorted motivations, such as craving (*tṛṣṇa*) and grasping (*upādāna*). These depictions are not meant to be in conflict, however, and we can find other depictions with different combinations and emphases.

Generalizing a bit, we can discern a process that has sensory, affective, perceptual, cognitive, and conative phases. First, sensory contact (*sparśa*) involves the meeting and correlation between a sense faculty, a sensible form, and a sensory consciousness. What one is able to sense is, of course, a function of one's environment and one's specific sensory faculties. Further, the sensory awareness (*vijñāna*) operates through discrimination or contrast ("this, not that"). Second, sensation leads to feeling (*vedanā*). The three basic affective modalities here are pleasure, displeasure, and indifference, but the key point is that now the sensory object is given as affectively salient. The sound is experienced not just as high-pitched but also as unpleasant. Third, the object is perceptually cognized (*saṃjñā*), which involves perceptual identification of the object—it is no longer a mere *that* but a *what*. Note that the object has sensory and affective salience even before it is fully perceptually identified. In addition, perceptual identification relies on prior experience and associations, that is, on sedimented conditioning (*saṃskārā*). Thus, while *vijñāna* is discriminating, *saṃjñā* is synthetic. Fourth, the affective valence and perceptual identification of the object lead to such impulses as desire (or aversion) and such motives as grasping. In phenomenological terms, we have a shift from what Husserl calls *affectivity*, the basic "pull" or "allure" of the object, to *receptivity*, the active orienting to the object. These impulses and motives in turn inform and guide one's action. An action, then, is conditioned by sensation, affect, perception, dispositions, and cognition and conditions each of these in turn. We do not merely perceive an object. Rather, the object is given in its sensory-affective salience and against the background of one's associations, habits, impulses, and motivations. Indeed, what we have here is a process in which each aspect conditions and is conditioned by the others (i.e., it is operationally closed). And the way in which our experience unfolds through time is largely a function of the ongoing operation of this *karmic* circuit.

The basic structure of the *karmic* circuit can be seen in the broader view of the Buddhist model of the twelvefold cycle of dependent origination discussed earlier:

1. Ignorance (*avidya*)
2. Conditioning (*saṃskāra*)
3. Consciousness or cognition (*vijñāna*)
4. The body-mind or sentient embodiment (*nāma-rūpa*)
5. The six sensory domains (*ṣaḍ-āyatana*)
6. Sensory contact (*sparśa*)
7. Feeling (*vedanā*)
8. Desire (*tṛṣṇa*)
9. Grasping (*upādāna*)
10. Becoming (*bhava*)
11. Birth or arising (*jāti*)
12. Death or ceasing (*maraṇa*)

The twelvefold cycle is a model of the perpetuation of *saṃsāra*, both across lifetimes and within a lifetime.[4] Moreover, it is important to note that these factors or links (*nidāna*) are viewed as mutually conditioning, interdefined, and related in complex ways, both synchronically and diachronically.

The first four factors can be seen as the enabling and constraining conditions of our sentient embodied being. As living, sentient beings (*nāma-rūpa*), we are of course embodied and conscious. Further, as we have seen, our bodies and minds are structured by conditioning (*saṃskāra*) from both our own past actions and experiences and those beings with whom we are physically or psychologically continuous (i.e., through rebirth or biological evolution). On this view, the human body-mind is a condensed, embodied history of past patterns of action.

If we refer to the twelvefold cycle of dependent origination, then we see that a human being is understood in terms of a specific form of sentient embodiment (4), which presupposes consciousness or cognition (3) as well as conditioning (2). This seems fairly unproblematic, considering what I have discussed thus far, but what of the first factor of ignorance? As mentioned previously, the existentially primordial ignorance referred to here is the instinctive sense of oneself as a substantial entity (*ātma-dṛṣti*) and its close cousin, the reification of both the self and worldly objects (*satkāya-dṛṣti*). This ignorance is the root problematic of human existence—leading as it does to the dissatisfaction (*duḥkha*) that pervades *saṃsāra*—and is therefore existentially primary. Indeed, we can see this more clearly when we take up the enactive perspective. Thompson explains,

> Individuality in this case [i.e., of an autopoietic system] corresponds to a *formal self-identity*—to an invariant dynamic pattern that is produced, maintained, and realized by the system itself, while the system undergoes incessant material transformation and regulates its external boundary conditions accordingly. An autopoietic system is thus an individual in a sense that begins to be worthy of the term *self*. (2010, 75)

On this interpretation, then, the emergence of bounded identity through organizational closure, in a sense, sets into motion the entire cycle, from ignorance and conditioning to death and rebirth.

The coemergence of organism and environment, of interiority and exteriority, is reflected in the transition from the first four factors to factors 5 through 9. The fifth factor, the six sensory domains (*ṣaḍāyatana*), includes both the sense faculties—the five external senses and the inner sense—and their correlative sensory objects (e.g., sights and sounds). These sensory fields are central to the constitution of the organism's milieu or lived environment (*loka*). The actual process of sensation, in turn, emerges from ongoing sensory contact or coupling (*sparśa*; 6) with the environment. This coupling is not merely causal but also intentional—it involves the organism's most basic sensory directedness toward objects. Along with sensory coupling, there emerges feeling or affective tonality (*vedanā*; 7). These modalities in turn condition factors 8 and 9, desire (*tṛṣṇa*) and appropriation (*upādāna*). Thus, the sensory-affective coupling with the environment feeds into the basic conative orientation in that milieu. A sentient being's milieu involves not just actual conditions but also conditions that must be effected or procured—that is, objects (potential or actual) of desire and appropriation. Therefore, with the coemergence of an organism and its lived environment, there emerges a dynamic sensory-affective-conative *karmic* circuit that is enabled by and reinforces prior body-mind conditioning (*saṃskāra*). The recursive, self-reinforcing aspect of this circuit, if successful, drives the continued existence or becoming (*bhava*; 10) of the sentient organism. The final two factors, birth (*jāti*) and death (*maraṇa*), have different connotations depending on the context of analysis. When the twelvefold cycle is used to analyze the moment-to-moment dynamics of a sentient being, the terms mean "arising" and "ceasing," respectively. As phases in a complex process, each factor, and indeed the being itself, is dependent and impermanent. However, when the target of analysis is a longer time frame, these factors indicate both the mutual entailment between birth and death (i.e., life and mortality) and the fact that death leads to rebirth (and ignorance) and a continuation of the entire cycle.

In sum, the enactment of identity through organizational-operational closure and body-mind conditioning are at the root of sentient being (1–4); organism and environment, or interiority and exteriority, are correlative and coemergent (5); the sentient being is coupled with and oriented toward the environment through a dynamic and self-reinforcing sensory-affective-cognitive-conative circuit (6–9), which, when effective (survival), perpetuates the existence of the sentient being (10); and, finally, this process feeds into the larger dynamic of birth and death that is the existential situation of all sentient beings (11–12).

ENACTION, EMPTINESS, AND REALISM

On my reading, the Indian Buddhist traditions developed a sophisticated account of the coemergence of the sentient being and its world out of a network of dependently related events and process, as well as an account of the ways in which prior cognitive, conative, and affective structures of the sentient being enable and constrain its ongoing living in its environment. The basic framework for understanding the existential situation of the sentient being, then, is the dynamic interdependence of mind, action, and world within a broader framework of a causally structured and impermanent reality. This interdependence is both causal and constitutive. It is causal in that the ongoing transaction or structural coupling between systems continuously regenerates the sentient being and its world. It is constitutive in that the mutual relations between sentient being and its world are part of the very nature of each—neither could exist nor be intelligible without the other. Given this constitutive entanglement of mind-action-world, the attempt to think about the entangled elements as if they were independent substances is misguided from the start. Moreover, for the Indian Buddhists, this fundamental interdependence rules out any form of naïve realism about the word of experience and calls into question traditionally realist accounts of cognition, such as those defended by the Nyāya school of Indian philosophy. Regarding early Buddhism, Noa Ronkin argues,

> According to this epistemology the range of whatever is conceived and apperceived is mediated by the cognitive apparatus as embodied in the operation of the five *khandhas* [Skt: *skandhas*]. Hence the boundaries of one's cognitive process are the boundaries of one's world: the latter is the world of one's own experience, dependent on the workings of one's cognitive apparatus. Under the aegis of this epistemology there follows a metaphysical framework that we have identified as an experientially oriented process metaphysics: the view that processes are fundamental to experience and cognition, and that all encountered phenomena are best portrayed and understood in terms of processes rather than of substances. (2011, 244)

Likewise, according to both proponents and opponents, the enactive approach has been taken to be incompatible with both naïve and sophisticated forms of realism. For instance, Varela and colleagues write,

> It is precisely this emphasis on mutual specification [of organism and environment] that enables us to negotiate a middle path between the Scylla of cognition as the recovery of a pregiven outer world (realism) and the Charybdis of cognition as the projection of a pregiven inner world (idealism). These two extremes both take representation as their central notion: in the first case representation is used to recover what is outer; in the second it is used to project what is inner. Our intention is to bypass entirely this logical geography of inner versus outer by studying cognition not as projection or recovery but as embodied action. (Varela et al. 2017, 172)

On this view, the enactivists, like many Buddhist thinkers, attempt to reject both realism and idealism in epistemology and ontology.[5] The enactivist alternative is the view that "organism and environment enfold into each other and unfold from one another in the fundamental circularity that is life itself" (Varela et al. 2017, 217). The broad point of agreement between the Indian Buddhists and the enactivists is that once one accepts (a) that the experienced world is not independent of the sensorimotor and cognitive capacities of the sentient beings that enact it and (b) that the primary role of cognitive states is to guide successful action (see Dharmakīrti's notion of *arthakriyā*), then the idea of cognition as accurately representing a metaphysically pregiven world drops out. Mind is not a mirror of nature. Furthermore, as mentioned in chapter 1, *The Embodied Mind* draws explicitly on Madhyamaka in its critique of objectivism and metaphysical realism and in its development of the enactivist alternative. In the final sections of the chapter, I explore some of these issues by drawing on the Madhyamaka analysis of emptiness (*śūnyatā*) and the Yogācāra analysis of the three natures of phenomena. The upshot of these considerations is, I think, a novel form of phenomenological-pragmatic antiabsolutism.

The relation between various forms realism and antirealism in Buddhist thought is a complex and contentious one. However, on my view, there is a strong strand of skepticism toward any absolutist metaphysical picture of the world—whether objectivist or subjectivist—that runs from the Pāli Nikāyas through later forms of Buddhist thought, especially Madhyamaka. I agree with Ronkin's assessment that, in the Nikāyas, "[w]hat the Buddha rejects is realism, conceptual and ontological alike: the notion that the encountered world is made up of distinguishable substances, and the linguistic theory that words refer to these substances which they represent; the conviction that our language corresponds to or mirrors a mind-independent reality" (Ronkin 2011, 245). Furthermore, the Madhyamaka school deepens and extends this rejection, including what it takes to be vestiges of metaphysical realism in Abhidharma reductionism and Yogācāra idealism.

As discussed in chapter 1, Buddhist reductionism constitutes a type of antirealism about everyday composite entities, including persons. Such entities may be pragmatically or conventionally real (*saṃvṛtisat*), but they are not ultimately real (*paramārthasat*). The being of these entities is fully accounted for in terms of more basic entities; they are fully analytically and ontologically decomposable. Thus, they have a merely derived nature (*parabhāva*) rather than their own irreducible intrinsic nature (*svabhāva*). Further, conventionally real entities must be epiphenomenal because if they were to have their own causal powers, then they would not be completely reducible. Hence, according to the Buddhist reductionists, all causation is microcausation—that is, real causation occurs only between simple, momentary *dharmas*.[6] Further, the genuine causal powers of these entities are determined by their intrinsic natures. Notice, then, that this two-tiered ontology rests on a radical dichotomy between the entities with a purely extrinsic nature (*parabhāva*) and those with a purely intrinsic nature (*svabhāva*).

It is this view that is forcefully criticized by Nāgārjuna and subsequent Madhyamaka thinkers. While it is not always clear which Abhidharma view is being targeted by Nāgārjuna, there can be no doubt that his primary philosophical target is the notion of *svabhāva*. An entity has *svabhāva* when it is ontologically independent of other objects, has an intrinsic and fixed nature or essence, and can be individuated mind-independently. Thus, the semantic range of "*svabhāva*" overlaps not only with our notions of "substance" and "essence" but also with our notions of a "thing in itself" and an absolutely or "really real" existent. Importantly, then, to say that an entity is (or has) *svabhāva* is not simply to claim that it exists but rather to specify its *mode* of existence: It is claimed to exist independently or absolutely. Mādhyamikas deny that anything could have this mode of existence and point out that the deep assumption that to be real is to be *svabhāva* inexorably leads to paradox. To say that an entity lacks *svabhāva* is just to say that the entity is empty (*śūnya*). Moreover, the emptiness of phenomena is said to be an implication of phenomena being dependently originated (*pratītyasamutpanna*; and vice versa). As we see in Nāgārjuna's *Mūlamadhyamakakārikā*,

> Dependent origination we declare to be emptiness.
> It [emptiness] is a dependent concept; just that is the middle path.
>
> There being no *dharma* whatsoever that is not dependently originated,
> It follows that there is no dharma whatsoever that is non-empty.[7]
> (*Mūlamadhyamakakārikā*, 24.18–19, in Siderits and Katsura 2013, 277–78)

Yet, if all *dharmas* are empty of *svabhāva*, then no *dharmas* are ultimately real. Indeed, because according to Nāgārjuna, *nothing* could have *svabhāva*, nothing could be ultimately real in the sense specified by Buddhist reductionists. And if nothing could be ultimately real, then what becomes of the distinction between ultimate and conventional? According to Buddhist reductionism, ultimately real entities are required to serve as the truth makers of ultimate truths and as the indirect basis for conventional truths. By pulling the rug out from under the Buddhist reductionist view, it would seem that the conventional-ultimate distinction collapses.

However, Nāgārjuna, too, is committed to the two-truths view:

> The Dharma teaching of the Buddha rests on two truths:
> Conventional truth and ultimate truth.
> Who do not know the distinction between the two truths,
> They do not understand reality in accordance with the profound teachings of the Buddha.
> The ultimate truth is not taught independently of customary ways of talking and thinking.
> Not having acquired the ultimate truth, nirvana is not attained.[8]
> (*Mūlamadhyamakakārikā*, 24.8–10, in Siderits and Katsura 2013, 272–73)

So, rather than reject it, the Mādhyamika must reinterpret the two-truths view. In his commentary on MMK, Candrakīrti gives three distinct glosses on "conventional" (*samvṛti*). The first is "concealing," that is, those ways of thinking and speaking (*vyavahāra*) that conceal the ultimate nature of things. The second is "mutual dependence," such as between cause and effect or part and whole. The third refers to the various customary practices of ordinary people in the world. As Sidertis and Katsura characterize it, "conventional truth is a set of beliefs that ordinary people (*loka*) use in their daily conduct, and it is conventional (*samvṛti*) because of its reliance on conventions concerning semantic and cognitive relations" (2013, 272).[9]

With regard to ultimate truth, it consists in the "faultless realization of the noble ones (āryas)" (Siderits and Katsura 2013, 272). Here Siderits and Katsura offer two possible ways to understand this idea. On the first interpretation, the realization is an insight into the true nature of things, namely that all *dharmas* are empty and therefore conventional. Ultimate reality, then, would be absent of all *dharmas*. On this view, there is a real way ultimate reality is, and the ultimate truth is the content of an enlightened being's grasp of this reality. On the second interpretation, the "ultimate truth according to Madhyamaka is just that there is no such thing as the way reality ultimately is. Or to put this in a somewhat paradoxical way, the ultimate truth is that there is no ultimate truth. On this reading, what the āryas realize is that the very idea of how things really are, independently of our (useful) semantic and cognitive conventions, is incoherent" (Siderits and Katsura 2013, 272–73).

Here I follow the second interpretation. On this view, the ultimate truth is not ultimate because it corresponds to the ultimately real (*svabhāvic*) entities or because it corresponds to the true nature of ultimate reality independently of our conventional modes of thinking and speaking. Rather, the ultimate truth is a kind of metatruth concerning the incoherence of the very idea of a transconventional way things are. On this reading, Madhyamaka is a form of metaphysical antirealism; that is, it constitutes a thoroughgoing rejection of metaphysical realism.

According to Hilary Putnam, metaphysical realism can be characterized as follows:

> On this perspective, the world consists of some fixed totality of mind-independent objects. There is exactly one true and complete description of "the way the world is." Truth involves some sort of correspondence relation between words or thought-signs and external things and sets of things. [We can] call this perspective *externalist* perspective, because its favorite point of view is a God's Eye point of view. (1981, 49)

Elsewhere Putnam elaborates on the first point by claiming that the metaphysical realist is committed to the belief in a "ready-made world": the idea that the world is uniquely and mind-independently partitioned into objects, properties, and relations. Moreover, these objects are "things in themselves" that have fixed intrinsic natures independently of our interest, concepts, and descriptions. As Putnam says of this view, the "world divides itself up into objects and properties in one definite unique way" (McCormick 1996, 190). There is a uniquely complete and correct description of reality, and the correctness of this description involves correspondence between the description and the metaphysically pregiven way the world is.

According to the antirealist reading of Madhyamaka, the view that all things are empty of *svabhāva* implies the rejection of each of the earlier claims. For Nāgārjuna and later Mādhyamikas, emptiness implies the absence of ontological independence and with it the idea that a phenomenon could have a fixed or absolute nature. Some Tibetan commentators on Madhyamaka philosophy have distinguished three dimensions of dependence relevant for understanding emptiness (Westerhoff 2009). First, there is *causal* dependence: An entity depends for its existence on its causes and conditions. Second, there is *mereological* dependence: A composite entity existentially depends on its parts. We may also include in this category other noncausal dependence relations, such as the interdependence between object and quality or agent and activity. The third, and according to these Tibetan commentators the most subtle form, is *conceptual* dependence: An entity is dependent on a basis of conceptual designation, a designating term or concept, and a designating cognitive event. Hence, to claim that an entity is dependently arisen (and therefore empty) is to do more than to point out its causal origin; it is to claim that it is constitutively embedded in a network of causal, ontic (including mereological) and conceptual relations.

On the antirealist interpretation, then, to hold that all things are empty is to give up the picture of a ready-made world. If all things are empty, then there is no unique, mind-independent partitioning of the world into objects, properties, and relations (or, for that matter, *dharmas*, *skandhas*, and *santānas*). Yet, pointing to an entity's causal and mereological dependence does not obviously tell us anything about its ultimate ontological status. To say that a tree depends on its causes and conditions and on its parts or constitutive processes does not seem to entail a rejection of metaphysical realism about trees. However, if trees are not ontologically fundamental phenomena, then we need to look elsewhere for the target of this line of reasoning. Indeed, a main target of the Madhyamaka dialectic is precisely those entities that are meant to provide the ontological foundation on which less fundamental entities rest. That is, the real candidates for being *svabhāva* are those entities, such as the Buddhist reductionists' *dharmas*, that are supposed to be at the terminus of a series of ontological dependence relations. Such entities are ontologically independent (*svabhāva*) precisely in contrast to all those other entities that are ontologically dependent (*parabhāva*). If they are to be ontologically foundational or ultimately real, then they must be ontologically independent; otherwise, one needs to keep following the chain of ontological dependence to its ultimate foundation elsewhere. Moreover, an ontologically independent entity needs to have an independent nature or essence, as well—it must be what it is independently of what other things are. Thus, the totality of *svabhāvic* entities constitutes the ultimately real foundation of the world, and it is a world that, as Putnam says, "divides itself up" in an absolute way.

On my reading, both Madhyamaka and enactivism reject metaphysical realism. However, in rejecting the picture of the ready-made world, both views, I think, contain an important internal tension that threatens to make them theoretically unstable. In Madhyamaka, the interminable process of dependent arising is fluid and divisible (or determinable) in various ways for various purposes. Likewise, in enactivism, worlds are relational domains correlative to the sense-making activity of the organism in environment. Worlds are therefore carved out of environments, and there is no uniquely correct way these carvings should go. Both views rest on a carving-carved or individuating-individuated contrast that threatens to reintroduce metaphysical realism at a different level. In criticizing the rejection of metaphysical realism, John Searle points out, "If conceptual relativity is to be used as an argument against realism, it seems to presuppose a language-independent reality that can be carved up or divided up in different ways, by different vocabularies" (1995, 165). What is the status of this reality that is being carved or divided differently? Is it (metaphysically) *really* interdependent and fluid or not?

In discussing the Mādhyamika's *śūnyavāda*, Paul Williams, Anthony Tribe, and Alexander Wynne raise a similar objection. They write,

> If all things were secondary existents [i.e., empty] then *all things would be constructs with nothing for them to be constructed out of*. This must mean that nothing exists at all. It is not sufficient to reply with Nāgārjuna that this ignores the two truths, since if all is merely a conceptual construct then there could be no foundation for the two truths. Everything is foam that dissolves into nothing. (Williams, Tribe, and Wynne 2012, 112)

From a Madhyamaka perspective, these objections are examples of the *svabhāvic* framework implicitly structuring our thinking. Searle seems to think that objectivity requires not just that reality is mind-independent in certain respects—causally and structurally or ontically—but *totally* independent. He also thinks that if we can draw a distinction between a domain and our various carvings of it, then there must at bottom be an *absolute* distinction between reality and our various representations of it. Williams, Tribe, and Wynne think that conceptual construction requires an absolutely unconstructed foundation.

However, I see no reason one must follow them in these assumptions. Rather, all that is required is a *relative* and *iterable* contrast between a domain and various partitionings. It must be admitted that such contrasts as representation-represented, construction-constructed, and partitioning-domain can be quite useful. Rejecting metaphysical realism should not involve absolutizing the first side of each contrast while denying the second side. Rather, it is based on a refusal to absolutize the contrast itself. Therefore, while the iteration of these relative contrasts can go on indefinitely, this process is not viciously regressive. It is a sign, not that we are merely chasing our tails, but that the process of inquiry is *open-ended.*

Sentient beings enact their worlds as relational domains of significance, carving them out of the larger environment through their sense-making. This account presupposes organisms in environments and a contrast between world and environment. Organisms are sensitive to some features of the environment and not others, and the environment constrains sense-making. When we describe the world of motile bacteria, we can make a distinction between the sugar as a causally independent environmental structure and its significance as food for the organisms we are describing. We say that sugar counts as food for bacteria in a situation. We thus take, to borrow John McDowell's phrase, a "sideways-on" view of the organism and its world. The organism's world is not independent of its sense-making, but that very sense-making depends on the causally and structurally independent features of is environment. We can also, to some degree, adopt a sideways-on view of different aspects of our own sense-making. But what we cannot do, because it ultimately makes no sense, is adopt an *absolute* sideways-on view, a view from nowhere on our sense-making. Thus, the sense that reality is always inexhaustibly *more* than any one way of making sense of it need not be grounded in the idea of a ready-made world *outside* (what would *outside* mean here?) all our sense-making. Rather, it can be grounded in the mundane recognition of causal independence and the more rarified image of reality as the open-ended horizon *within which* sense-making occurs. Furthermore, while we can make sense of our own sense-making partly in terms of how it is grounded in the ongoing interaction between autonomous systems and their environments (and here this includes autonomous systems interacting with one another), and we can describe both the systems and their environments physically, biologically, and cognitively, we must also recognize that these very descriptive schema are themselves forms of sense-making that arise from and presuppose the ongoing lived experience of the inquirers. Thus, while sense-making itself has intelligible causal underpinnings, *causal explanations* themselves are modes of sense-making that have no determinate sense (and are therefore not *ultimately* intelligible) apart from our conceptual frameworks, intersubjective interactions, and the implicit background of lived experience.

What emerges from these considerations, I think, is a broadly pragmatist view that has three key elements:

1. *Ontological parity*: There is no ontologically privileged level of reality.
2. *Conceptual-explanatory pluralism*: We use and *need* an irreducible plurality of conceptual and explanatory schemes.
3. *Epistemological pragmatism*: An embrace of fallibilism and grounding warrant in successful practice.

With regard to the first element, recall Nāgārjuna's claim, "There being no *dharma* whatsoever that is not dependently originated, It follows that there is no *dharma* whatsoever that is non-empty" (Siderits and Katsura 2013, 278). The point is that the ubiquity and interminability of dependent origination implies that all phenomena are empty of *svabhāva*.[10] Madhyamaka thus arrives at an ontological antifoundationalism in which there is no well-founded hierarchy of dependence relations bottoming out in an ultimate independent foundation. As inquirers, we find ourselves perpetually in the midst of an open-ended network of interrelated phenomena, no domain of which has absolute priority over all the others. *All* our explanatory work takes place within this horizon of dependent origination.

With regard to the second element, conceptual-explanatory pluralism, Mādhyamikas argue that phenomena are dependent not just on their causes and conditions and on their noncausal relations to other phenomena but also on their "conceptual designation." More specifically, one might say an entity depends on a basis of designation, a term or concept, and a cognitive event of designation. The basis of designation is a set of phenomena to which the concept can be applied. In the current context, we can think of the basis in terms of discernable features of the causal nexus. The concept brings the phenomena under some classification ("person," "object," "cause," "condition"). Finally, concepts don't apply themselves (if they did, then they would be *svabhāva*), so the cognitive event is the specific application of the concept within a specific domain. Hence, we have a kind of *triangulation* between a domain, a concept (or framework of concepts), and an agent using the concept to make sense of the domain. On this view, domains are not ready-made but are articulated or partitioned relative to a conceptual framework and the cognitive activity of agents.

This account of conceptual dependence suggests a form of conceptual relativity wherein such terms as *exist*, *object*, *relation*, and *cause* have no absolute or independent meaning or application. Rather, they are themselves, as Nāgārjuna says, "dependent designations" (*upādāya-prajñapti*). They are conventional (*samvṛti*) or transactional (*vyavahāra*) terms that get their sense and application from their role within a conceptual framework, which itself is grounded in ongoing cognitive activity by sentient beings. Even the concept of emptiness itself is not absolute but is itself empty. For both Madhyamaka and enactivism, the myth of the ready-made world is to be rejected—how we carve up the world is inextricably shaped by how minds like ours cognize that world. How then can we understand those cognitive enterprises we call the sciences? Here one might take Steven Horst's view that the sciences are cognitive "enterprises of modeling local features of the world (and of ourselves) in particular representational systems. Such models are local and piecemeal. They are also idealized in a variety of ways that can present principled barriers to their wholesale integration into something like a single axiomatic system" (2007, 5). The upshot here is that our ontology is inextricably bound to our modes of inquiring, modeling, and intervening in specific domains. Neither a naïve folk ontology nor the absolute ontology of metaphysical realism is to be accepted. Rather, one may adopt a critical pragmatic ontology, wherein ontological commitments are driven by the overall project of making sense of various aspects of the world. In this way, both the Mādhyamika and the enactivist can agree with Jay Garfield that in our inquiries we "pay attention to *pratītyasamutpāda*—to interdependence, and its multiple, multidimensional, inter- and intra-level character—and let a thousand entities bloom, requiring of each only that it genuinely toil and spin, accomplishing some real explanatory work" (2002, 75).

With regard to the third element, epistemological pragmatism, there are two features I want to emphasize. First, the epistemological pragmatist understands epistemic warrant in terms of (long-run) pragmatic success. From this perspective, the point of cognition is to facilitate adaptive engagement between the cognitive agent and its environment.[11] As the enactivist insists, sense-making is viable conduct. Relatively simple cognizers may cognize the world in fixed and simple ways. However, human cognizers have the ability to deploy a wide variety of cognitive systems. Moreover, we have the ability to both revise current and develop new modes of cognitive engagement. This leads to the second important feature of epistemological pragmatism, namely fallibilism. On the picture I sketch here, there is no certain foundation on which to build our knowledge. Further, the deep, conceptual, and explanatory pluralism of Madhyamaka and enactivism rule out global coherentism, as well. Our inquiries are plural, pragmatically constrained, and provisional, and so is the epistemic warrant that arises from those inquiries.

THE THREE NATURES OF PHENOMENA

What I find congenial in Indian Madhyamaka are its ontological antisubstantialism and antiabsolutism, as well as its emphasis on the dynamic interdependence of mind and world. However, it is within the Buddhist Yogācāra that I find perhaps the most detailed and philosophically rich account of the *experiential dynamics* whereby worlds are enacted. Historically, the Madhyamaka analysis based on emptiness (śūnyavāda) and the Yogācāra analysis based on cognitive experience (*vijñānavāda*) were distinct and often opposed strands (Garfield and Westerhoff 2015). However, in the syncretic thought of Śāntarakṣita, for instance, we find an important synthesis of the two modes of analysis. Śāntarakṣita's Yogācāra-Madhyamaka combines aspects of the phenomenological psychology of Yogācāra and the epistemology of *pramāṇavāda* with the antifoundationalism of Madhyamaka. What emerges is a nuanced analysis of the cognitive-experiential dynamics whereby subjects and worlds are brought forth, coupled with a refusal to take any account as absolute. Like Śāntarakṣita, then, my interest in the model of three natures of phenomena is not in service of an epistemological and ontological idealism, as it arguably was for the Yogācāra thinkers themselves. Rather, I am interested in the resources and insights of the model for understanding the coarising of self-making and world-making.

According to Vasubandhu's *Trisvabhāvanirdesa* or *Treatise on the Three Natures* (Gold 2014), experiential phenomena can be understood in terms of three natures (*svabhāva*) and three forms of naturelessness (*niḥsvabhāvatā*).[12] The three natures are the constructed nature (*parikalpita-svabhāva*), the dependent nature (*paratantra-svabhāva*), and the consummate nature (*pariniṣpanna-svabhāva*). The term *parikalpita* connotes mental construction, and to say that an experiential object has a constructed nature in this sense is to point to the way in which the object qua experienced depends on the constructive activities of the mind. Indeed, it is a core claim of the Yogācāra approach that objects of experience can only be given through the constructive activity of cognition and that this activity makes a nontrivial contribution to *how* the empirical object is given. Thus, to say that an object is mentally constructed is not to say that it is a mere hallucination because any object of experience is constructed in this way. Yet, the constructed nature is inherently misleading in that, in normal experience, we do not experience objects as mentally constructed. Rather, our default mode is a form of naïve realism that takes the mind to present objects as they really are independently of the contribution of the mind. This leads to the *paratantra-svabhāva*, the dependent nature of phenomena. Despite the fact we tend to experience objects as independent, they are, on the Yogācāra account, doubly dependent. Objects depend on their causes and conditions and on constructive mental activity. The rainbow qua experiential object depends on atmospheric conditions and on the sensory-cognitive systems of perceivers like us. Because the object as a construct is not pregiven in its conditions, our deep sense that cognition is the simple mirroring or recovery of pregiven objects of experience is mistaken. The deeper truth, on this analysis, is the *absence* of the constructed nature from the dependent nature. Finally, the *parinispanna-svabhāva*, the consummate nature, is the true or undistorted nature of phenomena. This is understood in terms of how an enlightened being would experience phenomena, namely, as the dependent nature absent the distortions inherent in the constructed nature, most fundamentally the subject-object dichotomy. Put simply, on the Yogācāra analysis, we start out as naïve realists about the experienced world (including our own subjectivity), but through careful analysis, we can come to see clearly the ways in which our experience of the world and ourselves is dependent on our own mental processes.

I now examine two distinct ways of fleshing out this framework. One way to flesh it out is in the direction of an internalist-representationalist account of mind. This account fits well the historical and conceptual connections between Vasubandhu's Yogācāra and the indirect-realist and representationalist views propounded in the Sautrāntika school. It also makes good sense of some of Vasubandhu's arguments against naïve and direct-realist accounts of the mind. Another way to flesh out the model of the three natures is in the direction of a more radically nondualist account of experience. This account makes good sense of Vasubandhu's emphasis on overcoming subject-object duality and on the flow of experience as fundamental. It also helps to make sense of Śāntarakṣita's Yogācāra-Madhyamaka synthesis.

The internalist-representationalist interpretation is based on a causal theory of experience, wherein the contents of experience are logically independent of their cause. So in the familiar fashion, an experience can be a visual presentation as of a shiny red apple, whether that experience is a dream, a hallucination, or a veridical perceptual experience. Indeed, what we are directly aware of in experience are not external objects but mental images or representations (*ākāra*), which can be caused in a variety of ways. Dreaming and perception alike involve the phenomenal presentation of experiential objects, but they differ in their causal constraints. Moreover, the character of a representation derives from the capacities and conditioning of the mind that creates it. The stream of consciousness, then, is a causal process, whereby virtual worlds of experience are brought forth moment by moment. Yet we are by default naïve realists about the virtual worlds our minds create. We do not recognize our mental constructs as mental constructs but take them to be mind-independent external objects. Thus, the constructed nature here refers to the mentally constructed objects within the virtual world of experience. The dependent nature refers to the fact that, despite appearances, experiential objects are mind dependent (both causally and constitutively). The dependent nature by extension also refers to those causal processes by which mental objects are constructed. Recognition of the absence of the constructed nature from the other dependent nature amounts to a recognition that the direct objects of experience are merely mental constructs or representations (*vijñāptimātra*) that continuously emerge from causal processes that we are not directly aware of. Seeing through to the true nature of experience, finally, is to experience the consummate nature.

On the Yogācāra account, this recognition of the true nature of experience is not a merely intellectual understanding but rather a transformation at the very basis of experience (*āśraya-parāvṛtti*). In the normal case, our mental representations are *transparent*—we do not see them as representations at all. As Thomas Metzinger writes, a "representation is transparent if the system using it cannot recognize it as a representation. A world-model active in the brain is transparent if the brain has no chance of discovering that it is a model" (2009, 42). He goes on to say that our various mental representations are

> seamlessly integrated into your overall conscious space of experience. Because it has been optimized over millions of years, this mechanism is so fast and so reliable that you never notice its existence. It makes your brain invisible to itself. You are in contact only with its content; you never see the representation as such; therefore, you have the illusion of being directly in contact with the world. And that is how you become a *naïve realist*, a person who thinks she is in touch with an observer-independent reality. (Metzinger 2009, 43)

On the internalist-representationalist interpretation of the three natures, various interconnected cognitive processes continually create an integrated internal world model that is transparent to the cognitive system that creates and uses it. Note, though, that Metzinger's account of transparency is stronger than the one I attribute to Vasubandhu because Metzinger asserts that the system itself *cannot* recognize its transparent representations as representations. Vasubandhu, however, holds that our representations are *in the normal case* strictly transparent but that this can change through the development of philosophical and meditative insight.

There are two types of case that lend support to Vasubandhu's position. The first type of case concerns persistent auditory hallucinations. People who suffer from persistent musical hallucinations often report that the music is experienced as if it were like any other music playing in their environment. It can be experienced as loud or quiet, as nearby or far away, as clear or muffled, and so on. While some people quickly realize that they are experiencing hallucinations, others remain for extended periods under the impression that their auditory experience is veridical. According to Paul Coates (2013), the transition process follows three stages. In the "deceptive phase," the music is experienced as externally produced, spatially located, and public. Here the auditory experience is constructed as an external sound event. Eventually, in the "transition phase," the subject realizes that the auditory experience does not correspond to bodily movements in the right way (moving "toward" or "away from" the sound does not change its sensory character) or that others can't hear it and so on. In the final "realization phase," the subject has come to fully recognize the hallucination as a hallucination. What this involves, according to Coates, is a shift in the way the auditory phenomenon is automatically conceptualized. So while the subject can still describe the various phenomenal features of the auditory phenomena (volume, pitch, timbre, etc.), they no longer take it to be an external sound event. It is important to see that, on Coates's view, this is not a merely intellectual change. Rather, because our experience involves an integration of sensory and cognitive aspects, a change in how a sensory phenomenon is automatically conceptualized is a change in the overall phenomenal character of the experience. What was transparently experienced as an objective event is now experienced as an internal subjective event. Hence, the auditory representation is no longer transparent in Metzinger's sense.

The second type of case is lucid dreaming. In cases of lucid dreaming, subjects are dreaming but are also aware that they are dreaming and also possess memory of both waking life and dream life, as well as the experience of attentional, thinking, and behavioral agency (Metzinger 2009). The lucid dreamer recognizes the dream world as a dream world and therefore recognizes the virtual world of experience as virtual. (It should come as no surprise that lucid dreaming played an important role in some Indian and Tibetan contemplative practices.) This type of global recognition of the mind-dependent character of the dream world can also carry over into waking life, such that waking is also experienced as dreamlike. On the internalist-representationalist interpretation of Vasubandhu's Yogācāra—and following an analogy used in the tradition itself—the transformation at the basis is similar to the global recognition found in lucid dreaming. To realize the consummate nature is to have not just lucid dreaming but also lucid experiencing as such.

Now despite the unfamiliar language, much of this should be fairly familiar. What we are directly aware of in conscious experience are not observer-independent features of the external world but mental images caused by the interaction between the world and our cognitive system. We are usually unaware of the constructive activity of the mind in producing these images, and we are unaware that they *are* images rather than external objects. The mind constructs a virtual world model that is transparent to us. But Vasubandhu's is more radical than many other internalist-representationalist views of the mind in that he applies the model of the three natures to the *subject* of experience, as well. For him, the fundamental structure of the *parikalpita-svabhāva* is the subject-object framework itself. Like the observed objects, the observing self is a virtual construct of a cognitive system. Indeed, Vasubandhu will agree with the Nyāya (and Kantian) point that there is a deep interdependence between grasping an objective world and grasping oneself as a persisting subject of experience. It's just that, on his view, this goes to show that *both* are mental constructs. As I have mentioned, on the Yogācāra view, the sense of self arises from the way the cognitive system models itself and draws the self-other distinction. This is the *kliṣṭa-manas* (afflicted mentation), which mistakes the selfless flow of the *ālayavijñāna* (base consciousness) for a persisting self. It is also the basis for the general sense of mental ownership and for thinking self-referential thoughts involving "I," "me," and "mine" (and their contrasts). Yet for Vasubandhu, there is no such *entity* as a self, only the self model of an impermanent cognitive system. What we take to be the self is like an avatar in the virtual world created by the mind. Again, the similarity to Metzinger is instructive:

> The brain is like a *total flight simulator*, a self-modeling airplane that, rather than being flown by a pilot, generates a complex internal image of itself within its own internal flight simulator. The image is transparent and thus cannot be recognized as an image by the system. Operating under the condition of a naïve-realistic self-misunderstanding, the system interprets the control element in this image as a nonphysical object: The "pilot" is born into a virtual reality with no opportunity to discover this fact. The pilot is the Ego. (Metzinger 2009, 108)

Of course, Vasubandhu takes the basis of the simulation to be the *ālayavijñāna*, not the brain (and he is, to put it lightly, much less sanguine about the idea that the ultimate causal basis of experience is an observer-independent physical reality). Moreover, as we have seen, he thinks it is possible to come to see both the experiential world and the experiential self as *vijñāptimātra*. The result is said to be a radical transcendence of the subject-object framework of understanding experience.

While this internalist-representationalist interpretation of the doctrine of three natures is a coherent and plausible one, I turn now to a quite different interpretation of the *trisvabhāva* view—one more in line with later

Madhyamaka appropriations and with the enactive approach to experience we have been exploring. On this "nondualist" interpretation, we start not from the constructed nature of experiential objects but from the perfected nature of mind-world nonduality. In this regard, Japanese philosopher Nishitani Keiji relates an interesting story from the Zen tradition:

> On a pilgrimage seeking the Way with two companion monks, Hōgen stopped to rest at the temple of a Zen priest named Jizō (Dicang) one rainy day. When the rain cleared and they were about to set off again, Jizō, who had come to see them off, remarked, "It is said you usually expound the doctrine that the three worlds are mind only." Then, pointing to a rock in the garden, he asked, "Is that rock inside your mind or outside it?" "Inside my mind, of course," was the answer Hōgen gave, typical of consciousness-only theory. Jizō, immediately retorted, "By what karmic fate I do not know, but a man is wandering around with a lump of stone in his mind. He must feel quite heavy." (Edelglass and Garfield 2009, 101)

Jizō's point here, I take it, is not to reinstate a naïvely realistic view of experience but rather to challenge Hōgen's phenomenologically and ontologically *internalist* view of Yogācāra. That is, the attempt to overcome the subject-object dichotomy by simply *internalizing* the phenomenal world—whereby the experienced rock is supposed to be in Hōgen's mind, which is implicitly in his head—is insufficiently radical. It tries to overcome the dichotomy by treating the mind as self-contained, and therefore it does not transcend the subject-object or inside-outside duality but rather absolutizes one side of it. Instead of the thoroughgoing interdependence of mind and world, the internalist-representationalist account of the three natures treats the mind as an autonomously intelligible domain. Indeed, it is precisely the tendency to treat the mind as being self-contained and ontologically fundamental (call it the myth of the "ready-made mind") that is at the basis of Candrakīrti's Madhyamaka critique of Yogācāra.

The nondualist alternative is to treat the distinctions between inside and outside, subject and object, mind and world as distinctions drawn *within* experience rather than *between* experience and something else. And *experience* here refers to the continuous dynamic interplay of (what we label) mental and physical factors constituting our sentient embodied (*nāma-rūpa*) being in the world. The *Dīgha Nikāya* states,

> Just this, namely *nāma-rūpa*, is the cause, ground, origin and condition of consciousness. Thus far, then, can we trace birth and decay, death and passing away and being reborn, thus far extends the way of designation (*adhivacana-*), of language (*nirutti-*), of concepts (*paññatti-*), thus far is the sphere of understanding (*paññāvacara*), thus far the round (of rebirth) goes as far as can be

> discerned here, namely *nāma-rūpa* together with consciousness. (DN, II.63–4, in Walshe 1995, 224)

Experience, then, is the *nāma-rūpa* process within which particular states of consciousness with their intentional objects arise. On this reading of Yogācāra, its distinctive features are a commitment to the radical primacy of experience and a fundamental rethinking of the nature of experience as nondual. In this respect, Yogācāra has affinities with the radical empiricisms of James and Dewey. In "Does Consciousness Exist?" James writes,

> As "subjective" we say that the experience represents; as "objective" it is represented. What represents and what is represented is here numerically the same; but we must remember that no dualism of being represented and representing resides in the experience *per se*. In its pure state, or when isolated, there is no-self-splitting of it into consciousness and what the consciousness is "of." Its subjectivity and objectivity are functional attributes solely, realized only when the experience is "taken," *i.e.*, talked-of, twice. . . . The instant field of the present is at all times what I call the "pure" experience. It is only virtually or potentially either object or subject as yet. For the time being, it is plain, unqualified actuality, or existence, a simple *that*. (2017, 11)

Moreover, in line with the Madhyamaka account of dependent coarising articulated earlier, experience is to be understood *transactionally*. Dewey writes,

> The structure of whatever is had by way of immediate qualitative presences is found in the recurrent modes of interaction taking place between what we term organism, on one side, and environment, on the other. This interaction is the primary fact, and it constitutes a transaction. Only by analysis and selective abstraction can we differentiate the actual occurrence into two factors, one called organism and the other, environment. (2008, 220)

On this nondualist interpretation of the three natures, the *paratantra-svabhāva* is the transactional flow of lived experience itself. From this flow we can construct (and reconstruct) the various distinctions between mind and world, subject and object, or inside and outside, but these categories should not be thought of as metaphysically prior to experience. As Dewey and Bentley characterize the transactional approach, "[s]ystems of descriptions and naming are employed to deal with aspects and phases of action, without final attribution to 'elements' or other presumptively detachable or independent 'entities,' 'essences,' or 'realities,' and without isolation of presumptively detachable 'relations' from such detachable 'elements'" (1949, 108). Furthermore, the construction of experiential objects and subjects is misleading in that we take the constructs to be prior to and independent of the experiential process itself. This does not mean that experiential objects are "inside us" rather than "out there" in the world where they appear to be. Rather, the point is that the very contrast between inside and outside emerges from and only makes sense within lived experience itself. Finally, the direct realization that there is no "sideways-on" view of the open-ended domain of experience and therefore no absolute dualities within it is the realization of the consummate nature.

According to the traditions I consider in this chapter, mind and world are constitutively bound together, and there is no point of view outside this interdependence. But, one might object, if we cannot step outside of lived experience and it is that from which "subject" and "object" and so on emerge, then hasn't experience itself been absolutized? The first response is that "experience" itself is a transactional notion, not an absolute one. Second, on my view, experience is primary insofar as it is the always-presupposed background of our more particular practices of understanding and explanation. But precisely insofar as it plays its role as background, it cannot also serve as an epistemic or ontological *foundation*. To try to employ experience foundationally would be to try to objectify that which makes possible and thus always recedes from objectification. In this sense, experience is both inescapable and ungraspable.

NOTES

1. *karmajaṃ lokavaicitrayam.*

2. Recall that, in chapter 1, I argue for a distinction between subjects and selves. Here I use the term *self* in Thompson's sense of a sentient being.

3. My interpretation here is much indebted to Waldron (2003), chapter 5.

4. Thus it is self-similar at different time scales.

5. Of course, the relation between later Buddhist thought and various forms of idealism and antirealism is a complex one. I appropriate aspects of these strands in order to develop a moderate phenomenological-pragmatic realism.

6. I include regularity theories of causation among accounts of real causation here.

7. *yaḥ pratītyasamutpādaḥ* śūnyatāṃ *tāṃ pracakṣmahe| sā prajñaptir upādāya pratipat saiva madhyamā* || 18 ||

apratītya samutpanno dharmaḥ kaścin na vidyate| yasmāt tasmād aśūnyo hi dharmaḥ kaścin na vidyate || 19 ||

8. *dve satye samupāśritya buddhānāṃ dharmadeśanā| lokasaṃvṛtisatyaṃ ca satyaṃ ca paramārthataḥ* || 8 ||

ye 'nayor na vijānanti vibhāgaṃ satyayor dvayoḥ| te tattvaṃ na vijānanti gambhīre buddhaśāsane || 9 ||

vyavahāram anāśritya paramārtho na deśyate| paramārtham anāgamya nirvāṇaṃ nādhigamyate || 10 ||

9. Note here that these glosses on the conventional are not based on the divisibility or mereological reducibility of conventional phenomena as in Buddhist reductionism.

10. This claim about the ubiquity of dependent arising does not imply that everything is connected to everything else but only that each phenomenon is related to at least one other phenomenon. See Siderits (2011) for further discussion of this point.

11. Both John Dunne (2004) and Laura Guerrero (2015) interpret Dharmakīrti's notion of *arthakriyā* in similarly pragmatist terms.

12. Note that the term *svabhāva* here simply means the nature of something and does not in this context refer to the type of "inherent existence" refuted in Madhyamaka thought.

Chapter Five

Cultivating Compassion

There is widespread disagreement between Buddhist thinkers and schools on important issues in metaphysics, epistemology, philosophy of mind, and philosophy of language. However, when it comes to Buddhist ethics, the tradition is very clear, and there is widespread agreement in the philosophical literature on what it recommends. Buddhist ethics counsels practitioners to overcome the three poisons of greed (*rāga*), hatred (*dveṣa*), and ignorance (*moha*) and to cultivate those states and traits of mind (and the actions that they motivate) that conduce to the genuine happiness and freedom of oneself and others.

Along with the cultivation of wisdom and meditative concentration, moral discipline (*śīla*) is central to the eightfold path to liberation from suffering. That is, right action, right speech, and right livelihood are integral aspects of the path. As for rules of conduct, lay practitioners commit to the five precepts of avoiding killing, stealing, lying, sexual misconduct, and intoxication. Monastics take the more stringent *prātimokṣa* vows (numbering in the hundreds). Vows, precepts, and rules are commonly justified as both means to and expressions of positive traits of mind, as well as ways to avoid harm to oneself and others and to facilitate harmonious social interaction. In terms of positive traits to be cultivated, the most widespread are the four *brahmavihāras*: loving kindness (*maitrī*), compassion (*karuṇā*), sympathetic joy (*muditā*), and equanimity (*upekṣā*). These can refer to both occurrent states and stable dispositions. Loving kindness involves the intention and motivation to benefit others. Compassion involves the intention and motivation to remove others' suffering. Sympathetic joy involves the tendency to take joy in the happiness of others. Equanimity involves a lack of bias or undue partiality in one's perceptions and interactions with others (and oneself). In the Mahāyāna tradition, the *bodhisattva* path is organized around the cultivation and exercise of the six perfections (*pāramitās*): generosity (*dāna*), moral discipline (*śīla*), patience or forbearance (*kṣānti*), vigor (*vīrya*), meditative stability (*dhyāna*), and wisdom (*prajñā*). The cultivation and exercise of these virtues is central to the Buddhist path.

Positive traits, such as these virtues, as well as positive actions are most commonly referred to as *kuśala* ("wholesome" or "skillful").[1] Actions and traits that are *kuśala* are conducive to the happiness (*sukha*) or well-being (śubha) of the agent or others, while *akuśala* ("unwholesome" or "unskillful") actions do the opposite. For instance, from the *Majjhima Nikāya*:

> When you reflect, if you know: "This action that I wish to do with the body would lead to my own affliction, or to the affliction of others, or to the affliction of both; it is an unwholesome bodily action with painful consequences, with painful results," then you definitely should not do such an action with the body. But when you reflect, if you know: "This action that I wish to do with the body would not lead to my own affliction, or to the affliction of others, or to the affliction of both; it is a wholesome bodily action with pleasant consequences, with pleasant results," then you may do such an action with the body. (Nanamoli and Bodhi 1995, 524–25)

Now, three fundamental questions immediately arise here. First, does Buddhist ethics rest on a form of hedonism? Second, what are the guidelines for dealing with conflicts between benefit to oneself and benefit to others? Third, what is the relation between virtues and their positive consequences?

With regard to the first question, while Buddhist texts often take pleasure and pain, as well as happiness and suffering, as salient values or disvalues, it is unwarranted to interpret Buddhist ethics as hedonistic. Buddhist texts repeatedly warn against seeking pleasure for its own sake, while exhorting practitioners to seek virtue, wisdom, and tranquility. Furthermore, the operative notion of *sukha* ("happiness") here is clearly beyond mere pleasure. Following Dambrun and Ricard (2011), we may distinguish two types of happiness. Hedonic or "fluctuating happiness" is stimulus driven, contingent on circumstances, and part of a larger cycle of periods of satisfaction and dissatisfaction. *Sukha*, or "authentic-durable happiness," in contrast is

> understood here as an optimal way of being, a state of durable plenitude based on a quality of consciousness that underlies and imbues each experience, emotion and behavior, and . . . [is] not intrinsically dependent on the positive and negative feedback that we are constantly receiving, but rather give[s] one the inner resources to deal with the variability of the world and be a source of continuous optimal adaptation to external conditions. (Dambrun and Ricard 2011, 139)

With regard to the second question, compared to contemporary ethical discourse, there is relatively little discussion of potential conflicts between self-interest and the interests of others. To be sure, the critique of selfishness or egocentrism is absolutely central to Buddhist thought and practice. However, egocentrism is thought to be harmful to both oneself and others, while selfless altruism is thought to be beneficial to oneself and others. Śāntideva puts the point starkly: "All those who suffer in the world do so because of their desire for their own happiness. All those happy in the world are so because of their desire for the happiness of others" (2008, 99).[2] I discuss this connection more extensively later, but for now, let us note that there are two interwoven aspects of the Buddhist view here. The first and most fundamental aspect is that the *perception* of a fundamental conflict between (genuine) self-interest and (genuine) other interest is based in the very egocentric frame of mind that creates and perpetuates it. The second aspect is that the operation of *karma* (both intra- and interlifetime) is thought to ensure that there is no ultimate conflict because the causal order of the world is such that our well-being is partly a function of the moral quality of our mental states and actions. Thus, on the Buddhist view, the more clearly one sees oneself and others, the more one overcomes the false perception of fundamental conflict between what is beneficial to oneself and what is beneficial to others. Moreover, the pragmatic function of precepts and rules is partly to smooth out potential conflicts among the unenlightened.

Regarding the third question, contemporary interpreters of Buddhist ethics are in broad agreement on the tight connection between virtue and beneficial consequences for oneself and others, even when they disagree on the nature of the connection. Damien Keown (1992), for instance, argues that early and Theravāda Buddhist ethics can be understood in terms of a teleological virtue ethics, structurally similar to *eudaimonism*. On this account, the ultimate goal is *nirvāṇa*, and the virtues are defined in terms of the relation to achieving and expressing awakening. The goal is one's own awakening, and cultivating the virtues of loving kindness, compassion, sympathetic joy, and equanimity is integral to the achievement of that goal. The primarily other-regarding virtues are then understood in terms of the role they play in achieving individual awakening. Similarly, I suggest elsewhere that Mahāyāna ethics can be understood as a virtue ethics of wise universal compassion (MacKenzie 2018).

In contrast, several interpreters (Clayton 2006; Goodman 2014; Siderits 2016) interpret Mahāyāna ethics in consequentialist terms. On this view, Buddhist ethics is based on promoting the welfare and diminishing the suffering of all sentient beings, and the virtues are understood in the context of that goal. Mark Siderits (2016) takes Mahāyāna ethics (at least) to be a form of aretaic utilitarianism in which wholesome states and virtue are a means to the impartial and agent-neutral promotion of happiness and the reduction of suffering. Therefore, the connection between virtue and happiness and the reduction of suffering is instrumental. Charles Goodman (2014), however, interprets the Mahāyāna ethics of Śāntideva as a form of character consequentialism. On this view, the ultimate goal of Buddhist ethics is understood in terms of the welfare of sentient beings, but the operative notion of welfare includes both happiness and virtue. This form of perfectionist consequentialism combines the idea of an internal relation between virtue and happiness characteristic of many forms of virtue ethics with the universalistic altruism characteristic of utilitarianism. Finally, others argue that Buddhist ethics is pluralistic (Edelglass 2006) or that we should resist the temptation to reconstruct Buddhist ethics in terms of current normative theories (Garfield 2014).

In this chapter, I do not presuppose a specific, full, theoretical reconstruction of Buddhist ethics. I do, however, return to the question of a Buddhist virtue ethics later. For now, I presuppose three key ideas. First, there is an internal connection between virtue (or the moral quality of states, traits, and actions) and genuine well-being. Second, certain traits of character are good in themselves (*svabhāvataḥ kuśalam*) independently of their consequences. These include, according to Vasubandhu, the three roots of *kuśala* (nongreed, nonhatred, and nonignorance); self-respect (*hrī*); and concern for others (*apatrāpya*) (Goodman and Thakchoe 2015). Third, the cultivation of altruistic universal compassion in particular is central to Mahāyāna ethics.[3]

The focus of this chapter, then, is not on the normative theoretical structure of Buddhist ethics but rather on Buddhist ethics as a transformative-developmental *path*. That is, Buddhist ethics is fundamentally concerned with the progressive dismantling of the greed, aversion, and ignorance that condition our minds and actions and the progressive cultivation of the nonattachment, compassion, and wisdom of an enlightened character. In particular, I focus on the delineation of the *bodhisattva* path in Śāntideva's *Bodhicaryāvatāra* because it is in his work that we find a rich and nuanced moral phenomenology of the path of ethical cultivation and awakening (Garfield 2014). My aim in this chapter, then, is to unpack the cognitive, affective, perceptual, bodily, and intersubjective dimensions of this path in dialogue with the enactive approach.

THE *SAṂSĀRIC* FRAMEWORK

In the first chapter of *Bodhicaryāvatāra*, *Śāntideva* gives a striking and memorable characterization of the *saṃsāric* predicament of sentient beings:

"Hoping to escape suffering, it is to suffering that they run. In the desire for happiness, out of delusion, they destroy their own happiness, like an enemy" (2008, 7).[4] *Saṃsāra* here is a kind of existential catch-22, a mode of functioning wherein our attempts to attain happiness and avoid suffering are self-defeating. The three poisons of greed, hatred, and delusion are dysfunctional forms of our basic impulses of attraction, aversion, and indifference, on the basis of which we respond to changing circumstances, seeking happiness and avoiding suffering. Because these basic forms of reaction are distorted or dysfunctional, as long as we are bound to them, our attempts to secure the lasting happiness we desire are doomed to fail.

More specifically, the *saṃsāric* predicament has deep roots in our cognitive, affective, and motivational systems. In terms of affect, we are subject to pleasant, unpleasant, and neutral sensations and feelings (*vedanā*) as well as such negative emotions (*kleśa*) as fear, anger, and craving. These affective states condition and are conditioned by our conative and cognitive states. That is, negative affective states of fear and anger may arise based on contact with that which we perceive as threatening (or we may perceive something is threatening based on feelings of fear and anger), and we may act to avoid or destroy that which elicits these feelings and perceptions. In addition, on the Buddhist account, even pleasant states are entangled with the *saṃsāric* framework. For instance, that which is pleasant can elicit craving (*tṛṣṇa*) or restless desire. Craving can bring about grasping (*upādāna*), the anxious attempt to maintain or protect the perceived source of pleasure. Further, affective states are thought to play an important role in reinforcing dysfunctional conative and cognitive states.

Corresponding to the three basic hedonic states (pleasant, unpleasant, neutral) are three basic motivational states: attraction, aversion, and indifference. These are basic impulses that drive the specific behavioral responses of approach, avoid, and ignore. In the *saṃsāric* framework, the approach-avoid-ignore system is oriented toward seeking pleasant stimuli, avoiding unpleasant stimuli, and ignoring that which is not perceived as relevant to this orientation (Dambrun and Ricard 2011).

At the root of the *saṃsāric* framework are various cognitive distortions (delusions) involving perception, conception, belief, and self-understanding. These distortions are based in a failure properly to recognize the three marks of conditioned existence: impermanence (*anitya*), unsatisfactoriness (*duḥkha*), and no-self (*anātman*). On my view, these are not simple failures to grasp these concepts or see their application in the world. Rather, they are forms of cognitive bias or distortion, wherein we misconstrue key aspects of experience in ways that perpetuate and reinforce the style of psychological function I have been calling the *saṃsāric* framework. Thus, at one level we may know full well that things change or are impermanent, but at a deeper level, we still operate with the belief that grasping after impermanent stimuli is an effective means to lasting happiness, even though the stimulus, by its nature, cannot provide such happiness. In fact, it is part of the definition of grasping that it involves a misconstrual or false projection onto the object of attachment. On the Buddhist account, the most fundamental form of cognitive distortion is the belief that one is a fixed, enduring self and the self-centeredness and self-cherishing that go along with this belief. As Dambrun and Ricard summarize,

> In the end, all of these processes generate fluctuating happiness which is characterized by the alternation of phases of well-being and ill-being. It seems to us that this type of happiness, if it can be qualified as such, also has a tendency to be self-reinforcing. Because the phases of well-being are of short duration, the individual runs the risk of finding himself in a state where he or she is perpetually seeking new gratifications to maximize his or her well-being. In other words, a self-centered style of functioning produces a circular effect in which the individual is, in a way, the prisoner of an "egoistic and hedonic" spiral. (2011, 146)

Saṃsāra, in this sense, is this dysfunctional, unsatisfactory bondage to the egoistic and hedonistic spiral.

In sum, the *saṃsāric* framework is a psychophysical mode of functioning that is characterized by distorted and dysfunctional cognitive, affective, and motivational states and traits. It is cyclical and self-reinforcing and constitutes the basic framework within which human beings tend to pursue happiness and attempt to avoid suffering. Yet insofar as the *saṃsāric* framework involves being bound to a false sense of self and such maladaptive impulses as greed, envy, fear, and aggression, authentic-durable happiness is unachievable within the framework. Moreover, on the Buddhist view, living within the framework obstructs the cultivation and exercise of our capacities for more accurate insight and the development of such virtues as compassion, generosity, and equanimity. Given this analysis, then, awakening is not simply an inner state but rather an optimal mode of being in the world, enacted in and through body, speech, and mind (in the standard Buddhist phrase) and always embedded in a context. The Buddhist path, including ethics, must involve the progressive dismantling of the *saṃsāric* framework and the development of this more wholesome or awakened cognitive, affective, and motivational-behavioral framework. On my view, this is the project of Śāntideva's guide to the awakened way of life.

BODHICITTA, EMPATHY, AND OPEN INTERSUBJECTIVITY

We may now distinguish between two frameworks or modes of living: *saṃsāric* and awakened. The *saṃsāric* mode, as just discussed, is characterized by self-centeredness, the three poisons, and fluctuations of happiness and suffering. The awakened mode is characterized by selflessness, authentic-durable happiness, and the perfection of virtue. But what is the basis of this optimal mode of being? What makes it possible (if it is possible)? For Śāntideva and his fellow Mahāyānists, the foundation of the awakened life is the cultivation and expression of *bodhicitta*, the "awakening mind," which Śāntideva calls the "seed of pure happiness in the world and the remedy of suffering in the world" (2008, 26).

The term *bodhi* here means "awakening" or "awakened," while *citta* is traditionally translated as "mind." However, *citta* here has a broader semantic range and encompasses cognitive, affective, and motivational factors, such that it is sometimes translated as "heart" or "heart-mind." It is the mind-set and existential commitment that forms the basis of the awakened life, and its cultivation is the path of the *bodhisattva*, the "awakening being" that is the spiritual ideal of Mahāyāna Buddhism. Following Garfield, I understand *bodhicitta* to be the "commitment to attain and to manifest full awakening for the benefit of others" (Garfield 2014, 299). It is centrally a motivational state or disposition but involves cognitive and affective aspects, as well. Its cultivation involves the development of deep insight; skillful moral responsiveness; and such virtues as compassion, generosity, and fortitude. On the Mahāyāna view, what separates the *bodhisattva* path from other forms of Buddhist practice is the centrality of an *altruistic* motivation for pursuing the path. The aim, then, is complex: One aims to fully develop one's potential for awakening in order ultimately to release all beings from the suffering of *saṃsāra*.[5] Indeed the *bodhisattva*, Śāntideva proclaims, "longs to remove the unequalled agony of every single being and make their virtue infinite" (2008, 7). It is noteworthy—beyond the grandiosity of the claim—that the aim is to relieve suffering *and* perfect virtue for all beings.

Śāntideva distinguishes two types of *bodhicitta*, the "mind resolved on awakening and the mind proceeding toward awakening" (2008, 6). The first, aspirational *bodhicitta* involves the genuine altruistic aspiration to spiritual development for the sake of all sentient beings, while the second, engaged or active *bodhicitta*, involves the long, sometimes-arduous walking of that path. Śāntideva goes on to remark that even aspirational *bodhicitta* is powerful, presumably because it marks the beginning of a break with the egoism of *saṃsāric* existence. He goes on to say that "worship of the Buddha is surpassed merely by the desire for the welfare of others; how much more so by the persistent effort for the complete happiness of every being?" (Śāntideva 2008, 7). The key to moving beyond the *saṃsāric* framework, then, is the cultivation of altruism within the context of a path of moral-spiritual development.

But if human beings are bound to the egoistic and hedonistic cycle of the *saṃsāric* framework, then how can altruism be evoked and cultivated in the first place? On the Mahāyāna view, the defilements of greed, hatred, and delusion are adventitious, and human beings have the natural capacity or potential for developing both nonegoic self-understanding and altruistic motivation. Indeed, it is often claimed that the capacities for wisdom and compassion are more fundamental than the defilements. What, then, is the basis of this capacity for altruism? On my view, the basis for the cultivation of *bodhicitta* is the fundamental empathy and intersubjectivity of human consciousness introduced in chapter 3.

The earliest forms of empathy can be seen in what developmental psychologists term "primary intersubjectivity" (Trevarthen and Bullowa 1979). Primary intersubjectivity involves sensorimotor capacities that enable relations and interactions with others (Gallagher 2012a). These capacities, which are innate or early developing, manifest in the ability to perceive another's feelings and intentions through their movements, facial expressions, gestures, and so on and to respond with our own movements, expressions, and the like. Newborn infants, for instance, can perceive and imitate facial expressions (Meltzoff and Moore 1989), a capacity that is both sensorimotor and interpersonally interactive. At around two months, infants develop the ability to follow the gaze of another, sense what the other is looking at, and even anticipate the other's intentions Baron-Cohen 1995; Barrera and Maurer 1981; Gallagher 2012a). Primary intersubjectivity continues to develop so that, by the end of the first year of life, "infants have a non-mentalizing, perception-based, embodied and pragmatic grasp of the emotions and intentions of other persons" (Gallagher 2012b, 197). At around nine months, children begin to develop forms of secondary intersubjectivity. Through the development of joint attention, children are able to engage in triadic interaction between the child themself, another, and an object or event. Secondary intersubjectivity involves the development of two processes. Gallagher summarizes,

> (1) They refer to others (in social referencing) and enter into joint actions where they learn how objects are used by using them and from seeing others use them, and they begin to co-constitute the meaning of the world through such interactions with others in a process of "participatory sense-making"; and (2) they build upon theses interactions to makes sense of the other's behavior in specific contexts. (2012b, 197).

Building on the classical phenomenological understanding of empathy as well as contemporary work in the mind sciences, the enactivist approach distinguishes four types or processes of empathy (Thompson 2010, 392–402). The first type of empathy involves the dynamic coupling of living, sensing, feeling bodies. This form of empathy is passive (i.e., not voluntary or deliberate) and is thought to operate at the level of the implicit or unconscious body schema. As Thompson characterizes it, "bodily coupling or pairing allows empathy to be not simply the comprehension of another's particular emotions . . . but on a more fundamental level the experience of another a living bodily subject like oneself" (2010, 393). Underpinning this fundamental type of empathy are the various cortical mirror systems, made up of interconnected mirror neurons. For instance, certain mirror neurons constitute a system that matches perceived motor actions by another with activation of brain areas that subserve those same actions in oneself (Buccino et al. 2001). As Gallese states, "when we observe actions performed by other individuals our motor system 'resonates' along with that of the observed agent" (2001, 38). Furthermore, this type of resonance occurs in cases of pain and emotion. Perceived unpleasant stimuli in another (e.g., watching another receive a pinprick) activates areas of the anterior cingulate cortex that are also activated when one feels an unpleasant stimulus (Hutchison et al. 1999). Likewise, perception of emotion in another activates neural mechanisms that are involved in the generation of one's own emotions. This type of empathy also includes affective resonance in which two or more individuals affect each other's emotions (Thompson 2010, 395). Infants will cry in response to the cry of other infants. And we may also include here the complex sensory, affective, and emotional resonance between an infant and a caregiver (e.g., skin-to-skin contact and breastfeeding).

The second type of empathy is the more active and cognitive process of imaginatively transposing oneself into the place of another—putting oneself in another's shoes. This form of cognitive perspective taking ranges from the tailored helping and consolation behavior observed in great apes (Preston and de Waal 2002) to the highly sophisticated ability displayed when "one individual can mentally adopt the other's perspective by exchanging places with the other in imagination" (Thompson 2010, 397). In human children, the beginning of this ability—a form of secondary intersubjectivity—is linked to the development of joint attention (Tomasello 2001).

The third type of empathy involves mutual self and other understanding. In this type of empathy, a person is able not only to put themself in another's shoes but also to see themself from the perspective of the other. In cases where the other also uses this kind of empathy, there can develop a mutual empathetic exchange, as in a conversation. This reflexive and reiterated form of empathy, then, helps to constitute an intersubjective point of view that transcends any single point of view. This type of empathy begins to develop between nine and twelve months in infants. When another directs attention at the infant, the infant can monitor and even direct the other's attention. Tomasello describes,

> From this point the infant's face-to-face interactions with others—which appear on the surface to be continuous with her face-to-face interactions from earlier infancy—are radically transformed. She now knows she is interacting with an intentional agent who perceives her and intends things toward her. . . . By something like this same process infants at this age also become able to monitor adults' emotional attitudes toward them as well—a kind of social referencing of others' attitudes to the self. This new understanding of how others *feel* about me opens up the possibility for the development of shyness, self-consciousness, and a sense of self-esteem. (2001, 89–90)

This "social-cognitive revolution," in Tomasello's terms, opens up the intersubjective world of objects, activities, contexts, and others as intentional agents in this shared world. Moreover, this type of reiterated empathy drives more sophisticated forms of self-understanding as one comes to see oneself as an intentional agent in interaction and mutual recognition with other intentional agents.

The fourth type of empathy involves a form of moral perception wherein one perceives the other as an object of concern and respect. It is the fundamental capacity for other-directed feelings of concern and is, in this sense, the "basic cognitive and emotional capacity underlying all the moral sentiments and emotions one can have for another" (Thompson 2010, 401). According to Tomasello, this basic form of moral understanding develops around the same time as the child understands others as mental agents and is based on the child's ability to see and feel things from the other's point of view.

It is important to see that these types of empathy (as forms of primary and secondary intersubjectivity) are deeply intertwined in human experience. The more sophisticated forms of empathy to do not replace the more basic, bodily, and sensorimotor forms. Our intersubjective interactions deploy these forms of empathy simultaneously and interconnectedly. Moreover, human beings come into the world primed for intersubjectivity and develop through intersubjective interaction. Indeed, Thompson states,

> This dialogical dynamic [of empathic interaction] is not a linear or additive combination of two preexisting, skull-bound minds. It emerges from and reciprocally shapes the nonlinear coupling of oneself and another in perception and action, emotion and imagination, and gesture and speech. In this way, self and other bring forth each other reciprocally through empathy. (2010, 402)

On my interpretation, then, the core human capacity of empathy is the root of *bodhicitta*, and the *bodhisattva* path involves both clearing away obstructions to empathic awareness and developing and extending the capacity toward all sentient beings. Further, if the psychological and phenomenological understanding of empathy sketched here is on the right track, then egoistic self-understanding is deeply mistaken. We are not fundamentally separate, alienated egos but rather empathic, social beings. Our very personhood is constituted from the beginning in intersubjective (bodily, sensory, affective, and cognitive) interaction, and therefore open, empathic intersubjectivity is both existentially and developmentally more fundamental than our egoistic self-understanding. Indeed, this, we think, is crucial to Śāntideva's understanding of the path of cultivating *bodhicitta*, and as I show in the rest of this chapter, the *bodhisattva* path works with and cultivates all four types of empathy.

MEDITATIVE CONCENTRATION

In chapter 8 of *Bodhicaryāvatāra*, "The Perfection of Meditative Absorption," Śāntideva lays out a path to overcoming egoism and the defilements and cultivating and expanding the altruistic compassion of *bodhicitta*. This includes both meditative techniques and the deployment of philosophical reasoning to undermine the entrenched egoism of the *saṃsāric* framework. Further, the notion of "perfection" (*pāramitā*) here includes in its semantic range both the idea of improving or perfecting something and the idea of perfection as a *virtue*, similar to the Greek idea of a virtue as an excellence of character. Thus, in the context of the perfection of meditation, we see an emphasis both on perfecting the attentional techniques and skills of meditation and on embodying the virtues of deepened and extended moral perception and motivation.

Śāntideva begins by emphasizing the need to develop the attention regulation and stability of *śamatha* ("calm abiding" or "tranquility"). He writes,

8.1 Increasing one's endeavor in this way, one should stabilize the mind in meditative concentration, since a person whose mind is distracted stands between the fangs of the defilements.

8.2 Distraction does not occur if body and mind are kept sequestered. Therefore, one should renounce the world and disregard distracting thoughts.

8.4 Realizing that one well-attuned to insight through tranquility can destroy the defilements, one should firstly seek tranquility, and that by disregarding one's delight in the world. (Śāntideva 2008, 88)[6]

So, while the ultimate goal of the *bodhisattva* path is compassionate moral engagement with all sentient beings, Śāntideva first recommends the cultivation of tranquility and solitude. On his view, worldly attachment within the *saṃsāric* framework prevents the development of *bodhicitta* both by reinforcing the framework and by distracting one from the development of the virtues. Also, one must develop both tranquility (*śamatha*) and penetrating insight (*vipaśyanā*) before one can begin to practice the more advanced and more demanding practices associated with overcoming egoism and developing altruism. In support of this basic idea, I point to the large and growing body of literature showing that the practice of forms of "mindfulness" meditation are associated with reduced negative emotion, greater attentional stability, greater sense of subjective well-being, more prosocial behavior, improved moral attention, improved psychological flexibility, and a greater emphasis on intrinsic/self-transcendence values (Goleman and Davidson 2017).[7] Moreover, the cultivation of calm abiding has been associated with a reduction of the stress-reactive cycle and an increase in vagal tone, which is in turn related to feelings of compassion and prosocial behavior. Indeed, Loizzo (2012) argues that one main function of these forms of meditation is to calm the stress-reactive cycle and its accompanying negative emotions and motivations (the defilements) in order to clear the way for cultivation of our more advanced social-empathetic capacities.

The calm and focused mind developed through the practice of *śamatha* becomes the basis for the development of insight (*vipaśyanā*). The practice here seems to be a form of analytical meditation in which one explores Buddhist insights and teachings in one's own experience. This includes both internalizing the teachings and working to penetrate them and apply them in one's conduct and thinking. For instance, the teaching of impermanence can be explored phenomenologically with regard to various processes of body and mind. Yet, one may also simply evoke the teaching of impermanence in the face of, for instance, desire for and attachment to bodily pleasures. Indeed, throughout the text, Śāntideva deploys core Buddhist teachings as *cognitive strategies* for defusing or counteracting the defilements and their associated vices, such as craving, envy, and anger. In chapter 6, for example, Śāntideva discusses a variety of strategies for defusing the anger that arises upon experiencing some perceived harm or transgression:

6.22 I feel no anger towards bile and the like, even though they cause intense suffering. Why am I angry at the sentient? They too have [causes] for their anger.

6.25 Whatever transgressions and evil deeds of various kinds there are, all arise through the power of conditioning factors [*saṃskāras*], while there is nothing that arises independently.

6.31 In this way everything is dependent on something else. Even that upon which each is dependent is not independent. Since, like a magical display, phenomena do not initiate activity, at what does one get angry like this?

6.33 Therefore, even if one sees a friend or an enemy behaving badly, one can reflect that there are specific conditioning factors that determine this, and thereby remain happy.[8] (2008, 52–53)

On the basis of these and other passages, some suggest that Śāntideva is arguing for a form of hard determinism (Goodman 2014). However, on my view, it would be a mistake to take these and other passages primarily as detached theoretical assertions or arguments. Rather, Śāntideva is employing key Buddhist ideas as cognitive strategies to deal skillfully with unskillful emotions, thoughts, and behaviors. Throughout the text, he recommends changing one's perspective in the face of negative events or unwholesome states of mind. Here he recommends shifting one's perspective from the normal interpersonal level to a more impersonal causal-psychological level as a way of defusing the destructive emotion of anger and maintaining happiness and compassion in the face of harm inflicted by another. In particular, the change in perspective here seems to mitigate angry reactions by counteracting an attribution error or bias in which one perceives the harm from another as (simply) motivated by ill intent or vicious character. By shifting to an impersonal perspective, one comes to see that personal agency is a multifactor causal-psychological process and that there is no absolute central controller of this process. Moreover, Śāntideva reminds the reader (and himself) that sentient beings interacting within the *saṃsāric* framework are bound by their own conditioning and that this is as true of others as it is of oneself. The intended effect of this perspective shift, it seems, is to defuse anger at the perceived harm by moving from the interpersonal harm-blame perspective to a perspective that emphasizes the many factors that constrain and condition personal agency and the shared plight of sentient beings as bound by the dysfunctional framework of *saṃsāra*. Ultimately, for Śāntideva, this change in point of view can lead to greater compassion even for those who cause harm. Yet he does not recommend that one always adopt this impersonal perspective in dealing with others. Indeed, he couldn't do so without falling into the error of nihilism, wherein—upon realizing that there is no substantial self and all phenomena are dependently originated—one rejects personal agency and moral responsibility entirely. What Śāntideva does here and elsewhere in the text, on my reading, is use the teachings (teachings he no doubt believes to be true) as ways to develop a kind of cognitive-affective flexibility that underpins the ability to respond skillfully and spontaneously to circumstances.[9]

THE FOUR-POINT MIND TRAINING

Now, once the aspiring *bodhisattva* has developed a sufficient degree of meditative concentration and insight, they can begin to cultivate *bodhicitta* directly. In the Tibetan tradition (Tegchok 2006), Śāntideva's instructions are organized as the "four-point mind training": meditating on (1) the equality of self and other, (2) the limits of egocentrism or self-cherishing, (3) the benefits of altruism, and (4) the exchange of self and other. This system of cognitive-affective training is designed to arouse and extend the altruistic concern of *bodhicitta* as well as the moral perception and responsiveness requisite for the path of the *bodhisattva*.

Equality of Self and Other

Śāntideva instructs,

> 8.90 At first one should meditate intently on the equality of self and others as follows: "All equally experience suffering and happiness. I should look after them as I do myself."
> 8.91 Just as the body, with its many parts from division into hands and other limbs, should be protected as a single entity, so too should this entire world which is divided, but undivided in its nature to suffer and be happy.
> 8.92 Even though suffering in me does not cause distress in the bodies of others, I should nevertheless find their suffering intolerable because of the affection I have for myself.
> 8.93 In the same way that, though I cannot experience another's suffering in myself, his suffering is hard for him to bear because of his affection for himself.
> 8.94 I should dispel the suffering of others because it is suffering like my own suffering. I should help others too because of their nature as beings, which is like my own suffering.
> 8.95 When happiness is liked by me and others equally, what is so special about me that I strive after happiness only for myself?
> 8.96 When fear and suffering are disliked by me and others equally, what is so special about me that I protect myself and not the other?[10] (2008, 96)

This meditation on the equality of self and other has as its explicit goal overcoming the narrow egoism of self-cherishing—that is, the deep-seated sense that one's own happiness and suffering are the only things that are really important—and the extension of altruistic concern for others. Those who fully realize the equality of self and other are ones "to whom the suffering of others is as important as the things they themselves hold dear" (Śāntideva 2008, 97).

In order to facilitate this realization, this meditation directly employs multiple empathic capacities. Recall that the four types of empathy are

1. the passive association of my lived body with the lived body of the other
2. the imaginative transposal of myself to the place of the other
3. the interpretation or understanding of myself as an other for you
4. ethical responsibility in the face of the other

First, the cultivation and extension of empathy here presupposes that one possesses basic (type 1) empathy. As mentioned previously, the cultivation of *bodhicitta* is typically understood as the cultivation of an innate potential of the human mind. On my view, empathy is an evolved biological capacity of humans and some other animals, such as great apes. The capacity to experience another as a living bodily subject like oneself is the background condition of cultivating *bodhicitta*. Moreover, Śāntideva here directly appeals to the suffering of other sentient beings, something that has the potential to elicit a powerful empathetic-affective response in the meditator.

After evoking the fact that it is the nature of sentient beings to experience suffering and happiness, Śāntideva then deploys imaginative transposition (type 2 empathy). Starting with the recognition of one's affection for oneself, one then imaginatively adopts the perspective of other sentient beings. This, of course, is a common form of perspective taking used to extend empathy and moral perception. We ask our young children to see the distress of another child and then ask, "How would you feel if he came and took *your* toy away?" And yet, this basic recognition of one's shared condition as sentient beings can be distorted and biased in a variety of ways. The focus on the most basic desire to be happy and avoid suffering here, it seems, is meant to counteract these forms of bias. As Śāntideva remarks, the world is "divided, but undivided in its nature to suffer and be happy" (2008, 96). Further, we see here that while simply recognizing that the suffering of others is as bad for them as one's own suffering is bad for oneself is important, it is not enough. One must also cultivate the desire actively to respond to other's suffering. Indeed, the *bodhisattva* is one who responds to the suffering of others as naturally and spontaneously as one's hand responds to a pain in one's foot (Śāntideva 2008, 96).

Next, the meditation moves from a recognition of the suffering of others to an interrogation of oneself: "When fear and suffering are disliked by me and others equally, what is so special about me that I protect myself and not the other?" (Śāntideva 2008, 96). This requires the ability not just to imaginatively transpose oneself to another's perspective but also to adopt a distinct perspective on oneself. One must be able to see oneself as just one sentient being among others rather than as the center of the universe. This might involve adopting an impartial, third-person point of view on oneself—a perspective perhaps made easier by the intense self-observation of *śamatha* and *vipaśyanā* meditation. But in this context, it is the second-person point of view that is more relevant. One must adopt the perspective that another might have of you: a fellow sentient being but no one special. Here, then, we see the deployment of both imaginative transposition and mutual intersubjective recognition (type 3 empathy).

The point of meditating on the equality of self and other, of course, is not to correct some mere factual or theoretical error. We *know* that others also want to be happy and don't want to suffer, that we are but one being among others. The problem of egocentrism addressed here is, at bottom, a failure of *moral perception* (and thus motivation, too). Egocentrism dampens and distorts the moral salience of others' suffering and happiness, such that—despite what we know—we are able to ignore the suffering of others and strive for happiness only for ourselves. The task of cultivating *bodhicitta*, then, begins with correcting these distortions of moral perception through our innate empathic capacities. One can then *see* the happiness and suffering of others as morally salient and therefore as something for which we bear some responsibility. Indeed, on my reading of Buddhist ethics, it is absolutely crucial that moral training involves working with the emotions, empathy, and imagination as well as reason. Negative states, such as fear, craving, and hatred, as well as various forms of delusion (including forms of cognitive bias and failures of imagination and empathy) obstruct our capacities for moral perception and responsiveness. Arne Johan Vetlesen argues,

> We experience the objects of moral judgments through emotion. . . . Judgment presupposes perception in the sense that perception "gives" judgment its object; we pass moral judgment on things that are already given, or disclosed, to us through acts of perception. . . . It is on this level, which logically precedes that of judgment . . . that we locate the emotions. Emotions anchor us to the *particular* moral circumstance, to the aspect of a situation that addresses us immediately, to the *here and now*. To "see" the circumstance and to see oneself as addressed by it, and thus to be susceptible to the way a situation affects the weal and woe of others, in short, to identify a situation as carrying *moral significance* in the first place—all of this is required in order to enter the domain of the moral, and none of it would come about without the basic emotional faculty of empathy. (1994, 4)

On this view, emotions and empathy are not merely the motivational oomph behind what is an otherwise theoretical or rational moral sense. Rather, empathy and the emotions (as value feelings or felt appraisals) are at the root of moral disclosure and significance. Bondage to the defilements and to egocentrism within the *saṃsāric* framework, then, constitutes a deep distortion in moral perception. Moreover, we can also see why, on this kind of view, moving beyond an egocentric structure of moral perception through cognitive and affective training can yield greater prereflective and spontaneous moral responsiveness. The *bodhisattva* is one who is naturally able "to 'see' the circumstance and to see oneself as addressed by it, and thus to be susceptible to the weal and woe of others" (Vetlesen 1994, 4).

Of course, there would be no point in engaging and extending the human capacity for empathy if there weren't a basic, perhaps ineliminable asymmetry between one's own experience of suffering and the suffering of others. This asymmetry might be one of the psychological underpinnings of egocentrism, but can it provide any justification for the refusal to take the suffering of others as morally on par with one's own? Śāntideva asserts,

> 8.97 If I give them no protection because their suffering does not afflict me, why do I protect my body against future suffering when it does not afflict me?
> 8.98 The notion "it is the same me even then" is a false construction, since it is one person who dies, quite another who is reborn.
> 8.101 The continuum of consciousness, like a queue, and the combination of constituents, like an army, are not real. The person who experiences suffering does not exist. To whom will that suffering belong?
> 8.102 Without exception, no sufferings belong to anyone. They should be warded off simply because they are suffering. Why is any limitation put on this?
> 8.103 If one asks why suffering should be prevented, no one disputes that! If it must be prevented, then all of it must be. If not, then this goes for oneself as for everyone.[11] (2008, 96–97)

I naturally do things in the present in order to protect myself against future (and therefore currently unfelt) suffering. So the moral importance of an instance of suffering can't be a simple function of my currently undergoing it. The obvious rejoinder here is that the future suffering in question will be *mine*, so I still have reason to prevent it in a way that I do not have reason to prevent the suffering of others. It is at this point that Śāntideva appeals to the doctrine of no-self. On Śāntideva's view, egocentrism rests on a robust conception of the self as a stable, independent, enduring entity of unique moral importance. Buddhist thinkers, of course, utterly reject the existence of this kind of separate self and therefore the justification of egocentrism. In 8.98 and 8.101, he claims that this notion of personal identity ("it is the same me even then") is a false construction, and neither the stream of consciousness nor the system of *skandhas* is ultimately real. Moreover, beyond the question of justification, the full realization of the truth of no-self is meant to elicit a radical transformation in one's sense of self, and this new mode of experience is thought naturally to lead to altruistic compassion.

Yet, in these passages, Śāntideva does not simply deny the reified substantial self but also goes further to say that the person who suffers does not exist and that suffering belongs to no one. That is, he moves from the cultivation of an *impartial* perspective to an *impersonal* perspective that affirms suffering but denies the sufferer. This strongly impersonal reductionism introduces two related problems for his view. First, 8.98–103 seem to reflect the view of Abhidharma reductionism, whereby what ultimately exist are fleeting, simple *dharmas*, such as pain events. On this view, discussed in chapter 1, complex entities, such as persons, are mere conventional constructions, while *dharmas* are ultimately real and have intrinsic existence. Śāntideva, however, is a Madhyamaka in his philosophical orientation. Thus, it is not at all clear that he can consistently avail himself of the reductionist move here, as it rests on the notion that suffering has *svabhāva* and on an understanding of the two truths rejected by Madhyamakas. That is, the strong reductionist route to undermining egocentrism reifies suffering and denies the sufferer while also privileging the impersonal perspective over the interpersonal perspective. Neither of these aspects of Buddhist reductionism sits well with Śāntideva's commitment to the Madhyamaka idea that *all* things are empty and conventionally real.

Second, the shift from cultivating the recognition of the moral equality of self and other to the recognition of the *nonexistence* of self and other threatens the moral point of view itself. The home ground of morality here is the interpersonal point of view, but by attacking egocentrism with the claim that the subjects of suffering do not exist and that suffering does not belong to anyone, we may begin to lose our grip on the moral importance of suffering and on how it is to be prevented. Put simply, if an instance of pain doesn't really *hurt anybody* (there is no one to be hurt!), then why does it matter? Of course, it is *conventionally* true that suffering hurts particular sentient beings. But the appeal to the conventional point of view here is problematic for two reasons. The force of the reductionist move derives from a contrast between the moral significance of the conventional and ultimate levels of reality—the distinction between persons and diachronic personal identity are not morally significant because they are merely constructions, while suffering remains morally significant because it is ultimately real. But if that is the case, then an appeal to the conventional truth of suffering harming particular beings also lacks moral significance. In addition, appeal to the conventional level of persons and their suffering is problematic because it reintroduces the very distinction between beings (and therefore their suffering) that the move to reductionism apparently rejects.

In response to these kinds of objections, it could be argued that Śāntideva is provisionally endorsing reductionism here as an improvement over the naïve realism about the self that is characteristic of common sense. That is, while Śāntideva ultimately holds that all things are empty and that even *dharmas* are not ultimately real, at the conventional level, the viewpoint of Buddhist reductionism is both theoretically and morally better than that of common-sense realism. On this interpretation, while a Madhyamaka rejects the metaphysical realist notion that any theory corresponds to ultimately reality, they may still differentiate better and worse views within the domain of the conventional truth. However, it is not clear that this move solves the problem for Śāntideva. This is because his reductionist move here does not simply replace the view of a substantial self with the reductionist account of persons (including the conventional distinctness and diachronic identity of persons). Rather, it treats suffering as ownerless and diachronic identity as a *false* construction. Thus, it looks like the moral force of the reductionist move derives not from the moderate reductionism of much Buddhist philosophy but from a basically eliminativist form of reductionism. And that form of reductionism is hard to square both with Madhyamaka philosophy and with the preservation (at the conventional level) of the moral point of view.

On my view, in order to understand Śāntideva's deployment of the no-self doctrine to undermine egocentrism, we must see this move as a specific cognitive strategy within the larger context of this chapter and within the text as a whole. As argued earlier, I don't think Śāntideva's remarks on anger and responsibility commit him to hard determinism as a philosophical view. Likewise, I don't think his comments here commit him to an eliminative reductionist account of no-self. Rather, the reductionist move is part of a larger movement to first deconstruct our default sense of personhood and then *reconstruct* a sense of personhood that is consistent with the altruistic ethics of the *bodhisattva*. After deconstructing both the reified notion of a substantial self and even the more moderate conventional notion of persons as distinct and persisting, Śāntideva writes,

> 8.110 Therefore, just as I protect myself to the last against criticism, let me develop in this way an attitude of protectiveness and of generosity towards others as well.
> 8.111 Through habituation there is the understanding of "I" regarding the drops of sperm and blood of two other people, even though there is in fact no such thing.
> 8.112 Why can I not also accept another's body as my self in the same way, since the otherness of my own body has been settled and is not hard to accept?
> 8.114 In the same way that the hands and other limbs are loved because they form part of the body, why are embodied creatures not likewise loved because they form part of the universe?

8.115 In the same way that, with practice, the idea of a self arose toward this, one's own body, though it is without self, with practice will not the same idea of a self develop towards others too?[12] (2008, 98)

Notice here that Śāntideva has returned from the impersonal perspective of reductionism to the interpersonal perspective of self and others. But now, having fully realized that it is a habitual *construction*, the self is not abandoned in favor of seeing the moral landscape as simply an impersonal distribution of suffering and happiness. Instead, the self, as an empty, malleable construct, is *reconstructed* nonegocentrically. Through practice, one comes to extend one's sense of identity and therefore one's moral concern to all other sentient beings as parts of an interdependent reality. Note also that this reconstruction does not simply erase the distinction between self and other but rather situates the distinction within the deeper insight into the impermanence and interdependence of selves and others. Moreover, within this new perspective of thoroughgoing interdependence, the egocentric view of self looks both alienating and absurd. Again, this is not because the interpersonal domain of self and other is *really* a false construction and *really* there are only events of suffering and happiness. Rather, on my reading of *bodhisattva* ethics, it is because the interpersonal domain of self and other has always been interdependent. Indeed, it is interdependent, not just causally—that is, it is not just that the *skandhas* are casually interdependent with the rest of the world's causal nexus—but also interpersonally. The emergence of a sentient being with a stable sense of self is based on the shared matrix of interpersonal interaction. Primary intersubjectivity is more fundamental than the sense of an ego self, and stable human selves are dependent on interpersonal dynamics of secondary intersubjectivity as well as the shared scaffolding of social practices, language, and culture. On this view, the supposedly independent and enduring ego self is indeed an illusion, not because subjects are reducible to impersonal *dharmas*, but because the matrix of interdependence is the condition of the possibility of being a subject in the first place. The reconstructed self here is one that is no longer bound to the delusion of independence and whose moral concern and perception naturally extends to others as if all were part of the same living body.

But why not simply abandon any notion of self, no matter how impermanent or interdependent it is taken to be? In one sense, the reconstruction of a postegological sense of self is merely a skillful means (*upāya kauśalya*)—other sentient beings are still trapped in the delusion of self, and the *bodhisattva* maintains a sense of self in order to benefit them. However, it may be that a sense of self is not simply an optional tool for the practitioner of the *bodhisattva* path. If the moral domain is constitutively interpersonal and the domain of empathy and empathic perception, then to abandon a sense of self (and other) is to abandon the moral domain itself. Some of the rhetoric of enlightenment suggests this kind of transcendence of the moral. Be that as it may, for one struggling to cultivate a wise and active altruism, abandoning self and other entirely does not seem to be a viable option, and it is not an option Śāntideva suggests here. Rather, recognition of the utter nonexistence of the substantial self and the emptiness of the conventional self opens up the possibility of a reconstruction of self on the basis of *bodhicitta*, as opposed to the afflictions.

The Limits of Self-Cherishing

Śāntideva claims,

> 8.129 All those who suffer in the world do so because of their desire for their own happiness. All those happy in the world are so because of their desire for the happiness of others.
> 8.130 Why say more? Observe this distinction: between the fool who longs for his own advantage and the sage who acts for the advantage of others.
> 8.134 The calamities which happen in the world, the sufferings and fears, many as they are, they all result from clinging onto the notion of self, so what good is this clinging of mine?
> 8.136 Therefore, in order to allay my own suffering and to allay the suffering of others, I devote myself to others and accept them as myself.
> 8.137 "Hey Mind, make the resolve, 'I am bound to others'! From now on you must have no other concern than the welfare of all beings."[13] (2008, 99–100)

As already discussed in the section on the *saṃsāric* framework, egotism, or self-cherishing, involves deep-seated cognitive, affective, and motivational biases. It involves a failure of impartiality—that is, a false sense that one is somehow uniquely morally important, despite being in all relevant respects the same as others. It involves a failure of sentiment and moral perception, whereby one ignores or underplays the moral salience of others' suffering and happiness. It also involves a failure to appreciate the fact of our deep interconnectedness with others and of the merely constructed nature of all claims to personal identity over time. Finally, egocentrism is implicated with bondage to destructive or unskillful habits and states of mind as well as such negative emotions as fear, jealousy, and anger. These negative states and emotions undermine the well-being of the possessor and have harmful consequences for others. In the end, then, despite the strong pull of egocentrism as a style of psychological functioning and strategy for achieving stable happiness, it is ultimately self-defeating. Genuine recognition of this fact is supposed to lead to the genuine desire to benefit others and oneself through the altruistic action.

The Benefits of Altruism

As Śāntideva emphasizes throughout the text, one key benefit of altruism is that it leads to one's own happiness. The poisons of delusion, compulsion, and aggression are mutually reinforcing and have at their center the excessive self-preoccupation of egoism. By shifting one's concerns to the happiness and suffering of others, one thereby displaces the excessive self-focus that, in turn, propels the oscillation between grasping and aversion characteristic of the *saṃsāric* framework. Psychological research supports the basic supposition here: Concern for and service to others is well correlated with increased happiness and contentment (at least up to a point) (Gilbert 2014). The developmental path of *bodhisattva* ethics is premised on the possibility of a positive feedback loop between other concern, the cultivation of virtue, and enhanced personal well-being, including the reduction of negative emotions.

And yet, Śāntideva raises and addresses an important objection to the cultivation of compassion:

> 8.104 You may argue: compassion causes so much suffering, why force it to arise? Yet when one sees how much the world suffers, how can this suffering from compassion be considered great?
>
> 8.105 If the suffering of one ends the suffering of the many, then one who has compassion for others and himself must cause that suffering to arise.[14] (2008, 97)

One way that compassion might cause suffering is through empathic distress. When confronting the suffering of others, one may experience an intense form of empathic resonance where one is caused pain by perceiving the pain of others. This form of empathic resonance is associated with increased negative affect and decreased helping behavior (Batson, Fultz, and Schoenrade 1987; Eisenberg et al. 1989). Repeated experiences of empathic distress can also lead to empathic burnout, a not uncommon experience among those working in helping professions, for example. Śāntideva's response here is that one's own empathic distress is small in comparison to the suffering in the world, and therefore, one should cause that suffering to arise as a side effect of cultivating compassion. Yet, this is a problematic response for two reasons. First, if it is correct that empathic distress is aversive and can lead to reduced helping behavior, then cultivating compassion in this way could be self-defeating. Second, Śāntideva says that one who has compassion for *himself* and others must allow this suffering to arise. But if compassion involves the motivation to help reduce suffering even toward oneself, then it seems odd to cause it to arise in this way.

Ultimately, it seems, Śāntideva thinks that the benefits of altruism for oneself outweigh the increased distress at facing the suffering of others. Some resent research bears this out, but also complicates the picture here. Klimecki and colleagues (2013) differentiate empathy and compassion and studied the differential effects of empathy training and compassion training. Empathy here involves perceiving and sharing the pain of others through empathic resonance. According to Lamm, Decety, and Singer (2011), empathy for pain is usually experienced as aversive and involves the anterior insula (AI) and anterior midcingulate cortex (aMCC), activation of which is associated with negative affect. In contrast, compassion—defined here as a "feeling of concern for the suffering of others that is associated with the motivation to help," as it is in Buddhist thought—is associated with positive emotions (Klimecki et al. 2013) and prosocial behavior (Leiberg, Klimecki, and Singer 2011). Moreover, compassion is accompanied by activations in the insula, ventral striatum, and medial orbitofrontal cortex (mOFC) (Beauregard et al. 2009; Immordino-Yang et al. 2009), areas associated with reward, love, and affiliation (as part of the mammalian "care" system). Klimecki and colleagues studied the effects of training in empathy and compassion, respectively (the control group trained memory). They found

> evidence for different patterns of emotional experiences and neural plasticity associated with the sequential training of these two social emotions within the same participants: a short-term training in empathy increased empathic responses and negative affect in response to others' distress. . . . Importantly, compassion training reversed these effects: it decreased negative affect back to baseline levels and increased positive affect. On the neural level, compassion training increased brain activations in mOFC, pregenual ACC and striatum—a network previously associated with positive affect (Kringelbach and Berridge, 2009), affiliation (Strathearn et al., 2009) and reward (Haber and Knutson, 2010). (2013, 5)

Therefore, there is evidence that Śāntideva may cede too much to this objection. It may be the case that compassion and some form of compassion training actually reduce the negative affect associated with witnessing the suffering of others and increase positive affect even in the face of suffering. When combined with the growing literature showing that compassion and compassion training is associated with increased emotional well-being, positive affect in daily life, and prosocial behavior, a strong case can be made that cultivating altruism is indeed beneficial to both self and others.

Exchange of Self and Other

Having realized both the basic equality and the interdependence of self and other, the harms of egotism, and the benefits of altruism, Śāntideva states, "Whoever longs to rescue quickly both himself and others should practice the supreme mystery: the exchange of self and other" (2008, 99).[15] This meditation involves a further extension of empathy and moral perception through a more sophisticated use of imaginative transposition and perspective taking, including the use of forms of perspective reversal. Śāntideva instructs, "[C] reating a sense of self in respect of inferiors and others, and a sense of the other in oneself, imagine envy and pride with a mind free from false notions!" (Śāntideva 2008, 100) That is, one is to imagine occupying the position of a person one deems inferior in some respect. One then attempts to imagine and feel what it is like to be looked down on by others and what it is like to feel envy toward those considered superior. Moreover, one is to imagine how you yourself look from the point of view of the "inferior" person. Imagine the arrogance and self-centeredness they perceive in your behavior toward them. Śāntideva also recommends exchange with one you perceive as superior to yourself in some way. Again, one is to deploy one's empathic imagination and understanding of different points of view to see how the defilements are at play in our interpersonal interactions.

Like the previous forms of contemplation I have discussed, this form of meditation focuses on counteracting various cognitive and affective biases, expanding empathy, improving moral perception, and reorienting the individual toward greater altruistic engagement. The distinctive feature of this modality is that it radically decenters one's own limited point of view by imaginatively "walking a mile in another's shoes." Further, it is crucial that one imagines not just others' circumstances but also their feelings, perceptions, and attitudes and in particular how you look from their point of view. The upshot of this training is to develop the insight and cognitive-affective flexibility to perceive the basic equality of self and other even across social and interpersonal difference, to perceive the emptiness and fluidity of the distinction between self and others, and to respond compassionately and effectively to others. Indeed, this is the fundamental path and fruition of *bodhisattva* ethics.

NOTES

1. The term *kuśala* (Pāli: *kusala*) is used in a variety of ways in Buddhist texts. It can mean "healthy," "good," "blameless," "skillful," "conducive to happiness," "harmless," or "conducive to liberation" (Cousins 1996).

2. *ye kecidduḥkhitā loke sarve te svasukhecchayā| ye kecitsukhitā loke sarve te'nyasukhecchayā.* ||129|| See Bhattacharya (1960) for the text in Sanskrit and Tibetan.

3. These presuppositions are widely but not universally shared in the current literature on Buddhist ethics. They are consistent with the views of Clayton, Garfield, Goodman, and Keown, for instance.

4. *duḥkhamevābhidhāvanti duḥkhaniḥsaraṇāśayā| sukhecchayaiva saṃmohāt svasukhaṃ ghnanti* śatruvat. ||28||

5. The "in order to" here should not be read merely instrumentally. One's own awakening is a constitutive part of the goal.

6.

*vardhayitvaivamutsāhaṃ samādhau sth*āpayenmanaḥ| *vikṣiptacittastu naraḥ kleśadaṃṣṭrāntare sthitaḥ.* ||1||

*K*āyacittavivekena *vikṣepasya na saṃbhavaḥ| tasmāllokaṃ parityajya vitarkān parivarjayet.* ||2||

śama*thena vipaśyanāsuyuktaḥ, kurute kleśavināśamityavetya|* śama*thaḥ prathamaṃ gaveṣaṇīyaḥ sa ca loke nirapekṣayābhiratyā.* ||4||

7. Following Dambrun and Ricard, we understand mindfulness to be "characterized by undistracted attention, free of distorting bias. Such mindfulness is oriented to the present moment, but is also combined with a meta-awareness, such that one remains aware of one's state of mind over time" (2011, 146).

8.

pittādiṣu na me kopo mahāduḥkhakareṣvapi| sacetaneṣu kiṃ kopaḥ te'pi pratyayakopitāḥ. ||22||

Ye kecidaparādhāśca pāpāni vividhāni ca| sarvaṃ tatpratyayabalāt svatantraṃ tu na vidyate. ||25||

evaṃ paravaśaṃ sarvaṃ yadvaśaṃ so'pi cāvaśaḥ| nirmāṇavadaceṣṭeṣu bhāveṣvevaṃ kva kupyate. ||31||

tasmādamitraṃ mitraṃ vā dṛṣṭvāpyanyāyakāriṇam| īdṛśāḥ *pratyayā asyetyevaṃ matvā sukhī bhavet.* ||33||

9. To clarify, I take Śāntideva to be more like a compatibilist rather than a hard determinist. Therefore, his shift to the impersonal causal point of view is not an abandonment of belief in personal agency and moral responsibility. I take it that he believes that all actions are part of the causal fabric of the world and that—to put it in contemporary philosophical terms—reminding ourselves of the determinist side of the compatibilist story can be a good strategy for defusing anger.

10.

parātmasamatāmādau bhāvayedevamādarāt| samaduḥkhasukhāḥ sarve pālanīyā mayātmavat. ||90||

*Hast*ādibhedena *bahuprakāraḥ kāyo yathaikaḥ paripālanīyaḥ| tath*ā *jagadbhinnamabhinnaduḥkha sukhātmakaṃ sarvamidaṃ tathaiva.* ||91||

*yadyapyanyeṣu deheṣu madduḥkhaṃ na prabādhate| tath*āpi *tadduḥkhameva mamātmasnehaduḥsaham.* ||92||

*tath*ā *yadyapyasaṃvedyamanyadduḥkhaṃ mayātmanā| tath*āpi *tasya tadduḥkhamātmasnehena duḥsaham.* ||93||

Mayānyaduḥkhaṃ hantavyaṃ duḥkhatvādātmaduḥkhavat| anugrāhyā mayānye'pi sattvatvādātmasattvavat. ||94||
yadā mama pareṣāṃ ca tulyameva sukhaṃ priyam| tadātmanaḥ ko viśeṣo yenātraiva sukhodyamaḥ. ||95||
yadā mama pareṣāṃ ca bhayaṃ duḥkhaṃ ca na priyam| tadātmanaḥ ko viśeṣo yattaṃ rakṣāmi netaram. ||96||
11.
tadduḥkhena na me bādhetyato yadi na rakṣyate| nāgāmikāyaduḥkhānme bādhā tatkena rakṣyate. ||97||
Ahameva tadāpīti mithyeyaṃ parikalpanā| anya eva mṛto yasmādanya eva prajāyate. ||98||
yadi tasyaiva yadduḥkhaṃ rakṣyaṃ tasyaiva tanmatam| pādaduḥkhaṃ na hastasya kasmāttattena rakṣyate. ||99||
*Ayuktamapi cedetadahaṃkārātpravartate | tadayuktaṃ nivartyaṃ tatsvamanyacca yath*ābalam. ||100||
saṃtānaḥ samudāyaśca paṅktisenādivanmṛṣā| yasya duḥkhaṃ sa nāstyasmātkasya tatsvaṃ bhaviṣyati. ||101||
asvāmikāni duḥkhāni sarvāṇyevāviśeṣataḥ| duḥkhatvādeva vāryāṇi niyamastatra kiṃkṛtaḥ. ||102||
duḥkhaṃ kasmānnivāryaṃ cetsarveṣāmavivādataḥ| vāryaṃ cetsarvamapyevaṃ na cedātmāpi sattvavat. ||103||
12.
*tasmādyath*āntaśo*'varṇādātmānaṃ gopayāmyaham| rakṣācittaṃ dayācittaṃ karomyevaṃ pareṣvapi.* ||110||
Abhyāsādanyadīyeṣu śukraśoṇitabi*nduṣu| bhavatyahamiti jñānamasatyapi hi vastuni.* ||111||
*tath*ā *kāyo'nyadīyo'pi kimātmeti na gṛhyate| paratvaṃ tu svakāyasya sthitameva na duṣkaram.* ||112||
Kāyasyāvayavatvena *yath*ābhīṣṭāḥ *karādayaḥ| jagato'vayavatvena tath*ā *kasmānna dehinaḥ.* ||114||
*yath*ātmabuddhirabhyāsātsvakāye*'sminnirātmake| pareṣvapi tath*ātmatvaṃ *kimabhyāsānna jāyate.* ||115||
13.
ye kecidduḥkhitā loke sarve te svasukhecchayā| ye kecitsukhitā loke sarve te'nyasukhecchayā. ||129||
*bahunā vā kimuktena dṛśyatāmidamantaram| svārth*ārth*inaśca bālasya muneścānyārthakāriṇaḥ.* ||130||
upadravā ye ca bhavanti loke yāvanti duḥkhāni bhayāni caiva| sarvāṇi tānyātmaparigraheṇa tatkiṃ mamānena parigraheṇa. ||134||
tasmātsvaduḥkhaśāntyarthaṃ paraduḥkhaśamāya ca| dadāmyanyebhya ātmānaṃ parān gṛhṇāmi cātmavat. ||136||
anyasaṃbaddhamasmīti niścayaṃ kuru he manaḥ| sarvasattvārthamutsṛjya nānyaccintyaṃ tvayādhunā. ||137||

14.

kṛpayā bahu duḥkhaṃ cetkasmādutpadyate balāt| jagadduḥkhaṃ nirūpyedaṃ kṛpāduḥkhaṃ kathaṃ bahu. ||104||

bahūnāmekaduḥkhena yadi duḥkhaṃ vigacchati| utpādyameva tadduḥkhaṃ sadayena parātmanoḥ. ||105||

15. *ātmānaṃ cāparāṃścaiva yaḥ śīghraṃ trātumicchati| sa caretparamaṃ guhyaṃ parātmaparivartanam.* ||120||

Conclusion

The three main aims of this work are to deepen and extend the dialogue between Indian Buddhist thought and enactivism, to engage with core issues in the philosophy of mind through that dialogue, and to develop a distinctive account of the embodied subject. By way of conclusion, I highlight some lessons that have emerged from the pursuit of these aims and point to some future directions of inquiry.

Regarding the Buddhist-enactivist dialogue, the first lesson is that Indian Buddhist thought presents, in many respects, a radical alternative to much current thinking about the mind. From early Buddhism through the later developments of Madhyamaka and Yogācāra, Buddhist thinkers challenged fundamental aspects of (what they themselves took to be) a common ontology and phenomenology of self and world. That is, they relentlessly challenged the ontology and phenomenology of unified, stable, and persisting selves in a world of unified, stable, and persisting entities. However widespread and deeply entrenched is this experience of self and world, Indian Buddhist thinkers argued that this is not how things are. Upon analysis, "self" and "world" are revealed to be conventional constructions based on the causal flux of momentary particulars or, in the case of Madhyamaka, without any ultimate basis at all. And yet, the brilliance of Buddhist thinkers is that they were able to develop rigorous accounts of how the constructions of "self" and "world" arise and are sustained and how they can be destabilized, transformed, and even transcended. Indian Buddhist ways of approaching philosophy of mind are based on rigorous analysis and are at once phenomenologically astute and deeply revisionist. What emerges are Buddhist accounts of mind that are dynamic, antisubstantialist, and constructivist and support a wide-spectrum phenomenology.

The second lesson, then, is that contemporary philosophers and others should pay attention to this rich tradition of thought. This book, I hope, highlights the importance and fruitfulness of engaging different philosophical traditions and frameworks. In doing so, we not only open up the possibility of new insights but also open ourselves to challenges to core assumptions that guide our thinking. For instance, in much of the current Anglophone work in philosophy of mind, reductionism about self, mind, or agency is strongly associated with a physicalist ontology and a scientific, even scientistic, approach to studying the mind. Yet we see in the Indian Buddhist tradition views that are at once reductionist (or antirealist or eliminativist or fictionalist, etc.) about self, mind, and agency while also being resolutely antiphysicalist in ontology and pluralist in method. Furthermore, the Buddhist use of a two-truths framework—in its Abhidharma, Madhyamaka, or Yogācāra variants—introduces a set of analytical tools that, I think, may shed new light on many current problems in contemporary philosophy.

Regarding enactivism, it, too, may present a radical alternative to current mainstream thinking about the mind. It is grounded in autopoietic biology and embodied phenomenology and skeptical of Cartesian, computationalist, and representationalist approaches to the mind. It is also resolutely realist and nonreductionist about consciousness and open to the exploration of a wide spectrum of phenomenological states and structures. Finally, its resonance with Buddhist thought is not merely accidental. Rather, Buddhist thought has influenced enactivism from the start. Hence, I think that enactivism provides an especially fruitful framework for engaging classical Buddhist thought about mind, self, agency, and world. And, on my view, an important lesson of this engagement is the power and depth of dynamic, nonsubstantialist, and embodied approaches to these phenomena. In particular, contemporary work on self-organization, dynamic systems theory, emergence, and (neuro-) phenomenological analysis can provide especially useful tools to deepen and extend Buddhist (or Buddhist-inspired) accounts of mind. In addition, the enactivist framework points to the possibility of a middle way between the more substantialist *ātmavāda* views of the Hindu schools and the strongly reductionist or antirealist *anātmavāda* approach of much Buddhist thought. Indeed, as this work shows, a Buddhist-enactivist approach has the potential to constitute a live research program in the philosophy of mind and related fields.

Turning to the core issues in the philosophy of mind, one upshot of this comparative inquiry is a reconfiguration of the problem space in light of the long history of Indian debates. In contemporary Anglophone philosophy of mind, we often approach (and introduce our students to) the field through a consideration of the Western mind-body problem, or the contemporary debate between physicalism and its rivals. Yet in the Indian context, this is not the central or organizing problem. Rather, as I show, Indian debates are much more commonly organized around the problem of the self, both in terms of its nature and existence. That is, arguably the main divide in this area of Indian philosophy is not between dualists and materialists (or idealists for that matter) but rather between *ātmavādins* and *anātmavādins*. Furthermore, as I discuss in chapter 2, another central controversy—which cuts across the self–no-self divide—is between *svaprakāśavāda* and *paraprakāśavāda* accounts of consciousness. As should be apparent, my inquiry into the nature of mind has been shaped by this classical Indian understanding of the philosophical terrain.

Regarding the self, the central question is whether mental life or experience is grounded in or organized around an enduring locus of consciousness, cognition, or agency. For all their many and important differences, the *ātmavādins* answer in the affirmative. In order to make sense of mental life, the coherence of experience, agency, and cognitive access to the world, one must affirm a unified self at the center of our being. In sharp contrast, as I show throughout this book, Buddhist thinkers decisively reject this core commitment. They therefore must develop and defend accounts of mental life in terms of multiplicity and flux, in terms of the causal connections between distinct, momentary particulars rather than the unity of the self. And this core difference ramifies through the rest of their thought on mind, knowledge, ethics, and more. In the contemporary context, I think this basic divide between models of the mind and mental life based on the self and those that reject the self is worth deeper examination. What might it mean to take the self-selfless divide as at least as fundamental as if not more fundamental than the physicalist-nonphysicalist divide? For a given model of the mind, how are its accounts of consciousness, cognition, agency, and embodiment shaped by a commitment to self or selflessness?

Regarding luminosity (*prakāśa*), I argue that the fundamental idea is of consciousness as (the power of) phenomenal presentation. The very nature of consciousness is to illuminate, present, or make manifest. The next and crucial question is whether the basic nature of consciousness is to present that which is other, to present itself, or to present some combination of the two. Other illuminationists argue that the nature of consciousness is to present that which is other. And on the basis of this commitment, they tend to argue for a higher-order view of self-consciousness, a transparent or aspectless (*nirākāravāda*) view of awareness, an externalist view of intentionality, and a direct theory of perception. Interestingly, this applies to both the resolutely metaphysical-realist *ātmavādin* Naiyāyikas and to the resolutely nonrealist *anātmavādin* Mādhyamikas. In contrast, self-illuminationists tend to argue for a reflexive or same-order view of self-consciousness, an aspectual (*sākāravāda*) view of awareness, an internalist view of intentionality, and an indirect or phenomenalist account of perception. Furthermore, as both Buddhists and Naiyāyikas argue, the concepts of an independent, persisting self and a mind-independent world of persisting objects are deeply intertwined. In this way, one's views of the self and of consciousness constrain one's view of the world and our access to and agency within it. Again, we may ask, for a given model of the mind, how are its views of self, agency, cognition, and world shaped by its commitment to other-illuminationism or self-illuminationism?

Throughout this book, I argue for a model of the mind as rooted in our nature as living individuals. Humans and other sentient beings are living, biological beings, and mindedness emerges from and remains rooted in the nature and structures of life. In particular, on my account, we are dynamic, self-organizing, and adaptive systems in a constant dance of stability and change. Moreover, we are sentient, conscious beings, and our consciousness, too, is rooted in our biological life. We are fundamentally embodied subjects, embedded in and in continuous interaction with a complex physical, biological, and psychosocial environment. And this ongoing adaptive interaction is a form of embodied sense-making, or what the classical pragmatists called simply *experience.*

So on this view, is mental life grounded in or organized around an enduring locus of consciousness, cognition, or agency? Is this view rooted in self or selflessness? In one sense, my view is clearly committed to an enduring (or persisting) locus of consciousness, cognition, and agency. It is the body—the dynamic, biologically autonomous system. But as Jonardon Ganeri persuasively argues, when it comes to the question of self, we must distinguish between base (*āśraya*) and place (*ādhāra*). That is, we must first distinguish the basis of individuation (the base) from the locus of subjective, mental life (the place). Only then can we ask what, if anything, may play these roles in a given account of the mind and self. In the view I develop in this book, the living body is the base of experience. It is not the self. Rather, the self emerges from deeper structures of life and mind and becomes the central locus, the place of subjective mental life. The self is neither an enduring substance nor a pure transcendental subject. Nor is it a mere fiction or convention. It is an enacted, emergent network of capacities—the embodied integration of subjectivity, ownership, agency, and valuation—within the life of a fundamentally biological individual. In this sense, the view is neither strictly *ātmavādin* nor *anātmavādin* but attempts to draw insights from both camps.

On the topic of consciousness, my account is squarely in the self-illuminationist or reflexivist camp. I have drawn on the dual-aspect reflexivist model of the Buddhist *pramāṇavādins*, according to which consciousness is by nature reflexive or self-presenting. And a typical act or moment of consciousness presents both an object aspect and a subject aspect, which I take to be phenomenal modes of presentation. Further, I combine this basic model with insights from Yogācāra thinkers regarding both base consciousness (*ālayavijñāna*) and the ultimately nondual nature of awareness. On the picture that emerges, reflexive nondual awareness is the nature of consciousness. It is rooted in the self-regulatory, sensory, affective, and conative functions of the body and forms the continuous background, or phenomenal-temporal, context for the ever-changing foreground contents of awareness. Furthermore, as reflexive, it is at the root of both creature subjectivity and the minimal phenomenal point of view in each moment of manifest consciousness.

My accounts of agency, intersubjectivity, and world crucially depend on the notion of the subject as constitutively embodied. On the issue of agency, I argue that it is best understood not as a mere convention or fiction but as a real, emergent capacity of living systems. Living beings are self-organizing, self-maintaining, and adaptive, and these core features ground the three key features of enactive agency: individuality, interactional asymmetry, and normativity. In this way, agency is a fundamentally biological and embodied capacity. Further, as I argue in chapter 3, this view of agency avoids both agent-causal substantialism and event-causal reductionism. On the issue of intersubjectivity and other minds, I argue that the form of life of embodied subjects like us is affective, conative, and expressive. The mental life of embodied subjects is neither entirely hidden from others in a private mental realm nor entirely transparent to the subject herself. Moreover, as I argue in chapter 5, empathy and intersubjectivity are deep features of minds like ours. On the issue of world, recall that sense-making is an ongoing way that a living, embodied, cognitive being engages its world. It is transactional and world involving from the start. Yet, as both Buddhists and enactivists point out, the world here is not something that can be specified in strict independence from sense-making. Indeed, on this view, sense-making is also self making and world making. Yet, as against strongly idealist or antirealist accounts, I argue that this insight can be understood in terms of pragmatic realism. This form of realism rejects metaphysical realism and affirms ontological nonfoundationalism, conceptual-explanatory pluralism, and epistemological pragmatism.

These strands of argument come together in my interpretation of *bodhisattva* ethics in Śāntideva's *Bodhicaryāvatāra*. On my view, Buddhist ethics in general and *bodhisattva* ethics in particular are fundamentally concerned with dismantling the greed, aversion, and ignorance that condition our minds and actions and cultivating the nonattachment, compassion, and wisdom of an enlightened character. And as Śāntideva's deep moral phenomenology shows, this path has cognitive, affective, perceptual, bodily, and intersubjective dimensions. Further, I think there is deep agreement between Buddhists and enactivists that we are not fundamentally separate, alienated egos but rather empathic, social beings. As embodied subjects, we are enmeshed from the beginning in intersubjective (bodily, sensory, affective, and cognitive) interaction, and therefore open, empathic intersubjectivity is both existentially and developmentally more fundamental than our egoistic self-understanding. On my interpretation, then, the human capacity of empathy is the root of the *bodhisattva* path, a path that involves clearing away obstructions to empathic awareness as well as developing and extending that capacity toward all sentient beings.

The richness and complexity of Buddhist and enactivist thought afford many possibilities for further exploration and constructive engagement. Here I mention just two. First, while I address the metaphysics of organism, self, and world, I do not directly address the hard problem of consciousness. Classical Buddhist thought is thoroughly antimaterialist, and such enactivists as Varela and Thompson embrace a naturalist but nonphysicalist emergentism about consciousness. Furthermore, in the current literature on consciousness, a number of other options are being explored, including panpsychism, cosmopsychism, neutral monism, and even idealism. Enactivism and Buddhist philosophy, indeed Indian philosophy generally, have much to contribute to this discussion. Second, as I explore in this book, Buddhism and enactivism offer deep and sophisticated accounts of intersubjectivity and social cognition. And there is excellent work being done in these areas (Durt, Fuchs, and Tewes 2017; Prueitt 2018; Tzohar 2017). Further critical and constructive engagement between these traditions of thought will certainly enrich our understanding of the social dimensions of mind, experience, and world.

As I discuss on the introduction to this work, Chakrabarti and Weber argue that contemporary comparative philosophy should be *borderless*. They write, "Good creative philosophy in a globalized world should spontaneously straddle geographical areas and cultures, temperaments and time-periods (mixing classical, medieval, modern, and postmodern), styles and subdisciplines of philosophy, as well as mix methods . . . whatever comes handy" (Chakrabarti and Weber 2015, 22). It is my hope that this constructive engagement between Buddhist philosophy and enactivism has made some small contribution to this creative, borderless philosophical enterprise.

Bibliography

Albahari, Miri. 2006. *Analytical Buddhism: The Two-Tiered Illusion of Self.* Houndsmills, NY: Palgrave Macmillan.

Aristotle. 1999. *Nicomachean Ethics.* Translated by Martin Ostwald. New York: Pearson.

———. 2014. *Brains, Buddhas, and Believing: The Problem of Intentionality in Classical Buddhist and Cognitive-Scientific Philosophy of Mind.* New York: Columbia University Press.

Ataria, Yochai. 2015. "Sense of Ownership and Sense of Agency during Trauma." *Phenomenology and the Cognitive Sciences* 14 (1): 199–212. https://doi.org/10.1007/s11097-013-9334-y.

Baker, Lynne Rudder. 2013. *Naturalism and the First-Person Perspective.* Oxford, UK: Oxford University Press.

Barandiaran, Xabier, Ezequiel Di Paolo, and Marieke Rohde. 2009. "Defining Agency: Individuality, Normativity, Asymmetry, and Spatio-Temporality in Action." *Adaptive Behavior* 17 (5): 367–86. https://doi.org/10.1177/1059712309343819.

Baron-Cohen, Simon. 1995. *Mindblindness: An Essay on Autism and Theory of Mind.* Cambridge, MA: MIT Press.

Barrera, Maria E., and Daphne Maurer. 1981. "The Perception of Facial Expressions by the Three-Month-Old." *Child Development* 52 (1): 203–6. https://doi.org/10.2307/1129231.

Batson, C. D., J. Fultz, and P. A. Schoenrade. 1987. "Distress and Empathy: Two Qualitatively Distinct Vicarious Emotions with Different Motivational Consequences." *Journal of Personality* 55 (1): 19–39. https://doi.org/10.1111/j.1467-6494.1987.tb00426.x.

Beauregard, Mario, Jérôme Courtemanche, Vincent Paquette, and Evelyne Landry St-Pierre. 2009. "The Neural Basis of Unconditional Love." *Psychiatry Research* 172 (2): 93–98. https://doi.org/10.1016/j.pscychresns.2008.11.003.

Bhattacharya, Vidhushekhara. 1960. *Śāntideva: Bodhicaryāvatāra [Sanskr. u. tibet.]* Calcutta: The Asiatic Society.

Bodhi, Bhikkhu. 2005. *In the Buddha's Words: An Anthology of Discourses from the Pali Canon*. 5th printing ed. Boston: Wisdom.

———. 2012. *The Numerical Discourses of the Buddha: A Complete Translation of the Anguttara Nikaya*. Annotated ed. Boston: Wisdom.

Braun, Niclas, Stefan Debener, Nadine Spychala, Edith Bongartz, Peter Sörös, Helge H. O. Müller, and Alexandra Philipsen. 2018. "The Senses of Agency and Ownership: A Review." *Frontiers in Psychology* 9 (April): 535. https://doi.org/10.3389/fpsyg.2018.00535.

Buccino, G., F. Binkofski, G. R. Fink, L. Fadiga, L. Fogassi, V. Gallese, R. J. Seitz, K. Zilles, G. Rizzolatti, and H. J. Freund. 2001. "Action Observation Activates Premotor and Parietal Areas in a Somatotopic Manner: An FMRI Study." *European Journal of Neuroscience* 13 (2): 400–404.

Buddhaghosa, Bhadantacariya. 1999. *The Path of Purification: Visuddhimagga*. Seattle, WA: Pariyatti.

Carpenter, Amber D. 2015. "Persons Keeping Their Karma Together." In *The Moon Points Back*, edited by Koji Tanaka, Yasuo Deguchi, Jay Garfield, and Graham Priest, 1–44. Oxford, UK: Oxford University Press. https://doi.org/10.1093/acprof:oso/9780190226862.003.0001.

Chadha, Monima. 2015. "Time-Series of Ephemeral Impressions: The Abhidharma-Buddhist View of Conscious Experience." *Phenomenology and the Cognitive Sciences* 14 (3): 543–60. https://doi.org/10.1007/s11097-014-9354-2.

Chakrabarti, Arindam, and Ralph Weber, eds. 2015. *Comparative Philosophy without Borders*. London: Bloomsbury Academic.

Chapple, Christopher Key. 1986. *Karma and Creativity*. Albany: State University of New York Press.

Christoff, Kalina, Diego Cosmelli, Dorothée Legrand, and Evan Thompson. 2011. "Specifying the Self for Cognitive Neuroscience." *Trends in Cognitive Sciences* 15 (3): 104–12. https://doi.org/10.1016/j.tics.2011.01.001.

Clayton, Barbra R. 2006. *Moral Theory in Santideva's Siksasamuccaya: Cultivating the Fruits of Virtue*. London: Routledge.

Coates, Paul. 2013. "Hallucinations and the Transparency of Perception." In *Hallucination: Philosophy and Psychology*, edited by Fiona Macpherson and Dmitris Platchias, 381–98.Cambridge, MA: MIT Press. https://doi.org/10.7551/mitpress/9780262019200.003.0017.

Cousins, L. S. 1996. "Good or Skillful? Kusala in Canon and Commentary." *Journal of Buddhist Ethics* 3: 136–64.

Damasio, Antonio R. 2000. *The Feeling of What Happens: Body and Emotion in the Making of Consciousness*. 1st Harvest ed. San Diego, CA: Harcourt.

———. 2003. *Looking for Spinoza: Joy, Sorrow, and the Feeling Brain*. Orlando, FL: Harcourt.

Dambrun, Michaël, and Matthieu Ricard. 2011. "Self-Centeredness and Selflessness: A Theory of Self-Based Psychological Functioning and Its Consequences for Happiness." *Review of General Psychology* 15 (2): 138–57. https://doi.org/10.1037/a0023059.

Deutsch, Eliot, and Rohit Dalvi. 2004. *The Essential Vedanta: A New Source Book of Advaita Vedanta*. 1st paperback ed. Bloomington, IN: World Wisdom.

Dewey, John. 2008. *The Later Works, 1925–1953*. Vol. 5, *1929–1930, Essays,* The Sources of a Science of Education, Individualism, Old and New, *and* Construction and Criticism, edited by Jo Ann Boydston. Carbondale: Southern Illinois University Press.

Dewey, John, and Arthur F. Bentley. 1949. *Knowing and the Known*. Boston: Beacon Press.

Di Paolo, Ezequiel. 2009. "Extended Life." *Topoi* 28 (1): 9–21. https://doi.org/10.1007/s11245-008-9042-3.

Di Paolo, Ezequiel A. 2005. "Autopoiesis, Adaptivity, Teleology, Agency." *Phenomenology and the Cognitive Sciences* 4 (4): 429–52. https://doi.org/10.1007/s11097-005-9002-y.

Dretske, Fred I. 1997. *Naturalizing the Mind*. Cambridge, MA: MIT Press.

Dreyfus, Georges B. J. 1997. *Recognizing Reality: Dharmakirti's Philosophy and Its Tibetan Interpretations*. Albany: State University of New York Press.

Duerlinger, James. 2003. *Indian Buddhist Theories of Persons: Vasubandhu's Refutation of the Theory of a Self*. London: Routledge.

Dunne, John. 2011. "Toward an Understanding of Non-Dual Mindfulness." *Contemporary Buddhism* 12 (1): 71–88. https://doi.org/10.1080/14639947.2011.564820.

Dunne, John D. 2004. *Foundations of Dharmakirti's Philosophy*. Boston: Wisdom.

Durt, Christoph, Thomas Fuchs, and Christian Tewes, eds. 2017. *Embodiment, Enaction, and Culture: Investigating the Constitution of the Shared World*. Illustrated ed. Cambridge, MA: MIT Press.

Edelglass, William. 2006. "Moral Pluralism, Skillful Means, and Environmental Ethics." *Environmental Philosophy* 3 (2): 8–16.

Edelglass, William, and Jay Garfield, eds. 2009. *Buddhist Philosophy: Essential Readings*. Oxford, UK: Oxford University Press.

Eisenberg, N., R. A. Fabes, P. A. Miller, J. Fultz, R. Shell, R. M. Mathy, and R. R. Reno. 1989. "Relation of Sympathy and Personal Distress to Prosocial Behavior: A Multimethod Study." *Journal of Personality and Social Psychology* 57 (1): 55–66. https://doi.org/10.1037//0022-3514.57.1.55.

Fotopoulou, Aikaterini, and Manos Tsakiris. 2017. "Mentalizing Homeostasis: The Social Origins of Interoceptive Inference." *Neuropsychoanalysis* 19 (1): 3–28. https://doi.org/10.1080/15294145.2017.1294031.

Frondizi, Risieri. 2011. *The Nature of the Self: A Functional Interpretation*. Whitefish, MT: Literary Licensing.

Fuchs, Thomas, and Sabine C. Koch. 2014. "Embodied Affectivity: On Moving and Being Moved." *Frontiers in Psychology* 5. https://doi.org/10.3389/fpsyg.2014.00508.

Gallagher, Shaun. 1998. *The Inordinance of Time*. Evanston, IL: Northwestern University Press.

———. 2000. "Philosophical Conceptions of the Self: Implications for Cognitive Science." *Trends in Cognitive Sciences* 4 (1): 14–21. https://doi.org/10.1016/S1364-6613(99)01417-5.

———. 2012a. "Empathy, Simulation, and Narrative." *Science in Context* 25 (3): 355–81. https://doi.org/10.1017/S0269889712000117.

———. 2012b. "In Defense of Phenomenological Approaches to Social Cognition: Interacting with the Critics." *Review of Philosophy and Psychology* 3 (2): 187–212. https://doi.org/10.1007/s13164-011-0080-1.

Gallagher, Shaun, and Daniel D. Hutto. 2008. "Understanding Others through Primary Interaction and Narrative Practice." In *The Shared Mind: Perspectives on Intersubjectivity*, edited by Jordan Zlatev, Timothy P. Racine, Chris Sinha, and Esa Itkonen, 17–38. Converging Evidence in Language and Communication Research (CELCR). Amsterdam, Netherlands: John Benjamins. https://doi.org/10.1075/celcr.12.04gal.

Gallagher, Shaun, and Dan Zahavi. 2012. *The Phenomenological Mind.* London: Routledge.

Gallese, V. 2001. "The 'Shared Manifold' Hypothesis: From Mirror Neurons to Empathy." *Journal of Consciousness Studies* 8 (5–6): 33–50.

Ganeri, Jonardon. 2012. *The Self: Naturalism, Consciousness, and the First-Person Stance.* Oxford, UK: Oxford University Press.

———. 2013. *The Concealed Art of the Soul: Theories of the Self and Practices of Truth in Indian Ethics and Epistemology.* Oxford, UK: Oxford University Press.

———. 2016. "Why Philosophy Must Go Global: A Manifesto." *Confluence* 4: 134–86.

———. 2017. *Attention, Not Self.* Oxford, UK: Oxford University Press.

Ganguli, Hemanta Kumar. 1963. *Philosophy of Logical Construction: An Examination of Logical Atomism and Logical Positivism in the Light of the Philosophies of Bhartṛhari, Dharmakīrti and Prajñākaragupta.* Calcutta: Sanskrit Pustak Bhandar.

Garfield, Jay. 2016. "Just Another Word for 'Nothing Left to Lose': Freedom, Agency and Ethics for Mādhyamikas." In *Buddhist Perspectives on Free Will: Agentless Agency?* edited by Rick Repetti, 45–58. New York: Routledge.

Garfield, Jay L. 2002. *Empty Words: Buddhist Philosophy and Cross-Cultural Interpretation.* Oxford, UK: Oxford University Press.

———. 2014. *Engaging Buddhism: Why It Matters to Philosophy.* Oxford, UK: Oxford University Press.

Garfield, Jay L., and Jan Westerhoff, eds. 2015. *Madhyamaka and Yogacara: Allies or Rivals?* Oxford, UK: Oxford University Press.

Gilbert, Paul. 2014. "The Origins and Nature of Compassion Focused Therapy." *British Journal of Clinical Psychology* 53 (1): 6–41. https://doi.org/10.1111/bjc.12043.

Gold, Jonathan C. 2014. *Paving the Great Way: Vasubandhu's Unifying Buddhist Philosophy.* Reprint ed. New York: Columbia University Press.

Goleman, Daniel, and Richard J. Davidson. 2017. *Altered Traits: Science Reveals How Meditation Changes Your Mind, Brain, and Body.* New York: Avery.

Goodman, Charles. 2009. "Vasubandhu's Abhidharmakośa: The Critique of the Soul." In *Buddhist Philosophy: Essential Readings*, edited by William Edelglass and Jay L. Garfield, 297–308. Oxford, UK: Oxford University Press.

———. 2014. *Consequences of Compassion: An Interpretation and Defense of Buddhist Ethics.* Reprint ed. Oxford, UK: Oxford University Press.

———. 2016. "Uses of the Illusion of Agency: Why Some Buddhists Should Believe in Free Will." In *Buddhist Perspectives on Free Will: Agentless Agency?* edited by Rick Repetti, 34–44. New York: Routledge. https://www.taylorfrancis.com/https://www.taylorfrancis.com/chapters/mono/10.4324/9781315668765-12/uses-illusion-agency-buddhists-believe-free-rick-repetti.

Goodman, Charles, and Sonam Thakchöe. 2015. "The Many Voices of Buddhist Ethics." In Moonpaths. New York: Oxford University Press.

Guerrero, Laura. 2015. "Conventional Truth and Intentionality in the Work of Dharmakīrti." In The Moon Points Back. New York: Oxford University Press.

Haken, Hermann. 2004. *Synergetics: Introduction and Advanced Topics*. Berlin, Germany: Springer.

Hanner, Oren. 2018. "Moral Agency and the Paradox of Self-Interested Concern for the Future in Vasubandhu's Abhidharmakośabhāṣya." *Sophia* 57 (4): 591–609. https://doi.org/10.1007/s11841-018-0642-0.

Horgan, Terry and Shaun Nichols. 2016. "The Zero Point and I." In *Pre-Reflective Consciousness: Sartre and Contemporary Philosophy of Mind*, edited by Sofia Miguens, Gerhard Preyer, and Clara Bravo Morando, 143–75. Abingdon, UK: Routledge. https://doi.org/10.4324/9781315681146-15.

Horst, Steven. 2007. *Beyond Reduction: Philosophy of Mind and Post-Reductionist Philosophy of Science*. Illustrated ed. Oxford, UK: Oxford University Press.

Hume, Robert E. 1921. *The Thirteen Principal Upanishads: Translated from the Sanskrit with an Outline of the Philosophy of the Upanishads and an Annotated Bibliography*. London: Milford.

Hutchison, W. D., K. D. Davis, A. M. Lozano, R. R. Tasker, and J. O. Dostrovsky. 1999. "Pain-Related Neurons in the Human Cingulate Cortex." *Nature Neuroscience* 2 (5): 403–5. https://doi.org/10.1038/8065.

Immordino-Yang, Mary Helen, Andrea McColl, Hanna Damasio, and Antonio Damasio. 2009. "Neural Correlates of Admiration and Compassion." *Proceedings of the National Academy of Sciences* 106 (19): 8021–26. https://doi.org/10.1073/pnas.0810363106.

Inami, Masahiro. 2001. "The Problem of Other Minds in the Buddhist Epistemological Tradition." *Journal of Indian Philosophy* 29 (4): 465–83.

Ismael, J. T. 2011. "Self-Organization and Self-Governance." *Philosophy of the Social Sciences* 41 (3): 327–51. https://doi.org/10.1177/0048393110363435.

———. 2014. "On Being Someone." In *Surrounding Free Will*, edited by Alfred R. Mele, 274–97. Oxford, UK: Oxford University Press. https://doi.org/10.1093/acprof:oso/9780199333950.003.0014.

Ismael, Jenann. 2016. *How Physics Makes Us Free*. Oxford, UK: Oxford University Press.

James, William. 2017. *Essays in Radical Empiricism*. N.p.: CreateSpace.

Janzen, Greg. 2008. *The Reflexive Nature of Consciousness*. Amsterdam, Netherlands: John Benjamins.

Jonas, Hans. 1996. Mortality and Morality: A Search for Good After Auschwitz. Northwestern University Press.

Josipovic, Zoran. 2014. "Neural Correlates of Nondual Awareness in Meditation." *Annals of the New York Academy of Sciences* 1307 (1): 9–18. https://doi.org/10.1111/nyas.12261.

———. 2019. "Nondual Awareness: Consciousness-as-Such as Non-Representational Reflexivity." *Progress in Brain Research* 244: 273–98. https://doi.org/10.1016/bs.pbr.2018.10.021.

Kapstein, Matthew. 2013. *Reason's Traces: Identity and Interpretation in Indian and Tibetan Buddhist Thought*. Boston: Wisdom.

Kellner, Birgit. 2010. "Self-Awareness (Svasaṃvedana) in Dignāga's Pramāṇasamuccaya and -Vṛtti: A Close Reading." *Journal of Indian Philosophy* 38 (3): 203–31. https://doi.org/10.1007/s10781-010-9091-y.

Keown, Damien. 1992. *The Nature of Buddhist Ethics*. Basingstoke, UK: Palgrave Macmillan.

Kiverstein, Julian, and Andy Clark. 2009. "Introduction: Mind Embodied, Embedded, Enacted: One Church or Many?" *Topoi* 28 (March): 1–7. https://doi.org/10.1007/s11245-008-9041-4.

Klimecki, Olga M., Susanne Leiberg, Claus Lamm, and Tania Singer. 2013. "Functional Neural Plasticity and Associated Changes in Positive Affect after Compassion Training." *Cerebral Cortex* 23 (7): 1552–61. https://doi.org/10.1093/cercor/bhs142.

Kriegel, Uriah. 2009. *Subjective Consciousness: A Self-Representational Theory*. Oxford, UK: Oxford University Press.

Lamm, Claus, Jean Decety, and Tania Singer. 2011. "Meta-Analytic Evidence for Common and Distinct Neural Networks Associated with Directly Experienced Pain and Empathy for Pain." *NeuroImage* 54 (3): 2492–2502. https://doi.org/10.1016/j.neuroimage.2010.10.014.

Larrabee, M. J. 1981. "The One and the Many: Yogācāra Buddhism and Husserl." *Philosophy East and West* 31 (1): 3–15. https://doi.org/10.2307/1399062.

Legrand, Dorothée. 2007. "Pre-Reflective Self-as-Subject from Experiential and Empirical Perspectives." *Consciousness and Cognition* 16 (3): 583–99. https://doi.org/10.1016/j.concog.2007.04.002.

Leiberg, Susanne, Olga Klimecki, and Tania Singer. 2011. "Short-Term Compassion Training Increases Prosocial Behavior in a Newly Developed Prosocial Game." *PLOS ONE* 6 (3): e17798. https://doi.org/10.1371/journal.pone.0017798.

Loizzo, Joe. 2012. *Sustainable Happiness: The Mind Science of Well-Being, Altruism, and Inspiration*. New York: Routledge.

Lusthaus, Dan. 2003. *Buddhist Phenomenology: A Philosophical Investigation of Yogacara Buddhism and the Ch'eng Wei-Shih Lun*. London: Routledge.

MacKenzie, Matthew. 2012. "Luminosity, Subjectivity, and Temporality: An Examination of Buddhist and Advaita Views of Consciousness." *Hindu and Buddhist Ideas in Dialogue: Self and No Self*, edited by Irina Kuznetsova, Jonardon Ganeri, and Chakravarthi Ram-Prasad, 181–98. Farnham, UK: Ashgate.

———. 2015. "Reflexivity, Subjectivity, and the Constructed Self: A Buddhist Model." *Asian Philosophy* 25 (3): 275–92.

———. 2016. “Dewey, Enactivism, and the Qualitative Dimension.” *HUMANA. MENTE Journal of Philosophical Studies* 9 (31): 21–36.

———. 2018. “Buddhism and the Virtues.” In *The Oxford Handbook of Virtue*, edited by Nancy E. Snow, 153. Oxford, UK: Oxford University Press.

Maiese, Michelle. 2016. *Embodied Selves and Divided Minds*. Oxford, UK: Oxford University Press.

Maturana, Humberto R., and Francisco J. Varela. 1992. *The Tree of Knowledge: The Biological Roots of Human Understanding*. Rev. ed. Boston: Shambhala.

McCormick, Peter J. 1996. *Starmaking: Realism, Anti-Realism, and Irrealism*. Cambridge, MA: MIT Press.

McGinn, Colin. 1993. *The Problem of Consciousness: Essays towards a Resolution*. New ed. Oxford, UK: Wiley-Blackwell.

Meltzoff, Andrew N., and M. Keith Moore. 1989. “Imitation in Newborn Infants: Exploring the Range of Gestures Imitated and the Underlying Mechanisms.” *Developmental Psychology* 25 (6): 954–62. https://doi.org/10.1037/0012-1649.25.6.954.

Mensch, James Richard. 2010. *Postfoundational Phenomenology: Husserlian Reflections on Presence and Embodiment*. University Park: Pennsylvania State University Press.

Merker, Bjorn. 2005. “The Liabilities of Mobility: A Selection Pressure for the Transition to Consciousness in Animal Evolution.” *Consciousness and Cognition* 14 (1): 89–114. https://doi.org/10.1016/S1053-8100(03)00002-3.

———. 2007. “Consciousness without a Cerebral Cortex: A Challenge for Neuroscience and Medicine.” *Behavioral and Brain Sciences* 30 (1): 63–81. https://doi .org/10.1017/S0140525X07000891.

Merleau-Ponty, Maurice. 2013. *Phenomenology of Perception*. Translated by Donald A. Landes. Abingdon, UK: Routledge.

Metzinger, Thomas. 2009. *The Ego Tunnel: The Science of the Mind and the Myth of the Self*. New York: Basic Books.

Montague, Michelle. 2016. *The Given: Experience and Its Content*. Oxford, UK: Oxford University Press.

Nagel, Thomas. 1974. “What Is It Like to Be a Bat?” *Philosophical Review* 83 (4): 435–50. https://doi.org/10.2307/2183914.

Nanamoli, Bhikkhu, and Bhikkhu Bodhi, trans. 1995. *The Middle Length Discourses of the Buddha: A Translation of the Majjhima Nikaya*. Clean and Tight Contents ed. Boston: Wisdom.

Nicholson, Daniel J., and John Dupre, eds. 2018. *Everything Flows: Towards a Processual Philosophy of Biology*. Oxford, UK: Oxford University Press.

Olivelle, Patrick. 1998. *The Early Upanishads: Annotated Text and Translation*. South Asia Research. Oxford, UK: Oxford University Press.

Panksepp, Jaak, and Georg Northoff. 2009. “The Trans-Species Core SELF: The Emergence of Active Cultural and Neuro-Ecological Agents through Self-Related Processing within Subcortical-Cortical Midline Networks.” *Consciousness and Cognition* 18 (1): 193–215. https://doi.org/10.1016/j.concog.2008.03.002.

Parvizi, J., and A. Damasio. 2001. “Consciousness and the Brainstem.” *Cognition* 79 (1–2): 135–60. https://doi.org/10.1016/s0010-0277(00)00127-x.

Perrett, Roy W. 1998. *Hindu Ethics: A Philosophical Study*. Honolulu: University of Hawaii Press.

Philippi, Carissa L., Justin S. Feinstein, Sahib S. Khalsa, Antonio Damasio, Daniel Tranel, Gregory Landini, Kenneth Williford, and David Rudrauf. 2012. "Preserved Self-Awareness Following Extensive Bilateral Brain Damage to the Insula, Anterior Cingulate, and Medial Prefrontal Cortices." *PLOS ONE* 7 (8): e38413. https://doi.org/10.1371/journal.pone.0038413.

Pradhan, P., ed. 1975. *Abhidharmakośabhāṣyam of Vasubandhu*. Rev. 2nd ed. Patna, India: K. P. Jayaswal Research Institute. http://archive.org/details/Pradhan1975.

Preston, Stephanie D., and Frans B. M. de Waal. 2002. "Empathy: Its Ultimate and Proximate Bases." *Behavioral and Brain Sciences* 25 (1): 1–20. https://doi.org/10.1017/S0140525X02000018.

Priestley, Leonard C. D. C. 1999. *Pudgalavada Buddhism: The Reality of the Indeterminate Self*. Toronto: University of Toronto, Centre for South Asian Studies.

Prueitt, Catherine. 2018. "Karmic Imprints, Exclusion, and the Creation of the Worlds of Conventional Experience in Dharmakīrti's Thought." *Sophia* 57 (2): 313–35. https://doi.org/10.1007/s11841-017-0618-5.

Putnam, Hilary. 1981. *Reason, Truth and History*. Cambridge, UK: Cambridge University Press.

Ram-Prasad, Chakravarthi. 2007. *Indian Philosophy and the Consequences of Knowledge: Themes in Ethics, Metaphysics and Soteriology*. Aldershot, UK: Routledge.

Ronkin, Noa. 2011. *Early Buddhist Metaphysics*. London: Routledge.

Rosenthal, David B. 1997. "A Theory of Consciousness." https://www.semanticscholar.org/paper/A-theory-of-consciousness-Rosenthal/a5422a0d823e1b752298f26e668fa770a5b63b1d.

Ruiz-Mirazo, Kepa, and Alvaro Moreno. 2004. "Basic Autonomy as a Fundamental Step in the Synthesis of Life." *Artificial Life* 10 (3): 235–59. https://doi.org/10.1162/1064546041255584.

Śāntarakṣita, and Jamgon Mipham. 2005. *The Adornment of the Middle Way: Shantarakshita's Madhyamakalankara with Commentary by Jamgon Mipham*. Translated by the Padmakara Translation Group. Boston: Shambhala.

Śāntideva. 2008. *The Bodhicaryavatara*. Edited by Paul Williams. Translated by Kate Crosby and Andrew Skilton. Oxford, UK: Oxford University Press.

Sartre, Jean-Paul. 2004. *The Transcendence of the Ego*. London: Routledge.

Searle, John R. 1995. *Construction of Social Reality*. New York: Free Press.

Shear, Jonathan, and Shaun Gallagher, eds. 1999. *Models of the Self*. Thorverton, UK: Imprint Academic.

Siderits, Mark. 2010. "Is Everything Connected to Everything Else? What the Gopīs Know," in *Moonshadows: Conventional Truth in Buddhist Philosophy*, ed. The Cowherds (New York, NY: Oxford University Press), 167–80.

Siderits, Mark. 2016. *Studies in Buddhist Philosophy*. Oxford, UK: Oxford University Press.

Siderits, Mark, and Shoryu Katsura. 2013. *Nagarjuna's Middle Way: Mulamadhyamakakarika*. Boston: Wisdom.

Smith, David Woodruff. 2016. "The Several Factors of (Self-)Consciousness." *Rivista Internazionale Di Filosofia e Psicologia* 7 (3): 291–302. https://doi.org/10.4453/rifp.2016.0032.

Sridharan, V. 2015. "The Enactivist Self—Virtual or Autonomous?" *Journal of Consciousness Studies* 22 (7–8): 183–200. https://www.ingentaconnect.com/contentone/imp/jcs/2015/00000022/f0020007/art00011.

Stapleton, Mog, and Tom Froese. 2016. "The Enactive Philosophy of Embodiment: From Biological Foundations of Agency to the Phenomenology of Subjectivity." In *Biology and Subjectivity: Philosophical Contributions to Non-reductive Neuroscience*, edited by Miguel García-Valdecasas, José Ignacio Murillo, and Nathaniel F. Barrett, 2:113–29. Historical-Analytical Studies on Nature, Mind and Action. Cham, Switzerland: Springer International. https://doi.org/10.1007/978-3-319-30502-8_8.

Stein, Edith. 1989. *On the Problem of Empathy: The Collected Works of Edith Stein.* Translated by Waltraut Stein. 3rd rev. ed. Washington, DC: ICS.

Steward, Helen. 2012. *A Metaphysics for Freedom.* Oxford, UK: Oxford University Press.

Tegchok, Jampa. 2006. *Kindness of Others: A Commentary on the Seven-Point Mind Training.* Translated by Stephen Carlier. Boston: Lama Yeshe Archive.

Thompson, Evan. 1996. "The Mindful Body: Embodiment and Cognitive Science." In *The Incorporated Self: Interdisciplinary Perspectives on Embodiment*, edited by Michael O'Donovan-Anderson, 127–44. Lanham, MD: Rowman and Littlefield.

———. 2010. *Mind in Life: Biology, Phenomenology, and the Sciences of Mind.* Cambridge, MA: Belknap Press.

———. 2011. "Living Ways of Sense Making." *Philosophy Today* 55 (Supplement): 114–23. https://doi.org/10.5840/philtoday201155Supplement14.

Thrangu, Khenchen. 2013. *Transcending Ego: Distinguishing Consciousness from Wisdom.* 2nd ed. Boulder, CO: Namo Buddha.

Tomasello, Michael. 2001. *The Cultural Origins of Human Cognition.* Reprint ed. Cambridge, MA: Harvard University Press.

Trevarthen, Colwyn, and M. Bullowa. 1979. "Communication and Cooperation in Early Infancy: A Description of Primary Intersubjectivity." In *Before Speech: The Beginning of Interpersonal Communication*, edited by Margaret Bullowa, 321–47. Cambridge, UK: Cambridge University Press.

Tsakiris, Manos, and Helena De Preester, eds. 2018. *The Interoceptive Mind: From Homeostasis to Awareness.* Oxford, UK: Oxford University Press.

Tzohar, Roy. 2017. "Imagine Being a Preta: Early Indian Yogācāra Approaches to Intersubjectivity." *Sophia* 56 (2): 337–54. https://doi.org/10.1007/s11841-016-0544-y.

Varela, Francisco J. 1999a. *Ethical Know-How: Action, Wisdom, and Cognition.* Stanford, CA: Stanford University Press.

———. 1999b. "The Specious Present: A Neurophenomenology of Time Consciousness." In *Naturalizing Phenomenology: Issues in Contemporary Phenomenology and Cognitive Science*, edited by Jean Petitot, Francisco J. Varela, Bernard

Pachoud, and Jean-Michel Roy, 266–314. Writing Science. Stanford, CA: Stanford University Press.

———. 2001. "The Emergent Self." Edge. https://www.edge.org/3rd_culture/varela/varela_index.html.

Varela, Francisco J., Evan Thompson, Eleanor Rosch, and Jon Kabat-Zinn. 2017. *The Embodied Mind: Cognitive Science and Human Experience*. 2nd ed. Cambridge, MA: MIT Press.

Velleman, J. David. 1992. "What Happens When Someone Acts?" *Mind* 101 (403): 461–81.

Vetlesen, Arne Johan. 1994. *Perception, Empathy, and Judgment: An Inquiry into the Preconditions of Moral Performance*. University Park: Pennsylvania State University Press.

Vireswarananda. 1982. *Brahma-Sutras: With Text, Word-for-Word Translation, English Rendering, Comments According to the Commentary of Sri Sankara and Index*. Calcutta: Vedanta Press.

Waldron, William S. 2003. *The Buddhist Unconscious: The Alaya-Vijñana in the Context of Indian Buddhist Thought*. London: Routledge.

Walshe, Maurice. 1995. *The Long Discourses of the Buddha: A Translation of the Digha Nikaya*. 2nd ed. Boston: Wisdom.

Wegner, Daniel M. 2003. *The Illusion of Conscious Will*. Cambridge, MA: MIT Press.

Wenzel, Christian, and Kai Marchal. 2017. "Chinese Perspectives on Free Will." In *The Routledge Companion to Free Will*, edited by Kevin Timpe, Meghan Griffith, and Neil Levy, 374–88. New York: Routledge.

Westerhoff, Jan. 2009. *Nagarjuna's Madhyamaka: A Philosophical Introduction*. Oxford, UK: Oxford University Press.

Williams, Paul, Anthony Tribe, and Alexander Wynne. 2012. *Buddhist Thought: A Complete Introduction to the Indian Tradition*. 2nd ed. London: Routledge.

Wong, David B. 1989. "Three Kinds of Incommensurability." In *Relativism: Interpretation and Confrontation*, edited by Michael Krausz, 140–58. Notre Dame, IN: Notre Dame University Press.

Zahavi, Dan. 2008. *Subjectivity and Selfhood: Investigating the First-Person Perspective*. Cambridge, MA: MIT Press.

———. 2010. "Inner (Time-)Consciousness." In *On Time—New Contributions to the Husserlian Phenomenology of Time*, edited by Dieter Lohmar and Ichiro Yamaguchi, 197:319–39. Phaenomenologica. Dordrecht, Netherlands: Springer. https://doi.org/10.1007/978-90-481-8766-9_16.

———. 2020. *Self-Awareness and Alterity: A Phenomenological Investigation*. 2nd ed. Evanston, IL: Northwestern University Press.

Index

Abhidharma Buddhism, 12–21, 23–25, 29–30, 65–67, 71, 114–15, 148, 160. *See also under* reductionism: Buddhist; Vasubandhu

Abhidharmakośabhāṣya (Vasubandhu), 16, 82–83

absolute consciousness (Husserl), 70–71, 100

action/actions, 6; central role of, 79, 106; and character, 6, 80; problem with causal-reductive accounts of, 85–86, 103. *See also specific descriptions, e.g.*, kuśala (wholesome or skillful actions and traits); *specific topics, e.g.*, altruism; karma

adaptivity, 30–32, 36–37, 83, 87–91, 99–100, 107, 121, 132, 162–63

Advaita Vedānta school of Indian philosophy, 18–19, 50–51. *See also* Śaṅkara

affect *(vedanā)*, 13–14, 27–28, 30, 34–35, 54, 63, 73, 76, 110–11, 135; positive/negative, 152–53

affectivity, 110

afflicted mentation *(kliṣṭa-manas)*, 67, 78n19, 126

agency, 143, 149, 155n9, 162–63; agentless, 6, 82–87; the author's account of, 163; enactivist approach to, 6, 87–90, 163; five aggregates as locus of (Vasubandhu), 82–83; and other minds, 79–103; psychological, 90–92; reality of conventional, 86

aggression, 136, 152

ahaṃkāra. *See* self-making

akuśala (unwholesome or unskillful actions), 80, 132

ālayavijñāna. *See* base consciousness

Albahari, Miri, 13, 44n20

alterity, 107

altruism, 8–9, 133–34, 137–38, 141–42, 144, 148–53; benefits of, 8, 152–53

anātman (no-self), 12–16, 81–82

anger, 54, 135, 142–43, 149, 151, 155n9

anticipation, 37, 71, 91, 138

antirealism, 2, 16, 39–42, 114, 116–17, 129n5, 160, 163

antisubstantialism, 16, 18, 20–21, 122, 159

appropriation *(upādāna)*, 86, 92, 112, 127

Aristotle, 81

arrogance, 154

arthakriyā, Dharmakīrti's notion of, 94, 114, 130n11

Asaṅga, 66–67

Ataria, Yochai, 34
ātman (self), 12–16, 21, 25, 46, 50, 56
attachment/nonattachment, 8, 134, 136, 142, 163
attentionalism, 91
attraction, 14, 79, 108, 135
"Authorship View" of self, 90–91
autonomy, 5; autonomous systems, 24; psychological and biological, 5, 91; as self-governance, 91; *See also* autopoiesis; self-governance
autopoiesis (self-production), 22, 38, 107–8
aversion *(dveṣa),* 8, 79, 81, 108, 110, 135, 152, 163
awakened life/mode of being, 7–8, 105, 136–37. *See also* bodhicitta
awareness: dynamic embodied nondual, 72–77. *See also* svasaṃvedana (self-awareness/reflexive awareness)

background consciousness, 6, 68, 71, 75–76
Baker, Lynne Rudder, 11
Barandiaran, Xabier, 87–88
Baron-Cohen, Simon, 138
Barrera, Maria E., 138
base consciousness *(ālayavijñāna),* 6, 18–19, 65–68, 71, 75–77, 126, 163
Batson, C. D., 152
Beauregard, Mario, et al., 153
Bénard cell, 23
Bentley, Arthur F., 128
Bhattacharya, Vidhushekhara, 155n2
biochemistry, 22
birth, 106, 109–12, 110–12, 127
bliss, 75
Bodhi, Bhikkhu, 26, 44n14, 80, 105–6, 108, 132
Bodhicaryāvatāra (Śāntideva), 8, 134–35, 141, 163
bodhicitta (the "awakening mind")/ the *bodhisattva* path, 8–9, 131, 134, 137–54 *passim,* 163–64; empathy as root of, 8
body, human: as base of experience, 162. *See also specific topics, e.g.,* autopoiesis; enactivism
body-mind, 18, 110–12. *See also* embodiment
borderless philosophy, 4, 164
boundaries, 15, 22–23, 88–89, 95, 97, 111, 113
Brahmanical tradition, 12, 25–26
brahmavihāras, four, 131
brain/human brain, 23, 31, 37–38, 76, 78n20, 92, 124, 139, 153; as like a total flight simulator, 126
Braun, Niclas, et al., 34
Buccino, G., et al., 139
Buddha, 80, 90, 103n2, 105, 108, 114–15, 137
Buddhaghosa, Bhadantacariya, 82, 91
Buddhism, 33, 162; Buddhist-enactivist dialogue, 5, 7, 159–60, 163–64. *See also specific topics, e.g.,* ethics; karma; reductionism; *specific traditions, e.g.,* Mahāyāna Buddhism; Yogācāra Buddhism

calm/tranquility (*śamatha),* 132, 141–42, 146
candle flame, 23
Candrakīrti, 6, 87, 116, 127
Carpenter, Amber D., 24–26
Cartesianism, 11–12, 21, 41–42, 50–51, 76, 160
causation, 120; Buddhist reductionism and, 114
Chadha, Monima, 71
Chakrabarti, Arindam, 3–5, 164
Chapple, Christopher Key, 79
character: actions and, 6, 80; traits the are good in themselves *(svabhāvataḥ kuśalam),* 134. *See also specific topics, e.g.,* karma
Christoff, Kalina, et al., 33–34
citta/caitta model of cognition, 54, 62, 137
Clayton, Barbra R., 133, 155n3

clinging *(upādāna),* 28, 106, 109, 151
Coates, Paul, 125
cognition: *citta/caitta* model of, 54, 62, 137; emergence of, 36. *See also* consciousness; metacognition; *saṃjñā*
cognitive-affective training, 8–9, 142–57
cognitive distortions, 74, 135–36
cognitive experience *(vijñānavāda),* 122
cognitive science, 1, 12, 105
cognitive strategies, 142–43, 149; four-point mind training, 8–9, 144–57
common sense, 149
comparative philosophy, 3–5, 164
compassion, 8–9, 131–57; empathy as differentiated from, 153; the four *brahmavihāra*s, 131; training, 153. *See also* altruism; loving kindness
complex systems, 21–22, 84
concern, 31. *See also* altruism; compassion
conditioning *(saṃskāra),* 13–14, 64, 73, 108, 110–12, 123, 142–43
consciousness, 2, 5–6, 46, 161; absolute (Husserl), 70–71, 100; the author's account of, 46, 161; background, 6, 68, 71, 75–76; base *(ālayavijñāna),* 6, 18–19, 65–68, 71, 75–77, 126, 163; dual-aspect reflexivist view of, 5, 46, 51–64, 72–75, 96, 162–63; as dynamic, embodied open presence, 46; eight modes/aspects of, 66–67; as light *(prakāśa)* or luminosity *(prakāśatā),* 2, 5, 45–48, 51, 57, 63–64, 161; modal model of, 57; as open presence, 46, 68; *paraprakāśavāda* account of (other-illumination), 2, 47–51, 161; plurality of, 100; pure, 50; reflexive awareness and, 5, 46, 51–64; and the self, 2, 11–12; as subjectivity, 50 (*see also* subjectivity); *svaprakāśavāda* account of (self-illumination), 2, 47–51, 161; *svasaṃvedana* as very nature of, 71, 74; two aspects of (object aspect and subject aspect), 6; unity of, synchronic and diachronic, 45–46, 73, 77n2. *See also* awareness; cognition; luminosity; stream of consciousness; time consciousness; *specific topics, e.g.,* empathy; intersubjectivity; phenomenology
contemplation/contemplative practice, 75, 125, 154. *See also* meditation
continuity: diachronic, 6, 23, 43n5, 64–72; and identity, 43n5
core self, 32
Cousins, L. S., 154n1
craving *(tṛṣṇa),* 109–10, 135
culture, 3, 5, 150

daily life, 116, 153
Dalvi, Rohit, 65–66
Damasio, Antonio R., 11, 30–32, 35, 44n19, 63, 76
Dambrun, Michaël, 132, 135–36, 155n7
death, 106, 109–12, 110–12, 127
Decety, Jean, 153
decomposability, 23
deliberation, 82, 92
delusion, 8, 29, 34, 79, 135, 138, 146, 150, 152. *See also* ignorance; three poisons
Dennett, Daniel, 39
dependent coarising (*pratītyasamutpāda*), 12, 20, 81, 121
dependent origination (*pratītyasamutpanna*), 12, 20–28, 81, 86, 115, 120–21; twelvefold chain of, 106, 109–12
desire/desires, 80, 85, 100; for happiness (see *saṃsāric* framework)
determinism, 143, 149, 155
Deutsch, Eliot, 65–66
Dewey, John, 99, 128
dharma/dharmas, 16–18, 20, 29, 41, 43, 64, 84, 86, 89–90, 114–18, 120, 148–50

Dharmakīrti, 2, 6–7, 53, 57–60, 63, 74, 77n5, 93–94, 103; and *arthakriyā,* notion of, 94, 114, 130n11
diachrony, 13–14, 23–26, 32–37, 44n23, 75, 110; diachronic continuity, 6, 23, 43n5, 64–72; diachronic identity, 14, 18, 20, 43n5, 44n27, 148–49; and unity of consciousness, 45–46, 77n2
dialogue, Buddhist-enactivist, 5, 7, 159–60, 163–64
Dīgha Nikāya, 127–28
Dignāga, 2, 51–57, 61–62, 77n8
Di Paolo, Ezequiel, 87–88
distinction between self and others, 9, 15
dreaming, 123; lucid, 125
Dretske, Fred I., 49, 52, 58, 60
Dreyfus, Georges B. J., 78n17
dual-aspect reflexivism (DAR), 5, 46, 51–64, 72–75, 96, 162–63
dualism, 100, 128, 161. *See also* Dharmakīrti
dualism, non-. *See* nondualism
Duerlinger, James, 24–25, 43n3
Dunne, John D., 63, 74, 75, 130n11
dynamic coemergence, 7, 23, 25, 105
dynamic embodied nondual awareness, 72–77
dynamic systems theory, 12, 21, 23–25, 28, 108, 160

Edelglass, William, 127, 134
egocentrism, 8–9, 133, 144, 146–49, 151. *See also* self-cherishing
egoism, 136–38, 141–42, 144, 152, 164
eightfold path to liberation from suffering, 131
eliminativism, 1–2, 5, 11–12, 37, 42, 149, 160
The Embodied Mind: Cognitive Science and Human Experience (Varela, Thompson, Rosch, and Kabat-Zinn), 1, 40, 114
embodiment, 1, 5, 7, 11, 75, 96, 99–101, 161; dynamic embodied nondual awareness, 72–77; sentient *(nāma-rūpa),* 13, 15, 110–11, 127–28. *See also* body-mind
emotion/emotions, 14, 30–32, 76, 98, 100, 132, 138–43; emergence of, 100; negative, 135, 151–52; positive, 153
empathy, 101, 137–41, 145–47, 150–54, 163–64; compassion as differentiated from, 153; earliest forms of, 138; and empathic distress, 152–53; failures of, 146; four types of, 145–46; and mirror neurons, 139; as root of *bodhicitta,* 8
empiricism, 12, 15–16, 50, 76, 81, 122, 128
emptiness *(śūnyavāda),* 7, 9, 37–38, 40–41, 71, 75, 112–22, 148–51, 154; concept of, 121; enaction, realism, and, 112–22. *See also* Madhyamaka Buddhism
enactivism, 1–2, 5–8, 73, 78, 87–91, 97–99, 134, 139; agency, approach to, 6, 87–90, 163; Buddhist-enactivist dialogue, 5, 7, 159–60, 163–64; enacting self, 5, 11–44; enacting worlds, 105–30; enaction, emptiness, and realism, 112–22. *See also* pragmatic realism
engagement, 97–99, 121, 142, 154, 160, 164
enlightenment, 8, 116, 123, 133–34, 151, 163. *See also* wisdom
environment, 162; agency, other minds, and, 87–90, 97–99; enacting selves and, 14, 17, 22–23, 27–40; enacting worlds and, 107–13, 118–21, 125, 128; luminosity and, 62–63, 73, 78n16. *See also specific topics, e.g.,* enactivism
envy, 136, 142, 154
epiphenomenalism, 16, 90, 114
epistemology, 7, 48, 62, 93, 96, 102, 113, 120–22, 131, 163. *See also* Dharmakīrti; Prajñākaragupta; Ratnakīrti

equality of self and other, 8, 144–51
equanimity *(upekṣā),* 131–33, 136
ethics: Buddhist, 8, 80, 131–38, 155, 163. See also *bodhisattva path*
eudaimonism, 133
evolution, 25, 28, 30, 33, 107–8, 111
exafference, 34
exchange of self and other, 8, 154
existence, human: recursive, autopoeitic character of, 108. *See also* human beings; life
existential, the, 13, 111–12, 117, 135, 137, 141, 164
experience, 162; cognitive *(vijñānavāda),* 122; immediate *(anubhava),* 54; phenomenal character of, 61–62; "pure," 128; the self and, 161–62; self-experience, 70; true nature of, 124
exteriority, 108, 111–12
externalist approach, 48, 52, 78n16, 116, 161

fallibilism, 7, 120–21
fear, 31, 98, 135–36, 144–46, 151
feeling *(vedanā),* 14, 30–32, 98, 100, 110, 135, 142. *See also* affect; emotions
fictionalism, 1, 6, 21, 39–40, 80, 160
first-person perspective, 11, 18–20, 28, 30, 40, 59, 62–63, 66, 83, 93, 103. *See also* givenness
flow. *See* stream
four *brahmavihāras*, 131
four-point mind training, 8–9, 144–57
freedom, 131; free will, 3. *See also* liberation
Froese, Tom, 88–89
Frondizi, Risieri, 36
Fuchs, Thomas, 167
Fultz, J., 152

Gallagher, Shaun, 13, 34, 64, 101–2, 138
Gallese, V., 139
Ganeri, Jonardon, 4, 7, 24–25, 29, 32, 41–44, 53–54, 90–96, 162
Ganguli, Hemanta Kumar, 95
Garfield, Jay, 8, 86–87, 92, 121–22, 127, 134, 137, 155n3
givenness, 19–20, 43n8, 69, 78n15, 101
global background consciousness. *See* background consciousness
goals, 63, 87–89
Goodman, Charles, 83, 86, 133–34, 143, 155n3
goodness/the good. *See* karma; virtue
grasping *(upādāna),* 109–10, 135–36, 152
greed, 8, 14, 131, 134–36, 138, 163. *See also* three poisons

hallucinations, 52, 122–25
happiness: and altruism, 152–53; *bodhicitta* as seed of, 8–9, 137–38, 141–42, 144, 151; and empathy, 8; two types of, 132
happiness, desire for. See *saṃsāric* framework
hatred, 8, 14, 131, 135, 138, 146. *See also* three poisons
hedonic states, 13, 63, 132, 135–36
hedonism, 132, 136, 138
Hinduism, 64, 160; Naiyāyikas, 50, 60, 161–62; *Upaniṣads,* 2, 46, 79 *See also specific traditions, e.g.,* Advaita Vedānta; *specific topics, e.g.,* nondualism
Hōgen, 127
Horgan, Terry, 63
Horst, Steven, 121
human beings, 2, 4, 8, 15–16, 20, 91, 140, 162; person *(pudgala),* 12–13, 24–26. *See also* sentient beings; *specific topics, e.g.,* autonomy; *saṃsāric* framework; self
human situation, 79
Hume, Robert E., 80
Husserl, Edmund, 68–71, 78n15, 110

idealism, 105, 113–14, 122, 129, 161, 163
identity, 22–23, 38, 66, 87–89, 111–12, 147–51; bounded, 111; continuity and, 43n5; diachronic, 14, 18, 43n5, 44n27, 148–49; and no-self, doctrine of *(anātman),* 12–16, 81–83; "virtual," 22, 38
ignorance, 8, 14, 54, 81, 110–12, 131, 163; and nonignorance, 134. *See also* delusion; three poisons
imagination, 37, 91, 101, 139–40, 154; failures of, 146
"I-making." *See* self-making/"I-making" *(ahaṃkāra)*
Inami, Masahiro, 93
independent self, sense of, 19, 56, 108
Indian philosophy, 1–2, 6, 45–47, 67, 81, 113, 164
individuality, 29, 88, 103n1, 108, 111, 163
individuation, 25–26, 40–41, 103; basis of, 162
infants, 138–40
intentions/intentionality, 2–3, 27, 31, 45–55, 62–64, 67–76, 81–86, 90–102, 111, 128; externalist view of, 161–62; internalist view of, 96, 162; as openness to the world, 97; of others, 101, 138, 140. *See also* karma; volition
interconnection/interconnectedness, 1, 17–18, 80, 124, 139–40; our deep interconnectedness with others, 151
interdependence, 6–7, 12–13, 18, 72, 80–81, 89, 105–13, 117–18, 120–22, 126–27, 129; of action and character, 6, 80; matrix of, 150; of self and others, 154. *See also* dependent origination
interiority, 7, 28, 44n16, 108, 111–12
internalist approach, 52–53, 96–98, 103, 161–62
internalist-representationalist view, 8, 93, 96, 123–27
intersubjectivity, 2, 8, 36, 96–97, 102, 120, 134; the author's account of, 8, 163; open, 137–39; a reflexivist theory of, 97
introspection, 15, 49–51, 54–55, 61, 77n7
Ismael, Jennan T., 36–37, 39, 91–92

Jainism, 4
James, William, 128
Janaka, King, 46–47
Janzen, Greg, 61
Japan, 127
jealousy, 151
Jinendrabuddhi, 61–62
jīva, 12
Jizō (Zen priest), 127
Jonas, Hans, 105
Josipovic, Zoran, 75
joy: of another, 101; sympathetic, 131. *See also* happiness

Kabat-Zinn, Jon, 1, 40, 114
Kant, Immanuel, 126
karma, 6–7, 25, 79–81, 105–10, 133
karuṇā. See compassion
Katsura, Shoryu, 115–16, 120
Keown, Damien, 133, 155n3
kindness: loving kindness *(maitrī),* 131, 133. *See also* compassion
Klimecki, Olga, et al., 153
kliṣṭa-manas (afflicted mentation), 67, 78n19, 126
Koch, Sabine C., 167
Kriegel, Uriah, 30
kuśala (wholesome or skillful actions and traits), 80, 132, 134, 154n1; three roots of (nongreed, nonhatred, and nonignorance), 134

Lamm, Claus, 153
language, 5, 37–38, 44n25, 114, 127, 131. *See also* diachrony; synchrony
liberation, 6, 79, 81, 154n1; eightfold path to, 131

life, 107; daily, 116, 153; emergence of, 32–33, 36–37; mental, 42, 90–91, 95–96, 99–102, 161–63; our nature as living individuals, 162. *See also entries beginning with* living; sentience
light *(prakāśa),* 2, 45–48, 57. *See also* luminosity
living as sense-making. *See* sense-making, living as
living systems, 5, 23, 28, 32–33, 35, 87, 89–90, 107, 163
"logical bootstrap" or "loop." See *autopoiesis* (self-production)
Loizzo, Joe, 142
loka (Buddhist concept of a world), 105–8, 111, 116
love, 149, 154; loving kindness *(maitrī),* 131, 133. *See also* altruism; compassion
lucid dreaming, 125
luminosity *(prakāśatā),* 2, 45–78; consciousness as, 2, 5, 63–64; self-luminosity and other luminosity, 2, 47–51, 161
Lusthaus, Dan, 14, 43n1

MacKenzie, Matthew, 44, 78n16, 78n19
Madhyamaka Buddhism, 41, 87, 92, 115–18, 120–21, 161. *See also* emptiness; Śāntarakṣita
Mahāyāna Buddhism, 8; ethics of, 131–38. *See also* Nāgārjuna; Śāntideva
Maiese, Michelle, 100
maitrī (loving kindness), 131, 133
Majjhima Nikāya, 26, 80, 132
materialism, 42, 162, 164
matrix, nondual, 74–75
Maturana, Humberto R., 22, 43n12
Maurer, Daphne, 138
McDowell, John, 119
McGinn, Colin, 53
meditation/meditative concentration, 75, 124, 131–32, 141–43, 154; four-point mind training, 8–9, 144–57. *See also* contemplation
memory, 16, 18–19, 35, 53–55, 57, 62, 65, 77n7, 83–84, 125, 153
Mensch, James, 70
mental events, 12, 15–19, 29, 42, 65–67, 71, 78n12, 83, 90, 93–94
mental life, 42, 90–91, 95–96, 99–102, 161–63
mental proliferation, 26
mental self, 13, 17
Merker, Bjorn, 30, 63
Merleau-Ponty, Maurice, 100–102
metacognition, 49–51, 54–55, 77n7. *See also* introspection
metaphysics, 1–2, 78n18, 105–6, 113–22, 131, 149, 161–64. *See also* ontology
Metzinger, Thomas, 124
mind, 162–64; the author's account of, 162; body-mind, 18, 110–12; other minds, 6–7, 97–103, 163; philosophy of, 1, 3, 12, 67, 131, 159–60; "ready-made," myth of, 127; and the self, 162. *See also* cognition; *entries beginning with* mental; *specific topics, e.g.,* enactivism
mindedness, 92, 96, 162
mindfulness, 142, 155n7
Mipham, Jamgon, 6, 67–68, 71, 73–75. *See also* temporality
mirror neurons, 139
momentariness *(kṣanikavāda),* 19
monastics, 131
Montague, Michelle, 52, 59, 96
moral discipline *(śīla),* 131–32
morality, 82, 148. *See also* karma; virtue
moral perception, 9, 140–41, 144–47, 151, 154
moral psychology, 8, 80. See also *Bodhicaryāvatāra* (Śāntideva); karma
moral significance, 146, 148
moral training, 146

Mūlamadhyamakakārikā (Nāgārjuna), 115

Nāgārjuna, 114–15, 117–18, 120–21
Nagel, Thomas, 77n1
Naiyāyikas, 50, 60, 161–62. *See* Nyāya
nāma-rūpa (sentient embodiment), 13, 15, 110–11, 127–28
naturalism, 164
negative actions and traits. *See* three poisons
negative states and emotions, 135, 146, 151–53; and empathic distress, 152–53. See also *saṃsāric* framework; suffering
networks, 12, 18, 22–24, 28, 31, 73, 81, 83, 86–87, 92, 108, 112, 117, 120, 153, 162
neuroscience, 30, 63, 75
Nichols, Shaun, 63
Nietzsche, Friedrich, 87
nihilism, 20, 24, 29, 43; error of, 143
Nikāyas, 114
nirākāravādins, 53
nirvāṇa, 81, 115, 133
nondualism, 8, 123, 127–28; dynamic embodied nondual awareness, 72–77
nonlinear systems/interactions, 23
norms, 27, 73, 87, 89, 97
Northoff, George, 31–32
no-self, doctrine of *(anātman),* 12–16, 81–82
Nyāya school of Indian philosophy, 19–20, 48–51, 57, 113, 126. *See* Naiyāyikas

object appearance *(viṣayābhāsa),* 52, 60–62
object aspect of consciousness, 6
objectivism, 7–8, 105–6
ontology, 1, 7, 159–64; agency, other minds, and, 81, 85–88, 97–99, 103; enacting selves and, 11–12, 15–20, 24–25, 29, 38–44; enacting worlds and, 105, 113–22, 127–29; luminosity and, 48, 55, 57, 66, 77; ontological parity, 7, 120; ontological status, 25, 44n22, 90, 103n1, 117; and reality, 7
organization, self-. *See* self-organization
orientation, 27–28, 31, 35, 63, 73, 97, 112, 135
other minds, 6–7, 79–103, 163; agency and, 79–103
ownership, 5, 28, 33–36, 39–42, 63, 67, 126

pain, 31, 54, 56, 101, 106, 109; and compassion, 132, 134, 139, 145, 148, 152–53. *See also* empathy; suffering
Pāli Nikāyas, 114
Panksepp, Jaak, 31–32
pāramitās (the six perfections), 132
paraprakāśa (other-illumination)/ *paraprakāśavāda* account of consciousness, 2, 47–51, 161
pariniṣpanna-svabhāva (the consummate nature), 123
pathology, 14, 44n21
patterns, 12, 22, 26, 33, 36, 38, 40, 81, 88, 90, 100, 111, 153
perception, 1. *See also* moral perception; *saṃjñā*
perfection, 137, 141; the six perfections *(pāramitās),* 132
Perrett, Roy W., 79
person *(pudgala),* 12–13, 24–26. *See also* human beings; sentient beings
personality, 13, 18
phenomena, three natures of, 8, 114, 122–29
phenomenology, 1–2, 5–6, 8, 97–101, 141–43, 159–64; enacting selves and, 11–12, 16, 19–21, 27–30, 33, 37, 42, 44n18; enacting worlds and, 106, 110, 113–15, 117, 120; luminosity and, 45–48, 51, 53–77 *passim,* 78n18, 78n20. *See also* Husserl, Edmund; Śāntideva

philosophy, 1–6, 160, 164; borderless, 4, 164; Buddhist, 1–2, 6, 37, 67, 81, 149, 164; comparative, 3–5, 164; contemporary, 4, 105, 155, 160; Indian, 1–2, 6, 45–47, 67, 81, 113, 164; of mind, 1, 3, 12, 67, 131, 159–60. *See also individual names/ philosophers, e.g.*, Śāntarakṣita; *specific schools of thought*
physical events, 12, 15–17, 83
physicalism, 160–61, 164
planning, 31, 35, 37, 91
pleasure, 31, 54, 109–10, 132, 135, 142
pluralism, 1, 4, 7, 120–21, 134, 160, 163. *See also* Śāntarakṣita
plurality of consciousness, 100
positive actions and traits, 131–32. *See also* virtue
positive emotions, 153. *See also* happiness; joy
pragmatic realism, 2, 8, 39–40, 106, 129n5, 163
pragmatism, 1–2, 7–8, 162–63; agency, other minds, and, 101–2; and cultivating compassion, 133, 138; enacting selves and, 16–18, 32, 36, 78n16; enacting worlds and, 114, 120–22, 129n5, 130n11; three key elements of, 120. *See also* pragmatic realism
Prajñākaragupta, 93, 95
pramāṇavādins, Buddhist, 5, 46, 51, 75, 77n6, 162; *See also* dual-aspect reflexivism
Pramāṇavārttika (Dharmakīrti), 63
prātimokṣa vows, 131
pratītyasamutpāda. See dependent coarising
pratītyasamutpanna. See dependent origination
pride, 154
primary intersubjectivity, 138
psychological agency, 90–92
pudgala (person), 12–13, 24–26
Pudgalavādins ("proponents of the reality of persons"), 24–25
Putnam, Hilary, 116–18

Ram-Prasad, Chakravarthi, 47–50
Ratnakīrti, 9, 93–99, 103
reafference, 34
realism: enaction, emptiness, and, 7, 112–22; metaphysical, 2, 7, 105–6, 114, 116–19, 121, 149, 161, 163. *See also* pragmatic realism
realism, anti-. *See* antirealism
reality: ontology and, 7; ultimate, 20–21, 116. *See also specific philosophies, e.g.,* substantialism
reason, 146
reasoning, 91
rebirth, 20, 80, 111–12, 127. *See also* karma
receptivity, 27, 73, 110
recognition, 18–19, 27, 64–65, 71, 92, 125–26, 140; mutual intersubjective, 145–46
reductionism, 6, 16–17, 26, 37, 43n6, 89–91, 103, 160, 163; Buddhist, 16–21, 23–25, 29–30, 35, 41, 43n10, 82–87, 90, 114–15, 130n9, 148–49; four problems with Buddhist, 18–21; mereological, 17–18, 20–21, 29, 93, 103; and nonreductionist accounts, 1, 21, 24, 41, 87, 160. *See also* Abhidharma Buddhism
reflexivism: dual-aspect, 5, 46, 51–64, 72–75, 96, 162–63; intersubjectivity, reflexivist theory of, 97; and the Transitivity Principle, 57, 59. See also *svasaṃvedana* (self-awareness/ reflexive awareness)
reification, 7–8, 18, 20–21, 43, 71, 75, 105–6, 111, 148–49
responsibility, 86–87, 143, 145–47, 149, 155n9
responsiveness, 9, 35–37, 44n15, 85, 98, 100, 137, 144, 146–47
Ricard, Matthieu, 132, 135–36, 155n7

ritual action, 79
Rohde, Marieke, 87–88
Ronkin, Noa, 113–14
Rosch, Eleanor, 1, 40, 114
Rosenthal, David, 57

ṣaḍāyatana (six sensory domains), 106, 110–12
sahopalambaniyama, 57–58
Śākyabuddhi, 74
śamatha (tranquility), 132, 141–42, 146
Saṃmitīyanikāyaśastra, 25
saṃsāra/saṃsāric framework, 13, 28, 108–11, 134–38, 141–43, 147, 151–52; deep sense of independent self as linchpin of, 108; liberation from/moving beyond, 8, 79, 134–35, 138, 141, 163
saṃskāra. See conditioning; volition
saṃvṛtisatya. See under truth: conventional
Śaṅkara, 18–19, 65–66, 71, 78n12
Santānāntarasiddhi (Dharmakīrti), 93
santānas, 13–14, 64, 67, 84, 93–94, 117
Śāntarakṣita, 57, 67–68, 71, 73–74, 122–23. *See also* dual-aspect reflexivism
Śāntideva, 8, 133–38, 141–54, 155n9, 163–64; *Bodhicaryāvatāra,* 8, 134–35, 141, 163
Sartre, Jean-Paul, 20
Sautrāntika Buddhism, 94, 123
Schoenrade, P. A., 152
Searle, John R., 118–19
second-person perspective, 101–3, 146
self, 2, 11–12, 41–42; *ātman*, 12–16, 21, 25, 46, 50, 56; Authorship View of, 90–91; the author's view of, 12, 19–20, 41–42, 90–91, 105, 129n2; the body and, 162; Cartesian view of, 41–42; consciousness and, 2, 11–12; as constructed, 38, 92; core, 32; as dependently originated (*see* dependent origination); distinction between self and others, 9, 15; as emergent (*see* self, emergence of *as separate entry, below*); enactive view of, 5, 11–44 (*see also* enactivism); equality of self and other, 8, 144–51; exchange of self and other, 8, 154; and experience, 161–62; functionalist account of, 36–37, 40; Ganeri's taxonomy of views of, 41–42; *I* consciousness/ first-person experiences and thoughts, 19; as I-making/self making *(ahaṃkāra),* 12, 19–20, 37–41; independent, sense of, 19, 56, 108; Mādhyamika view of, 92; mental, 13, 17; the mind and, 162; nonexistence of, 148, 151; No Place view of, 42; and no-self, doctrine of, 12–16, 81–82; person *(pudgala),* 12–13, 24–26; real existence of, 2; Real Self view of, 42; and selfhood, 5, 12, 14–15, 33, 76, 92; sense of (*see* self, sense of *as separate entry, below*); subjectivity and, 5, 12, 32–37, 129n2; "trans-species core self," 31–32; unity of, 37, 161. *See also* autonomy; first-person perspective; identity; *specific topics/schools of thought, e.g.*, emptiness; pragmatic realism; reductionism; substantialism
self, emergence of, 5, 7, 33, 36–37, 44n25, 91–92, 105, 150; and coemergence with world, 7, 106–8, 111–12
self, sense of, 2, 5–6, 15, 29–31, 33–35, 44n19, 67, 74, 83, 126, 136, 140, 147–48, 150–51, 154; self-making/ "I-making" *(ahaṃkāra),* 5, 12, 19–20, 37–41
self-awareness, 6–7, 11, 20, 27, 54–57, 63, 71–77, 102
self-centeredness, 136–37, 154
self-cherishing, 136, 144; limits of, 8, 151–52
self-control, 21–22, 36–37, 82, 90–91
self-experience, 70

self-governance/self-governing systems, 36–37, 39, 41, 91–92
selfhood, 5, 12, 14–15, 33, 76, 92
selfishness, 133. *See also* egocentrism
selflessness, 16, 33, 35–37, 84, 126, 133, 137, 161–62. *See also* altruism
self-making/"I-making" *(ahaṃkāra),* 5, 12, 19–20, 37–41
self-organization, 2, 5, 12, 21–28, 32, 36–41, 87–92, 105, 160, 162–63. *See also* self-making
self-preservation. *See* survival
self-protection. *See* survival
self-respect, 134
'self-specifying' processes, 33–34
self-transcendence, 142
sense-making, living as, 27–28, 30–31, 35, 68, 73, 97–99, 107–8, 118–21, 138, 162–63
sentient beings, 2, 5, 12, 44n15, 163; Buddhist accounts of, 26–27; dependent organization of, 21–26; as dynamic systems, 12, 21, 23–25, 28, 108, 160; and subjectivity, 5, 26–32. *See also* embodiment; human beings; life
service to others, 152. *See also* altruism
Shear, Jonathan, 13
Siderits, Mark, 17, 115–16, 120, 130n10, 133
significance, 27, 31, 35, 73, 97–98, 107–8, 119, 146–48. *See also* valuation
Singer, Tania, 153
six perfections *(pāramitās),* 132
six sensory domains *(ṣaḍāyatana),* 106, 110–12
skandhas, five, 13–15, 35, 84, 86, 113, 117, 147, 150
skill: cognitive-affective training, 8–9, 142–57. See also *akuśala* (unwholesome or unskillful actions); *kuśala* (wholesome or skillful actions and traits)
Smith, David Woodruff, 57
"social-cognitive revolution," 140
solipsism, 7, 44, 46, 66, 93, 95–98, 102–3
solitude, 142
soteriology, 80, 93
space, 2, 6, 74–77, 124, 160; of awareness, 77; nondual, 74–75
spiritual development, 8, 137–38
Sridharan, Vishnu, 40
Stapleton, Mog, 88–89
Stein, Edith, 101
Steward, Helen, 85–86, 89–90
Strawson, Galen, 12–13
stream *(santāna),* 13–14, 67, 84, 93–94, 117
stream of consciousness, 19, 64–65, 67, 69–71, 77, 80, 90, 123–24, 147
subjectivism, 6–8, 105–6
subjectivity, 162–63; bodily, 100; consciousness as, 50; enacting worlds and, 123, 128; and luminosity, 45–47, 50–51, 72–77, 77n2; minimal, 2, 5, 72; self/enacting selves and, 5, 12, 26–37, 39–42, 43n8, 44n18, 129n2; sentience and, 5, 26–32. *See also* first-person perspective
subject-object framework, 7, 74, 93, 105, 123, 126–27
substantialism, 5–6, 11–12, 18, 20–21, 24–26, 37, 42, 86, 89, 159–60, 163; and nonsubstantialist accounts, 2, 43n5, 67
substantialism, anti-. *See* antisubstantialism
suffering: as dependently originated *(pratītyasamutpanna),* 79; eightfold path to liberation from, 131; and empathetic distress, 152–53. *See also* compassion; empathy; pain; *saṃsāra*
śūnyavāda. See emptiness
survival, 31, 35, 108, 112
svābhāsa (self-appearance), 52–54, 62, 72

svaprakāśa (self-lumination)/ *svaprakāśavāda* account of consciousness, 2, 47–51, 161
svasaṃvedana (self-awareness/reflexive awareness), 6, 20, 54, 56–57, 77; as very nature of consciousness, 71, 74
synchrony, 6, 13, 24–26, 32–33, 35, 64, 67–68, 72–76, 110; and unity of consciousness, 45–46, 73
syncretism, 1, 122

temporality, 5–6, 13, 17, 37, 42, 46, 64–72, 75, 77, 163. *See also* stream of consciousness
Theravada Buddhism, 91, 133
third-person perspective, 103, 146
Thompson, Evan, 21–23, 27–28, 31, 35, 43n12, 62, 68, 73, 75–76, 88–89, 100–101, 105, 107, 111, 129n2, 139–40, 164; *The Embodied Mind,* 1, 40, 114. *See also* background consciousness
Thrangu, Khenchen, 71–72
three natures, doctrine of, 8, 114, 122–29
three poisons, 8, 14, 79, 131, 135, 137
Tibet/Tibetan Buddhism, 11, 117, 125, 144, 155n2. *See also* Mipham, Jamgon
time: momentariness *(kṣanikavāda),* 19; time consciousness, 68–72, 75, 97. *See also* temporality
Tomasello, Michael, 139–40
total flight simulator, brain as like, 126
tranquility *(śamatha),* 132, 141–42, 146
Transitivity Principle, 57, 59
"trans-species core self," 31–32
Tribe, Anthony, 118–19
Trisvabhāvanirdesa or *Treatise on the Three Natures* (Vasubandhu), 122
trisvabhāva view, 126–27
truth: conventional *(saṃvṛtisatya),* 17, 86, 115–16, 148–49; "two truths," Buddhist doctrine of, 17, 43n10, 115–16, 118, 148, 160
Tsongkhapa, 11
twelvefold chain/cycle of dependent origination, 106, 109–12
"two truths," Buddhist doctrine of, 17, 43n10, 115–16, 118, 148, 160

Uddyotakara, 19–20
unity of consciousness, synchronic and diachronic, 45–46, 73, 77n2
unity of the self, 37, 161
"unwholesome" or "unskillful" actions. See *akuśala*
upādāna, 28, 109–12, 135. *See also* appropriation; clinging; grasping
Upaniṣads, 2, 46, 79
utilitarianism, 133–34

valence, 13, 27, 31, 35, 63, 73, 97–98, 107–8, 110
valuation, 5, 33, 35–36, 39–42, 162
Varela, Francisco J., 1, 22, 37–41, 43n12, 78n20, 107–8, 113–14, 164. See also *autopoiesis*
Vasubandhu, 6, 15–16, 19, 23–25, 29, 32, 66–67, 81–93 *passim,* 105, 122–23, 126, 134; *Abhidharmakośabhāṣya,* 16, 82–83; *Trisvabhāvanirdesa* or *Treatise on the Three Natures,* 122
vedanā, 13–14, 27–28, 35, 54, 63, 109–11, 135. *See also* affect; feeling
Vedānta (Advaita Vedānta school of Indian philosophy), 18–19, 50–51
Velleman, J. David, 84–85, 89–90
Vetlesen, Arne Johan, 146–47
Vireswarananda, 18–19, 71
virtual identity, 22, 38
virtue: *pāramitās* (the six perfections), 132; virtue ethics, 133–34; and well-being, 134. *See also* karma
viṣayābhāsa (object appearance), 52, 60–62
Vissudhimagga, 82
volition, 6, 13–14, 35, 81, 94. *See also* intentions/intentionality; karma

Waldron, William S., 64, 109, 129n3
Weber, Ralph, 3–5, 164
Wegner, Daniel M., 83
Western thought/tradition, 2–3, 19, 33, 56, 160
"wholesome" or "skillful" actions and traits. See *kuśala*
will/free will, 3, 83. *See also* agency
Williams, Paul, 118–19
wisdom, 8, 131–32, 134, 138, 163. *See also* enlightenment
world/worlds: the author's account of, 7, 163; Buddhist concept of *(loka),* 105–8, 111, 116; coemergence of self and, 7, 106–8, 111–12; conventional, 103; enactivism and/enacting, 7, 105–30; ready-made, myth of, 117–19, 121. *See also specific topics/theories, e.g.,* dependent origination
Wynne, Alexander, 118–19

Yājñavalkya, 46–47
Yogācāra Buddhism, 6, 19, 65–68, 71, 75, 78, 103, 114, 159–60, 163; internalist-representationalist approach to, 8, 93, 96–97, 123–27; and stream of experience as based on horizontal/vertical dynamics, 68; and the three natures of phenomena, 8, 122–29; ultimate philosophical/soteriological aim of, 93. *See also specific topics, e.g.,* base consciousness

Zahavi, Dan, 11, 43n8, 53, 67, 69–71, 101
Zen Buddhism, 127

www.ingramcontent.com/pod-product-compliance
Lightning Source LLC
Chambersburg PA
CBHW020121010526
44115CB00008B/927
9781538160145